AUBREY COHEN COLLEGE LIBRARY
75 Varick St. 12th Floor
New York, NY 10013

SCIENCE FICTION, MYTH, AND JUNGIAN PSYCHOLOGY

Kenneth L. Golden

The Edwin Mellen Press
Lewiston/Queenston/Lampeter

Library of Congress Cataloging-in-Publication Data

Golden, Kenneth L., 1951-
　　Science fiction, myth, and jungian psychology / Kenneth L. Golden.
　　　　p.　　cm.
　　Includes bibliographical references and index.
　　ISBN 0-7734-9023-X
　　1. Science fiction--History and criticism.　2. Myth in literature.
3. Psychoanalysis and literature.　4. Jung, C. G. (Carl Gustav),
1875-1961--Influences.　I. Title.
PN3433.6.G65　1995
809.3'87620915--dc20　　　　　　　　　　　　　　　　　　　95-3015
　　　　　　　　　　　　　　　　　　　　　　　　　　　　　　　CIP

A CIP catalog record for this book is available from the British Library.

Copyright © 1995 Kenneth L. Golden

All rights reserved. For information contact

　The Edwin Mellen Press　　　　　　　The Edwin Mellen Press
　　　　Box 450　　　　　　　　　　　　　　　Box 67
　Lewiston, New York　　　　　　　　　Queenston, Ontario
　　USA 14092-0450　　　　　　　　　　CANADA L0S 1L0

　　　　　　　　The Edwin Mellen Press, Ltd.
　　　　　　　　　Lampeter, Dyfed, Wales
　　　　　　　　UNITED KINGDOM SA48 7DY

　　　　　　　Printed in the United States of America

To my parents

    Lacoy and Ruth Golden

and to my colleagues and friends

    Joseph K. Davis

    Joan Weatherly

TABLE OF CONTENTS

1. Contexts:
   The Individual Journey and the Cosmic   1

2. Jung,
   on the Mythological Symbolism of the UFO   29

3. The Literature on the Myth   53

4. Virgin Birth, Shadow, and Terrible Mother:
   Wyndham's *Midwich Cuckoos* and Archetypal
   Symbolism   63

5. Cosmic Life and Human Consciousness:
   Alien Visitors to the Solar System   73

6. The Shadow in Space   99

7. Colin Wilson's *The Mind Parasites*:
   Shadow, Self, and Evolution   131

8. Shadow/Self and the Dilemmas of the Ideal--
   Christian or Technological   141

9. Self, Overmind, and Evolution:
   Arthur C. Clarke's *Childhood's End*   151

10. Love, Psyche, and Transformations:
    The Anima and Farmer's *The Lovers*   163

11. The Occidental Hero in Transformation:
    Star Trek--"The Needs of the Many"/
    "The Needs of the One"   171

12. The Journey of the Hero:
    Clarke's *Space Odyssey* Novels
    and the Functions of Myth   181

13 . Mandalas, Evolution, and Disembodied Minds:
     The Inner Journey in Outer Space   191

14 . *Stranger in a Strange Land* as Myth:
     The Christ and the Self   197

15 . Inner and Outer Space/the Myth of the UFO:
     Self and Shadow in Crichton's *Sphere*   209

16. Myth and History in Novels
    by Hoyle and LeGuin   223

    Afterword   233

    Works Cited   235

    Index   245

PREFACE

Here at the end of the twentieth century, we really do live in a strange, strange land. With dire predictions from a variety of directions, and from the point of view of many on our planet, the world looks bleak in the extreme unless envisioned in radically new dimensions.

In the opinion of many, two interrelated radical points of view are 1) Jungian depth psychology and 2) the comparative approach to myth. Whether radical or actually conservative in the truest sense, both points of view *are* quite valid. This book sets out to show the validity both viewpoints to the study of science fiction and the closely related UFO phenomenon.

Chapter 1 offers information about the context in which postmodern individuals live. People live in the vast context of the starry heavens and of the infinitudes of the atom and of the human psyche. As a part of that context, an incredible amount of knowledge exists--both in the form of what is known about that universe and what is *not* known. Partly because of this context, individuals frequently are bereft of the ability to believe in anything like a traditional mythology which provides spiritual sustenance.

Chapter 2 discusses Jung's 1959 theory that UFOs are as much related to the psychology of humanity as they are to possible actual visitors from elsewhere in the cosmos. It discusses in particular Orfeo M. Angelucci's *The Secret of the Saucers* (1955). This work is an early UFO testimonial that Jung himself discusses briefly in his *Flying Saucers: A Modern Myth of Things Seen in the Sky* (1959).

Chapter 3 examines some of the critical literature on science fiction, noting primarily the lack of studies of the kind here presented.

Chapter 4 discusses Wyndham's *The Midwich Cuckoos* (1957), which Jung also treats briefly at the end of *Flying Saucers*. This chapter also deals with the virgin birth motif, treated somewhat ironically in Wyndham's novel as well as the archetypal shadow projected onto invading aliens.

Chapter 5 follows this line of investigation in treating the theme of aliens visiting the solar system. It touches on various aspects of the quest into outer space from the perspective of Jungian psychology. It concerns itself especially with archetype of the shadow and of the self. It treats mainly Sir Fred Hoyle's *The Black Cloud* (1957), Carl Sagan's *Contact* (1985), and Arthur C. Clarke's *Rendezvous with Rama* (1973).

Chapter 6 also deals with the shadow experience, which Jung calls the first stage of the individuation process. The chapter treats examples of science fiction from the late nineteenth century: Dostoyevsky's "The Dream of a Ridiculous Man" (1881); Maupassant's "The Horla" (1989); it then picks an example from the twentieth century, Philip José Farmer's "My Sister's Brother" (1960).

Chapter 7 discusses Colin Wilson's *The Mind Parasites* (1967) in relation to the shadow motif and the concept of psychic evolution, discussing some of Shaw's "creative evolution" materials as well.

Chapter 8 takes the combined theme of the shadow and the self, and of evolution of one sort or another one step further into a discussion of C.S. Lewis's *The Hideous Strength* (1945), the culminating novel of his space trilogy.

Chapter 9 deals with the archetypes of shadow and self in the 1953 science fiction perennial classic by Arthur C. Clarke, *Childhood's End*. Though its beginning is set in the 1970s, this apocalyptic tale continues into the next century or two.

Chapter 10 discusses the manner in which Philip José Farmer's *The Lovers* (1961) treats the motif of the archetypal anima in a story set for the most part on a distant planet in the far future.

iii

Chapter 11 primarily concerns the transformation of the ultra-masculine Captain Kirk in Gene Roddenberry's *Star Trek* phenomenon primarily in the 1983 motion picture, "Star Trek II: The Wrath of Khan."

Chapter 12 discusses the transformation, evolution motif regarding the human species and unknown aliens in Arthur C. Clarke's first two *Odyssey* novels. The archetype involved here is primarily that of the self.

Chapter 13 continues what is basically the same motif in a discussion of two episodes from the original *Star Trek* series, "Errand of Mercy" and "Charlie's Law."

Chapter 14 treats the hero motif in Heinlein's 1961 classic *Stranger in a Strange Land*. The story of the human reared on Mars and evolved well beyond the rest of humanity involves a modernization of the sacrificial god-hero story.

Chapter 15 covers a 1987 Michael Crichton novel called *Sphere* which deals with the self and the human ability to imagine; it is a story about those investigating an American space craft from the future which contains an alien artifact.

Chapter 16 treats the theme of history versus cyclical and paradisal myths regarding Hoyle's *October the First Is Too Late* (1966) and Ursula LeGuin's *The Lathe of Heaven* (1971). The chapter deals with the concept of progress in regard to myth.

I wish to acknowledge those who assisted me with a variety of important tasks regarding this book: Betty Bozeman, Dr. Joseph K. Davis, Anthony G. Farrington, Dr. Ted Frank, Paul Freeman, Ben Golden, Jim Golden, Jonathan Golden, Dr. Dabney Gray, Anne and Ernest Hilgeman, Mindy Holly, Angela Marsh, Vicky Long, Ernesto Muniz, Lisa Powell, Dr. Gregory Salyer, and Dr. Joan Weatherly.

CHAPTER ONE

CONTEXTS:

THE INDIVIDUAL JOURNEY--AND THE COSMIC

To stand outside alone on a totally clear night somewhere away from the lights of cities is potentially one of the most moving of all experiences. Anyone who stands there knows that the number of those beautiful and mysterious stars is only a tiny fraction of those that exist in the infinities of space. Who does not feel something profound before such a scene and the relationships and questions it represents? The mystery of the individual's existence in the context of such magnitude seems overpowering.

Even if we had the means--a telescope strong enough--to see every star, we would never see all of them, even if we paused on seeing each one just long enough to count it. Also, what we would see, in myriads of cases, would be not "what is" but "what was"--that is, what existed, in *that* way at least, countless lifetimes, ages, aeons, ago, when the light began its journey away from those "heavenly bodies."

We may, of course, contemplate the cosmic without the prop provided by a night in the country looking at the heavens. People, for example, sometimes ask themselves where (or how) the universe ends. Frequently, such questions bother adolescents in particular. Does it end with a solid wall? Yet a wall, by definition, has another side--for a wall is a divider between two portions of space, whether two rooms or the space inside a house and the space outside. So the wall would signal no ending, for the universe would not end with something comparable to a wall or a fence.

One might try saying that no wall "ends the universe" or that no "end of the universe" exists. The universe, then, seems to go on and on, forever and forever. That, then, would be one answer to the original question. Really, how *could* it go on forever? Yet what sort of question is it merely to ask about the *how* and the *where* with reference to the end point of the great "here, there, and everywhere" we call the universe? A question only for a divine being.

Influences from the context of one's own religious education always counselled extreme care regarding that line of questioning. God supposedly frowns harshly on anyone's even *asking* those metaphysical questions. As adolescents, many are given to understand that what might be called a difference of opinion might cause them to be damned, to be sent after death to be tormented in hell by horrible, horned devils--forever and ever. ("O, no end is limited to damnéd souls," says Faustus.[1]) Yet in the West, God--so churlish as to use His absolute power to punish weak human beings for all eternity for a mere difference of opinion--was supposed to be the very One who set up this whole universe and decided how, where, and *if* it was to end, both *spatially* and *temporally*.

The "facts" that the "truth" about God and about all ultimate concerns proves not equally available to everyone and could "ruin one's life" for all eternity-these and other "facts" made life look like a crazy dream of some sort from which I would love to awake, even if the awakening meant retiring into the great "never has been."

People have various sorts of brushes with these deepest questions of "the individual in the cosmos." Yet the "starlit night in the country" is a good *symbolic* point of departure for such questions in that it represents the broadest of contexts within which we live: it symbolizes the broadest of physical contexts

---

[1] The line is from Marlowe's *Doctor Faustus* (c. 1590): past half way through Faustus's final soliloquy.

reaching into the unlimited past and into the just-as-unlimited future, as well as into the depths of the human psyche.

As far as physical context is concerned, imagination and sheer fact, regarding the latest research in physics, today progress into even more dazzling realms. The subatomic world of the so-called "basic constituents of matter" presents the obverse of the infinitudes of the starry heavens--infinite in a different direction--mysterious, full of paradox the mind cannot fathom. Further, the physicists tell us that time, hardly a physical manifestation like the stars and gases of the magnificent nebulae, is relative. Einstein's theories and their proofs have banished Newton's constant context, the unified order in which time as a constant was a given.

Indeed, we are led to suspect that time is intimately bound up with consciousness, the reality which no one can explain and which must be related to, if it is not indeed one with, the life core of the universe. Once we broach the subject of consciousness, we find opening out the context of the possibilities of multiple dimensions--"planes," perhaps--of reality. We then see the possibility of the deep union of the infinite "material world" and the infinite "non-material" world of the psyche. These two realities, it now seems, are, somehow, behind the scenes *one* reality in the strangest and most wonderful of ways. Ultimately, their relationship is not fully understandable in terms of rational science.

However, such relationships *are* treated in the metaphorical manner of myth. Myths are stories or claims or symbols or images which arise out of the human collective unconscious, giving meaning to humanity, its life, and its pursuits. A myth gives harmony and meaning to the cosmos. It usually involves a supra-natural or symbolic, rather than a naturalistic or materialistic, approach to, or reading of, the universe. It gives people meaning and helps them to make sense of existence in the universe, their environment, because it turns it into a living cosmos, a world.

In regard to new experience, to growth, the human symbol-user/myth-maker thinks in terms of *journeys* quite habitually. In fact, the symbol of the journey is one of the most prominent ways in which we are able to see meaning in and to make sense of the various contexts of our lives. "Journey" is, most basically, a physical trip, a movement from one place to another on the face of the earth, as travelled physically. Yet also we speak of "a journey into the world of Dickens's characters" or "a journey into the world of the autistic child"; "a journey into the fabulous world of quarks" or perhaps "a journey toward self-awareness." "Journey" thus becomes a symbol, a metaphor for the process of encountering new experience, exploring new worlds, whether that act leads to sheer enjoyment or to new realizations or improved conditions for the individual.

Joseph Campbell's *The Hero With a Thousand Faces* is a seminal, and in many ways a definitive, work on the symbolic journey ubiquitous in myth. According to Campbell, the symbol of the journey works on two essential levels all over the world and in all times: the microcosmic level of the life of the individual represented by the hero; and the macrocosmic level of the entire cosmos, the totality in the context of which the individual lives. Furthermore, the two levels are joined and seen not only as parallel but, in a sense, as intersecting. Campbell (borrowing from Joyce) names the story of stories--that is, the mythic journey of the hero--"the monomyth," and shows us its two levels. The two parts of his book are entitled "The Adventure of the Hero," and "The Cosmogonic Cycle," respectively.

The ultimate stage of the hero's journey into his own depths involves an apotheosis in which the hero realizes that ultimately he is one with the god toward whom his quest leads him:

> The two--the hero and his ultimate god, the seeker and the found--are thus understood as the outside and inside of a single self-mirrored mystery, which is identical with the mystery of the manifest world. The great deed

of the supreme hero is to come to the knowledge of this unity in this multiplicity and then to make it known. (*Hero* 40)

Thus the psychological level of the symbolic journey is intimately wed to the metaphysical. It involves a realization of one's relationship to the whole or to the ultimate ground of all being.

The macrocosmic level of the journey regards the movement from what may look like nothingness into being and back into what may look like nothingness and so on forever. In one great mythic vision, the whole cosmos, all life and all space and all time, are the dream of the god Krishna who lies sleeping on a lily pad on the surface of the great cosmic ocean. Campbell explains the basis for myths of the "journey" of the cosmos into temporal manifestation and then again back into the void. This basis is the ubiquitous spiritual principle frequently called the "perennial philosophy." Campbell sometimes refers to it as the "traditional wisdom" (256):

> Briefly formulated, the universal doctrine teaches that all the visible structures of the world--all things and all beings--are the effects of a ubiquitous power out of which they rise, which supports them during the period of their manifestation, and back into which they must ultimately dissolve. This is the power known to science as energy, to the Melanesians as *mana*, to the Souix Indians as *wakonda*, the Hindus as *shaki*, and the Christians as the power of God. (*Hero* 257)

Thus the context against which the symbol-user lives is one held together in a consistent totality upheld by a power best termed "divine." The forms of phenomenal existence constantly bubble forth into being, reach their peaks, and then exit--again and again, *ad infinitum*. The One divine principle--whether we call it God, Brahman, Life, or It--plays on in a constant dance generating more of itself in more and more different forms--always producing again more of itself. Each new production is the One Itself one more time, in one more form. As the twelfth-century hermetic *Book of the Twenty-Four Philosophers* says, "God is an intelligible sphere, whose center is everywhere and circumference nowhere" (Campbell, *Creative* 31).

Myth, in traditional societies, with its central image of the journey, is the picture language of the soul--expressing at its best this perennial philosophy, a philosophical wisdom found everywhere and at all times down through history.[2] Myth, in its best sense, presents humanity with "*supra*-natural" meanings and realities, in a context, as it were, superimposed, over the context of the immensity of the mysterious universe in which it lives. A myth is a story, a pattern, a paradigm, a provisional construct to express or to deal with something too vast, too complex, or too opaque to be treated by any other means. Myth is only the pointer, the tool for placing the individual in a relationship with realities beyond names and forms. According to Alan W. Watts,

> Myth is to be defined as a complex of stories --some no doubt fact, and some fantasy--which, for various reasons, human beings regard as demonstrations of the inner meaning of the universe and of human life. Myth is quite different from philosophy in the sense of abstract concepts, for the form of myth is always concrete--consisting of vivid, sensually intelligible narratives, images, rites, ceremonies, and symbols. (*Myth* 7)

The phrase "inner meaning" here suggests such matters as the relationship of the individual to the whole--as in Campbell's thesis--and the whole question of the depths of psychological experience. Such matters can only be known in their real nature through direct experiences which can never totally logically be described in words: the literalistic and abstract language of science is of hardly any help.

---

[2] According to Aldous Huxley, in the preface to his classic anthology, *The Perennial Philosophy*:

> PHILOSOPHIA PERENNIS--the phrase was coined by Leibnitz; but the thing--the metaphysic that recognizes a divine Reality substantial to the world of things and lives and minds; the psychology that finds in the soul something similar to, or even identical with, the divine Reality; the ethic that places man's final end in the knowledge of the immanent and transcendent Ground of all being--the thing is immemorial and universal. (vii)

The closest approach is to such depths is through myth with its narratives, its symbols and analogies, and even its illogic.

Myth, then, is of the order of poetry in its presentation of meanings--concerning our various relationships with our contexts--in concrete form. A myth is, in its most primary sense, of the nature of an intuition arising spontaneously within the psyche as in a dream, a fantasy, or an act of the imagination.

We need myth in order to make sense of this world, and to find our way in this world into which we find ourselves thrown. One may have the sense of having been thrown into and even to be intriguingly confused by a situation that is in many ways quite pleasant. For the vast context in which we live is both fearfully baffling in its appalling horror and beautifully humbling in its strange beauty and the magnificent wonder it inspires in us--and that applies both to the outer universe and to the vast inner universe of the psyche.

Certainly, one area with which myths concern themselves is that of humanity's place in the context of the vast space of the heavens, magnificent but appalling in their mystery, beyond any ordinary rational measure--and of time, that reality which causes ordinary language to bend back against itself. Many creation myths are not so much cosmological--attempting to explain the physical shape of the earth and heavens--as they are metaphysical/psychological, attempting to give meaning to humanity's existence in that universe, that vast "Everything," which can be so extremely confusing unless we are able to give it a "local habitation and a name," to turn it into a cosmos through myth. Many such myths answer questions such as, "How did all this come to be?" or "Why does anything exist in the first place?" Myths of the apocalypse, of course, give symbolic answers to our wonderment regarding the future and to questions such as, "How and why will it all end, and (then) what, if anything, will happen?"

If, as many commentators agree, myths--in their metaphysical and psychological functions--express something about the "inner meaning" of "the universe," as well as about the depth of the individual's relationship with "the universe"--context in the largest sense--they have, then, turned a "universe" into a "cosmos," a coherent consistent whole that makes sense to us. Of course, science attempts in a different way to do something of the kind by questing for the "laws" of nature. However, the laws of nature, as generally conceived, speak to us only of the how of things, not of the why. It is left for myth in its metaphysical function to provide a buffer of *meaning* between humanity and the nakedness of the universe.[3]

Myths also relate to the universe within, "the inner meaning" of human life itself, that psychological universe which if given order and form is transformed into a cosmos by the alchemy of myth.[4] Indeed, according to Joseph Campbell, "Mythology . . . is psychology misread as biography, history, and cosmography" (*Hero* 256). Myth--much of it, at least--is psychology in symbolic form, and it sets forth the ego's relationships with its contexts: the depths of the unconscious and the external world. According to C.G. Jung, myths "are symbolic expressions of the inner, unconscious drama of the psyche which

---

[3]According to Campbell, in "Mythological Themes in Creative Literature and Art," four functions of mythology exist: 1) the mystical/metaphysical; 2) the cosmological; 3) the sociological; 4) the psychological. The last of these, the psychological, stands "at the root of all three as their base and final support" (141). Similarly to Jung, he speaks of "certain irreducible psychological problems inherent in the very biology of our species" which remain constant and give structure to myths/rituals. Campbell's comparative mythology parallels Jung's view of the archetypes: "there run through the myths of all mankind the common strains of a single symphony of the soul" (141).

[4]Though the terms *universe* and *cosmos* are generally synonymous, *cosmos* seems more often to hold meanings related to order; it is a reality, despite its vastness, containing a logic combined with sheer immensity. *Universe*, on the other hand, seems a more indifferent expression. Alan Watts somewhere suggests that it means *one-turn*, as in the sheer fact of a physical immensity that requires a second turn instigated *by the individual psyche* to cause it to make any sense.

becomes accessible to man's consciousness by way of projection--that is, mirrored in the events of nature" ("Archetypes" 6). In projection, what is within is seen as though it were outside, in the world, external to the individual. Here is an example of the functioning of the myth-making side of psychology. An individual projects the shadow, one of the archetypes of the collective unconscious containing repressed instincts and negative tendencies, onto his enemy or adversary. He sees, though, the very evil for which he himself is, in reality, responsible as residing in someone else other than himself. Over the eons, collective symbols of the shadow--devils, trolls, and other dark adversaries--have arisen as it were to accept some of this projection of the shadow. Many times in the past, if human beings had then had no devil on which to blame things, they might have blamed other people.

Down through the centuries, the symbolic figures of myth have acted as screens for the projection of the archetypes which reside in the collective unconscious and which are the *modus vivendi* of the self-regulating psyche. As Jung says, concerning the archetypes,

> The deposit of mankind's whole ancestral experience--so rich in emotional imagery--of father, mother, child, husband and wife, of the magic personality, of dangers to body and soul, has exalted this group of archetypes into the supreme regulating principles of religious and even of political life, in unconscious recognition of their tremendous psychic power. (*Portable* 43)

That is, myth provided a creative context to act as a screen erected between the ego and the mysterious natural context within, the strange forest of mystery within the unplumbed depths of the psyche with their dream creatures and fears and madnesses roaming about ready to devour anyone. According to Jung, "Religion is a vital link with psychic processes independent of and beyond consciousness, in the dark hinterland of the psyche." He notes that "A tribe's mythology is its living religion, whose loss is always and everywhere, even among the civilized, a moral catastrophe" ("Psychology" 261). For the tribe be to bereft of belief in its traditional mythology is for it to be left without meaning, without the answers and patterns provided by the inborn nature of the psyche. It no longer has the myth as creative context and is left with the vast context of mystery and the infinitude of the inner universe.

Today, though, as Campbell points out, in the age of science and technology, the traditional mythic structures have all collapsed and left Western humanity in a spiritually confused state: "The long inherited, timeless universe of symbols has collapsed. In the fateful, epoch-announcing words of Nietzsche's Zarathustra: 'Dead are all the gods.' One knows the tale; it has been told a thousand ways" (*Hero* 387).

So humanity finds itself, has more and more found itself, during the last two hundred years, confused. It feels alone and terrified, all the gods having fled. We are lost in the cosmos--or universe, really, since, in many instances, the individual has no myth to use in order to turn it into a cosmos. He is baffled by his ultimate context, that vast, appallingly indifferent universe--both within and without--lacking in meaning and significance except as it points up his own insignificance.

So a culture may find itself groping in the dark for meaning, pretending to live by dogma, patterns, or propositions that no longer really mean much, or running wildly after various pseudo-meanings, many of them couched in the rotten clothing of exploded myth. Rather than not have myth as a "creative context," humanity, in the mass, will--rather than live without meaning--make new gods out of the fabric of the classless society, the idea of progress through science, or the image of the heroic figure in the cinema.

Indeed, such pseudo-myths as Communism have become authoritarian religious structures in form and operation. Celebrities like Marilyn Monroe and Madonna; the Rolling Stones, the Monkees, and the Beatles; Elvis Presley and Michael Jackson--have sparked something like cults and have been adored, in all but name, as deities.

Jung somewhere suggests that to take away a person's gods is, necessarily, to give him others in return. The only one who is free of this principle is the individual who has gotten beyond all the gods and seen myth from the outside, as it were, from the viewpoint of the comparatist. Such a person is able to see that which is of universal human value in the world's various mythologies yet also to see some of their elements as mere wish-fulfillment and rationalization as well. He also knows that whatever of value they have provided humanity with can come as well through introspection and intuitive psychological experience. Hence the significance today of the disciplines of counseling and psychotherapy.

Yet, for the mass of humanity, a mythology by which the individual is enthralled in the true rapture of "otherness" and a sense of wonder in a totally unself-conscious manner seems to be necessary for psychological balance and social health. That is, in one way or another, the individual must "believe," or live within, the myth. If he does not consent to its literal truth, he consents to its symbolic or "as if" truth.

Perhaps in the "as if" manner is the way much of a living mythology operates anyway. In an important sense, individuals in primitive cultures make little distinction between "literal" and "symbolic." In scientifically advanced cultures, when the literal truth criterion--the matter of "fact," as in the nineteenth-century scientific mind-set--comes to be applied to the mythic structure of a religion born at an earlier stage of development, the myth has lost most of its power. The end of that religion as a vital force has begun. Thus enters the wasteland malaise, a age of transition, an age of great degradation and danger but also of great creativity and opportunity for positive development. It is, in a sense, an age waiting for new gods to emerge. The modern age is one in which myths are in the process of dying or at least of getting lost to make room for others to be born.

Always one of the reasons a myth gets lost, becomes no longer worthy of belief and allegiance, is that some elements of the myth simply wear out, lose their ability to speak forth the eternal truths of the perennial philosophy to the mass of individuals. In such a situation, a myth becomes susceptible of the sort of doctrinal encrustation that allows it to be misused in all sorts of ways, to become confused as well as confusing and contradictory, become a matter to alienate people from the eternal context out of which each is born rather than to link them back to It, as religion (*religere*) *should* do.

A religion with its mythology--to all intents and purposes--thus becomes "invalid" except perhaps in an aesthetic sense. This atrophying of power occurs despite the fact that for the individual--for the one here or the one over there--the myth may still represent all the perennial meanings.

Of the four functions of myth, that one the loss of which is usually the first to be involved in this process of atrophy, is what Joseph Campbell calls the cosmological function, which is concerned with

> formulating and rendering an image of the universe, a cosmological image in keeping with the science of the time and of such kind that, within its range, all things should be arranged as parts of a single great holy picture, an icon as it were: the trees, the rocks, the animals, sun, moon, and stars, all opening back to mystery. ("Mythological Themes" 140)

In many ancient cultures, of course, not much separate-from-myth "science of the time" existed; the myth itself came close to containing the only "science of the time." The medicine men, shamans, or priests were the only scientists. They gained their wisdom by way of deep psychic introspection--intuition, inspiration--and tried to set forth a healthy obedience to the Way, the Tao, Nature, God, or Reality. They pointed the way to the great "supra-natural" mythic context which gave meaning to the appalling natural context of mystery: 1) "out there" in the universe and 2) in the individual's dark internal forest of fears, instincts, and emotions.

An ancient culture would have myths setting forth the verities of perennial myth in the context of a picture of the physical universe based on what was currently believable about the universe given the state of science at the time.

Perhaps it would be said, for example, that the world is a great block resting on the back of a cosmic turtle or that the stars and all the heavenly bodies orbit this earth, which resides at the center of the cosmos. In each case, the cosmological image is what could have been expected in the context of the state of the development of technical knowledge at the time. Frequently ingenious, it usually contained definite psychological meanings, rendered in a metaphorical manner. Mythology thus operates on what Campbell calls the cosmological and also perhaps on the more vital mystical and psychological functions.

In some ages a sort of dual existence of "religion" and what is today called "science" goes on, the enmity between the two not being intense enough to cause complete and direct conflict. This situation usually involves cultures in which science is ascendent. During such times, the more creative individuals--who, like Galileo or Giordano Bruno, were branded as heretics--see no conflict between their ideas and conventional religion. Such heroic individuals can see the larger context, in more than one sense of the term. They are able to see that the myth, the symbol, is not absolute but only penultimate. They see that it points the way to realizations than the vast majority of society can not yet understand.

A great mass of humanity, actually--without that mixture of creative and analytical insights which accompanies true culture--easily can be thrown off the mark, can miss a point entirely, because they stubbornly concern themselves with questions of literal truth or falsity, with, for example, the cosmological aspect of a religion which may truly be in the process of becoming outdated. In such cases, the myth may still be able, understood rightly, to sound the eternal themes metaphysically and psychologically--yet, for all that, it may die anyway for lack of popular support of its cosmological, historical, and biographical aspects, in which people lose faith.

For example, the monk Copernicus never renounced his Roman Catholic religion. Yet the full implications of his astronomical discoveries were enough to pull the foundation out from under the cosmological aspect of medieval Christianity which to many more conventional minds would truly invalidate all aspects of Christianity.

According to Campbell's theory of the four functions of mythology, it is the cosmological and the sociological functions that over the centuries break down, wear out. Interestingly enough, though the mystical and psychological elements of a myth may be just as valid today as they were 3,000 years ago, the other two functions of myth--the cosmological and the sociological--are those clung to in the most vehement and fanatical way by the mass of humanity who may live lives of emptiness, inauthenticity, and tacit desperation once they no longer have a living myth, or one in which they can fully believe. It is against such a background that the living myth of the UFO and thus of science fiction gain their prominence.

The sociological function of myth is exemplified by the Hindu caste system, with its totally outmoded strictures on individuals, with its separate "castes" or classes, with its strange sense of justice. The same is true of the Hebrew dietary laws--which may have their true origin in health needs now long since served in other ways. The case may be similar with the codified ethical components of many religions--every situation in which the individual is required by his religion to turn the critical thinking part of the psyche off, as it were, and act according to petty *principles* that do not take living *contexts* into consideration. The sociological and cosmological elements, when outdated, are what cause a religion to be rejected both by the materialist and by the rationalist.

The comparative mythologist is of quite a different breed, one who values rationality but also recognizes the value of psychic depth and intuition. Many today have in one way or another begun that journey ubiquitous in myth, the journey toward wholeness, toward true enlightenment.

The new mythic material (or much of it) of visitors from outer space relates in general to cosmology, to the picture of the universe, an area where much disparity exists between the present and the past. Yet frequently one of the first messages of the fancied people in UFOs is an ethical one--that if human beings are not careful, they will commit mass suicide with their fast-developing weapons of mass destruction.

Science as we know it was born in the speculations of the pre-Socratic Ionian philosophers in fourth or fifth century, B.C.E. Greece. Though all the theoretical foundations of modern science existed in the Western world by the second century of the common era, the *Zeitgeist*, the creative urge for the development of science and technology as we know them today was somehow not there. About the same time, the force of the various Western mythologies from the Greek to the Norse was overcome, superficially at least, by Christianity.

Christianity gained from its Hebrew foundations the tendency to place great emphasis on the unique historical event. In important senses such a quality was, as it were, calculated to set religion up as a kind of pseudo-science, proclaiming that certain things really *did* happen at particular times and places and that their so happening had a specific bearing on all matters of depth and even on the individual's eternal destiny.

Despite this aspect of Christianity as a new religion, another of its major sources is to be found in the tendency of many Asian and Near-Eastern cults to have at their center the myth of the yearly and eternal death and resurrection of a god. This element in Christianity--through the central image of the crucifixion and resurrection as well as the ritual of the communion--linked it to the broadest mythological context possible, that of the *philosophia perennis*. According to Alan W. Watts, in *Myth and Ritual in Christianity*,

> That which has been held "always, everywhere, and by all [to be true]" is the one common realization, doctrine, and myth which has appeared with consistent unanimity in every great culture . . . . It was even obvious to St. Augustine, though he later retracted the statement, that "the very thing now called the Christian religion was not wanting among the ancients from the beginning of the human race . . . ." In the light of such a catholicity the Virgin-born One, who is both God and Man, is that

uncaused Reality which is both the timeless and the present, which is simultaneously the true life of man and of all. (*Myth* 136)

Yet--as Watts's reference to Augustine's retraction of his statement under the forces of institutionalism indicates--the path taken by orthodox Christianity was heavily influenced by the historical, legalistic, and institutional bent of its Hebrew foundations--even to the point that it turned the perennially authentic myth embodied in the death and resurrection of the Christ into a legalistic charade in which the death of God's son becomes (of all things) payment to God for Man's "sins."

From about the thirteenth century, the foundations of Christianity as a force having any appeal for the creative individual began to crumble. Vital inquiry and true inspiration lay in actions the Church could only term heresy, in figures like Roger Bacon, Nicholas Copernicus, Giordano Bruno, and Galileo. Further, the great Arthurian and Holy Grail myth cycles, heretical from an orthodox point of view, also held great spiritual depth. Also, the secret genius of much of the literary and philosophical thought in the West, positive and negative, the vital mythological image that unconsciously moved the culture toward where it is today, was that of Faustus.

The Faustian age, of which Oswald Spengler wrote in the early twentieth century, began in approximately the thirteenth century even though the literary symbol of the individual of learning who sells his soul to the Infernal Powers for infinite power arises as early as the fifteenth century. The high Renaissance and post-Renaissance ages were dominated by the idea of space. In one sense, it is space to be adventured into, to be filled with humanity's new ideas, its inventions, its fabulous cities, its materialized dreams.

The driving spirit of the Faustian age has been one, whether consciously or unconsciously, set free from the intellectual shackles of the orthodox Christian morality and worldview as well as from the more ancient standards of conduct and the informing patterns of the perennial philosophy set forth in the essential

Christian myth and in high myth the world over. But unconsciously Faustian humanity has been at the mercy of the Devil, God's hidden partner, especially in the form of the compensatory forces within which the ruthless rape of Nature in the process of discovery and conquest.

The Faustian spirit thrived both within Christianity, despite (or perhaps because of) its nominal orthodoxy, and outside of it as well. Many activities and tendencies purely Faustian in their overweening, hubristic, and heartless nature were condoned by the Church with the tacit agreement that they be conducted under disguise.

Yet that was not enough, for Faustian urges tended toward the destruction of the time-honored perennial mythic patterns. Christianity was at enmity with Nature. In fact, it saw Nature as ruled by the Devil. Yet Christianity had its own Faustian deal with Lucifer which can be seen portrayed in the "Grand Inquisitor" chapter of Dostoyevsky's *The Brothers Karamazov*.

After many intimations of conflict, a definite battle broke out in the nineteenth-century West between science and religion--Doctor Faustus and the monks. The two new scientific elements having the most sudden and direct effect on the status of belief in Christianity were the chain of discoveries in geology, during the eighteen-twenties made by Lyell, and the discoveries in biology and "evolution" made by Darwin and Wallace during the eighteen-fifties.

The discoveries in geology cooperated with those in biology to establish the fact that the earth is immensely old, much older than it would have to be if the accounts in the Old Testament were literally true. Humankind was swiftly being placed in that potentially terrifying context of material magnitude from which myth, as well as its own ignorance, had protected it. This dangerous move involved, the endangerment, for Western humanity, of a whole mythic cosmology, involving the "account" of God's creation of humankind in the Garden a rather short time ago, given present knowledge of the earth's history. In the medieval elaboration of the myth, at least, the earth was the center of the rather limited cosmos, and just outside the ring of the fixed stars lay God and heaven. Before the new discoveries, these accounts were believed literally by most everyone.

It was left for the twentieth century to continue laying humanity bare against the infinite *context* of the limitless reaches of space, now, as well as time. Here Faustus, in his desire to storm heaven and know all, has come up against what might seem the ultimate material *context* in the challenge, in the mystery, in the fascination with outer space.

One space age form of Faustianism is, as the opening words of every *Star Trek* episode puts it, "to bravely go where no man [sic] has gone before." Outer space is a context so terrifying that it has tantalized Faustian humanity with the desire to fathom it--or else. As that far voyaging nineteenth-century seafaring Faust, Captain Ahab, puts it, "All visible objects . . . are but as pasteboard masks." He then adds that (like twentieth century UFO enthusiasts) he sees out there behind the mask something mysterious yet human-like in having the ability to reason. The egoistical Ahab encourages himself on his voyage into the unknown: "If man will strike, strike through the mask!" He thinks of himself as a prisoner of sorts in a walled-in situation. Perhaps it is *metaphysically* that really he is walled-in, by his rationalistic insistence on the eradication of all mystery. That is perhaps one of the worse difficulties of our scientific modernity. Ahab's feelings may be similar to those of some believers in UFOs: "To me, the white whale is that wall, shoved near me. Sometimes I think there's naught beyond." Ahab's attitude toward the whale is a militaristic one, the reflex of the attitude of some of those today who see the aliens they have been abducted by as an invasion force: "He tasks me; he heaps me; I see in him outrageous strength, with an inscrutable malice sinewing it. That inscrutable thing in chiefly what I hate . . . I will wreak that hate on him." In that Ahab has no reverence for Nature or God in the whale, he is not unlike much of science in our century, which sometimes does things of an utterly unholy (non-holistic) nature, taking a very short view of things and in fact thinking (like a fanatic) of only one thing: "Talk not to me of blasphemy, man; I'd strike the sun if it insulted me. . . . Who's over me? Truth hath no confines" (139).

Modern humanity--in its fascination with its own ego, with utility, materialism, and technology--takes, in essence, just such an attitude as Ahab does toward nature and all its sacred mysteries. Frequently, outer space is, to the modern individual, just the new frontier in his quest for supremacy of some sort over nature, over the overarching context.

Indeed, for Faustian humanity the call of the stars is infinitely fascinating, tantalizing, inviting. Thus, a new secular mythology has arisen to give contemporary meanings to humanity's existence in the *context* in which it exists. Humanity has found, in the new symbology of the quest "out there" among the stars a myriad of targets for the projection of the elements of his internal unconscious psychological drama.[5] It is a mythology enough in keeping with at least the popular version of the accepted science of the time that it begins to function in the cosmological, psychological, and mystical respects as a living myth.

For there emerges more and more, until it has proliferated fantastically by the end of the twentieth century, an almost universal, according to some,[6] fascination with space, with the final frontier. This fascination exists with time,

---

[5]The archetypes, if repressed and not recognized in some way or another, are *projected* or seen and dealt with "out there" (frequently in a negative way) in someone or something else. Likewise, their energy and sometimes their hypnotic power come to reside, for the individual, in whoever or whatever carries the projection.

[6]David Lavery's *Late for the Sky* (1992) is an excellent and insightful discussion of a number of rather flagrant failings and difficulties related to the trivialization of the myth here being discussed. However, it dwells primarily on silly, dangerous, or simply negative embodiments of the "extraterrestrial imperative." Though certainly completing a worthwhile task, essentially it fails to look at the myth from the valuable point of view of the Jungian comparatist.

as well. Human beings speculate concerning the far future and imagine the possibilities for conquest and discovery in the future. Some fantasize of time travel in the sense of Einstein's theory of relativity. Carl Sagan gives expression to this new myth in the "legitimate" scientific sense thus: "The surface of the Earth is the shore of the cosmic ocean," adding that "The ocean calls," for "Some part of our being knows this is from where we came" (*Cosmos* 5).

As the stars send their light to us, so we strive toward, so we quest for, the stars. Human beings exist on one planet in the solar system. If other stars do have planets, as we must assume that many of them possibly do, no evidence exists yet to prove that anything like *human* life exists on any of them or anywhere in the universe. Yet the strangeness, the mystery, even the danger, calls--just as the overweening fervor called Ahab to his quest after the white whale. Various ways of hearing and answering this call exist.

A basic dream today, a very popular image, sees the universe "out there" as a place into which we may some day journey with ease, seeking "truth," seeking the answer to ultimate questions, or seeking something unconsciously some more questionable fate. This dream is growing, despite the tentative, limited, and faltering characteristics of our voyages into space in the latter half of the twentieth century. Why is modern humanity--with its space programs, its countless literary and video fantasies, its "science" of "futurology," its UFO sightings, and its UFO cults--so fascinated by this new image?

Though it *is* quite likely that life of a kind we would recognize *as life* probably does exist elsewhere in the universe, it is not sensible to suppose that it operates in any sense by our standards. It might be quite strange and possibly lethal in a purely innocent way. Many of the fantasies about benevolent or even "humanoid" aliens, on the one hand, or devious monsters, on the other, are clearly examples of projection, wishful thinking--or of projecting our shadow sides in the form of the BEM (bug-eyed monster) image.

To hold to that kind of anthropomorphism which sees humanity as a nation or as a kind of political party--which must make Empire and Colonies of the universe--is certainly to be naively Faustian. In the twentieth century we live in a world--just on this planet--which is less and less malleable to our provincial preconceptions and our human dreams. Though the individual in the street may not have caught on to it yet, the successes of the physical sciences have made the universe look more majestic in its infinite immensity, more mysterious in the vastness of time and space with their strange conundrums, than ever it did to savages crouching in rain forests afraid of the gods of the sun and the moon. And yet somehow that very strangeness lures us on.

Indeed, the new myth *is*, in a sense, science itself. At least a great deal of it involves the *results* of science and technology or experiences which are contingent on those results. (The key is perhaps the power the ego expects to receive *from* science.) The new mythology is not unified around a single specific mythological story as is, for example, Christianity around the life of Christ. Rather, the unifying element is the general theme of the journey "out there" into new realms, usually into space, or into time, into the future or into the past. Frequently, the journey into new experience, into discovery or change occurs *in reverse*. It occurs in regard to visitors having journeyed *from* deep space or *from* another time to the earth of the present.

This new mythology appears in several places: in the fantasy or "science fiction" genre in literary form as well as in cinematic and television forms; in the news media and rumors and the vast "literature" on UFO's; and in cults and prophets related to the UFO phenomenon. Each is fueled by and encouraged by dreams and intimations arising out of the space industry, man's actual voyages into outer space, or the speculations surrounding them--as well as by the current lack in the vast majority of individuals--of living religions. It is our project here to treat for the most part literary manifestations of the myth.

Space is the new frontier--that, and time, time in various senses, especially in the sense of the future or at least our ideas about what it may be like or what we wish it would or would *not* be like. In a sense, the whole myth of space (and time) is like many myths. It is a symbol for humanity's questing into the mysteries of the contexts in which it finds itself--the external world of vast unknowns, as well as the inner world of perhaps even deeper mysteries.

In the past, humanity's gods were frequently modeled on ideas of kingship, fatherhood, or spiritual authority. Now, as Jungian analyst Robert A. Johnson says, in the twentieth century,

> We have yet another myth, another symbol. Spaceships bring extraterrestrial beings from far-off galaxies and planets, civilizations more advanced and powerful than our own, from which we learn new and wondrous things. (26)

The new and wondrous things we learn, or of which we have intimations, are frequently in the same category at least as what human beings have always learned from the myths embodying the depths of the psyche. The same old themes of myth in its psychological and mystical functions are played through yet again and again.

Really, most of what is new is the clothing and the futuristic setting. For example, instead of the gods coming down from the heavens, we have superior alien beings arriving from, or human beings journeying "out there" into, outer space. Instead of the hero's voyaging about in the realms of magic, the region of the gods, we have him--or her--going out to confront one's own depths metaphorically in the mythic context of the journey to the stars, "out there," "where no man [sic] has gone before." Indeed, frequently "out there," like "up there," is really "in there," here within the individual. Again and again, elements of the space mythology are metaphorical representations of elements of the inner drama of the psyche. Humanity confronts the archetypes of the collective unconscious, the universal patterns, in its mythic conceptions as they take the form of the confrontation with the unknown universe "out there," "where no one has gone before."

The archetype in question may be, for example, the shadow, representing the morally negative element, the repressed aspects of experience; or it may be the anima/animus, the contrasexual side of experience which is frequently repressed; or it may be the Self, the archetype of the whole, frequently appearing in myth as the God figure with whom the hero comes to realize his essential oneness. Each story is related to--or is a fragment of--the general theme, the monomyth, the journey of the hero toward transformation, enlightenment, individuation, apotheosis. As always, the symbols of myth represent meanings relating us to the baffling mysteries of the whole universe outside of us as well as the psyche within--in both cases, to our *context*.

For, with the external context--the infinities of space and time, as with the psyche--it is the *supra*-natural, the symbolic reading of the universal contexts that is presented in myth. The modern myths of the quest into outer space and of the arrival of aliens constitute a new symbolic setting, a new myth--yet another way of finding meaning in the universe and in human possibilities both present and future. The myths of the UFO's and the future voyages of men to the stars are based either on conscious or unconscious speculations about the final frontier, the real and fantastical possibilities which modern science enables us to glimpse.

The projection of contents of the unconscious into the symbols of myth is directly related to the insights of poets and other creative individuals such as, for example, William Blake, who held that all gods live within the human heart. The gods come from within and function as mediators between consciousness and the unconscious. They may assist us in the journey toward maturity and enlightenment. They place us in a symbolic context, show us our relationship metaphysically to the whole--the *context*--both "outside" us and "within" us.

I place these expressions in quotation marks because, ultimately, we cannot know to what extent they are really accurate descriptions. It is clear that "external events" are never fully external. The whole question of the relation of the "inner" to the "outer," of subjective to objective has been an open one in philosophy since the time of Kant. At any rate, the whole, the ultimate context, from the points of view both of Jungian psychology and of the perennial philosophy, contains both the "external" and the "internal."

Jung, in his later years, was working at questions concerning the (only seemingly chance) coincidental events related to what he called "synchronicity"--which demonstrates the underlying union of the physical and the psychological, the worlds of nature and of the psyche (*Portable* 505-18). Myth is related to vision and to dream, and tends itself to unify these two contexts. What is within is seen out there in the external world as the gods--or as the occupants of UFO's--who visit man. This theory is a definite possibility for accounting for at least part of the UFO phenomenon. If we project our internal archetypes into social interaction, why might we not project them in the form of such psychoid fantasies? Other possibilities exist but certainly this is one good working hypothesis.[7]

---

[7]Stanislav Grof, in *The Holotrophic Mind* (1993), cites Jung's theories (182-86) and seems also to agree with the conclusion of Jaques Vallee that UFOs are psychoid experiences, perhaps related to other dimensions existing in the same physical space as the so-alled ordinary universe (*Dimensions* xiii-xvii, 246 ff). Grof speculates that if UFO's came from inhabited planets, those planets might be so far off in space (and therefore time) that they would have to be equipped to travel through "hyperspace." Thus, it would not be illogical to entertain the possibility that they might even have the ability to use transpersonal levels of human consciousness in unknown ways and that their visits might indeed appear as fantasies, archetypal events, or visions (188). The late Michael Talbot, in *The Holographic Universe* (1991), comes to the same rather Jungian conclusions, also mentions Vallee, but adds his concept of the hologram-like nature of such events (274-85); he cites many sources in support of this particular aspect of this fascinating and somewhat convincing holographic theory.

Accounts, theories, and stories of UFO's with their wise and mysterious aliens are, like "all the gods who play in the mythological gardens,"[8] representative of the workings of what Jung called the transcendent factor. The world of what Jung terms the Self transcends such distinctions as subjective and objective.

Even for one who is open to the possibility that, one fine day, "They" just might really arrive, all UFO stories can not be true in the ordinary, literal, objective sense. If they were, earth would have to be "Grand Central Station" for this arm of the galaxy. The forms and capabilities of space craft, despite some typical elements, are quite numerous, as are those of the aliens inhabiting them. The stories are not *all* true--how likely is it that any *one* can be true? Beyond that, if the aliens have been here at least since the present series of UFO sightings began in 1947,[9] why is it taking them so long to finish with whatever it is that they came to do? Questions of this sort could be multiplied.

An interesting parallel can be drawn regarding the gods of older myths. *All* of the reports of the existence of supernatural beings or contacts of men with gods could never have been literally true. Also, it would have made little sense for any objective person having access to several sets of myths to believe that one set was true, in a literal sense, while all the others were false. In fact, despite the endless variation, such reports are in essence all the same. As regards the question of literal truth, it is best to view all supernaturalistic belief systems with the unbiased eye of the comparatist. None of the gods exist literally, yet all exist as long as does anyone does who has a living faith in them or a receptivity to

---

[8]From the popular ballad, "Atlantis," written and recorded by Donovan Leitch in the late 1960s. "Atlantis" figures prominently in many of the "non-fiction" writings of self-appointed UFO prophets too numerous to name here.

[9]According to *Time/Life Mysteries of the Unknown: The UFO Phenomenon*, the 24 June 1947 experience of Kenneth Arnold above the Cascade Mountains of Washington marks the start of the "modern flying saucer era" (37-36).

their symbolism. All gods are symbolic projections of these elements within the psyche Jung calls the archetypes.

Jung notes that what the archetype, on which the myth is based, is *in itself* is ultimately a matter of mystery. In no way do his findings rule out the possibility of other planes of existence in which time and space as we know them are non-existent. Indeed, we may come closest to experiencing what such unknowable, possibly infinite worlds are like, in dreams and at times when our intuitive faculties are most awake--when we are, according to Jung, closest to thinking is the manner of the unconscious, in the way that perhaps primitive humanity thought all the time.

The institutionalized aspect of all traditional mythologies is dead for anyone who lives today in a fully contemporaneous sense.[10] Yet, even now in the twentieth century, spontaneous unconscious human creativity is very much at work fashioning mythic materials which offer new avenues of meaning. Certainly, one aspect of this phenomenon is represented by what Jung, in the 1958 monograph, calls "a modern myth of things seen in the sky" (*Flying Saucers*). Jung's subtitle, of course, refers to the rumors, dreams, and literary phenomena centered on the theme of the arrival of aliens from outer space. Yet an attempt to explore living myth in this century further than Jung did leads to much more than the UFO motif in its primary form in the television report or *National Inquirer* article. Indeed, the task of this book is to explore the symbolism of the new mythology in fiction (and, to a lesser degree, television drama and cinema) of the sort involving space/time fantasy.

---

[10]For example, a certain Christian lives her faith in the Christ and has no thought for what the Pope says or for what this or that evangelist says. She does what she does out of *her* own depths to live a life beyond fear and desire, empowered and activated by the life, death, and resurrection of Jesus, the Christ. Such a person would be a vessel of active love and mercy ministering to others with no concern for whether they *believed* what she believed or not. She would certainly not be trying to save people from any *burning hell*.

One "mythogenetic zone"[11] is the futuristic novel or story--whether or not it contains aliens arriving on the earth in UFOs. At their, best such works provide fantasies containing mythological symbols relating humanity to universal spatial, temporal, metaphysical, and psychological contexts. One species of this kind of novel is the apocalyptic novel, based structurally on the mythic theme of the apocalypse, which has taken many forms all over the world. The question embedded in the myth is "How will the world, or the present age, end? And what does its ending or transformation mean?" An example of such an apocalyptic novel is Arthur C. Clarke's *Childhood's End*.[12] Of course, the novel set in the future has its popular counterpart in the world of strange religious sects, cults, and prognosticators. Again the attempt is to find meaning in the future, a meaning both acceptable in a scientific age yet, and the same time, serving the same purposes as perennial myth.

The space travel story is, of course, most easily related to "things seen in the sky." Almost always, such a story is of a journey of some kind, as are the time stories, although frequently the point of view is that of the "thing seen in the sky." Sometimes the types are somewhat combined as in the Clarke example mentioned above, which embodies both. Indeed, many of these space journeys are also future stories as well, as they are usually set in an imaginary future in which space travel has become fairly easy. Such a story might be a narrative concerning how a fictitious astronaut in some fairly near future is picked up from a space station by aliens who show him a world which cherishes meanings representing and elaborating upon themes related to the perennial philosophy and the universal "monomyth." He will presumably (beyond the scope of the narrative) then be able

---

[11]A mythogenetic zone is a place giving birth to myth. Campbell says that today it "*is the individual in contact with his own inner life, communicating through art his art with those 'out there'*" (*Creative* 93).

[12]See Chapter 9.

to bring back meaning and wisdom (Campbell's "eternal boon") to his fellow human beings on earth. In this example, as in many others, the pattern is mythic--the journey of the individual into a strange, mysterious, or "other" zone where he becomes enlightened in one way or another and is enabled to return the boon of such realizations to the everyday world.

One version of the myth is of course the simple rumor of the encounter with the UFO. Indeed, many presumably credible people have "seen" UFO's.[13] Yet, as Jung argues, it may be more likely that they have seen and heard, and even (in many instances) touched, psychic projections. (Jung's 1958 monograph is discussed in more detail in the next chapter.) Sometimes witnesses come together to form cults of a sort, with intricate mythical narratives ultimately treating the same questions about context--time and space--as do the ancient myths and the religions they support.

Always, whether in the novel or short story, in the movie, or in the rumor or cult, fragments of the myth of the journeying hero recur. In space and time, as in the forests and deserts of ancient earth, his journey goes on. He continues to seek realizations about the face of mystery, the depth of infinity, his relationship to the context of the vast unknown--both "out there" and deep within.

---

[13]Even two American presidents claim to have seen UFOs: Jimmy Carter (1976-80) and Ronald Reagan (1980-88).

CHAPTER TWO

JUNG, ON THE

MYTHOLOGICAL SYMBOLISM OF THE UFO

C.G. Jung, in his monograph *Flying Saucers: A Modern Myth of Things Seen in the Sky* (1959), discusses quite seriously the unidentified flying objects phenomenon. Not only are UFOs of great popular interest, but masses of human beings in the second half of the twentieth-century are fascinated at some deep level by images and narratives of space travel and of the future. Jung finds such matters to involve clear elements of the perennial human quest for meaning and wholeness. Such cultural phenomena involve what is central to both Jung's process of individuation and to Joseph Campbell's concept of the monomyth of the hero's journey.

Humankind in the late twentieth century is in the process of symbol re-evaluation. Human beings are finding new symbols for the inner realities Jung calls "archetypes"[1] in the context of the new frontier of space and of extrapolations concerning the future. Indeed, in response to modern humanity's dissociation from nature, the collective unconscious is projecting images of new possibility, even of unification and of the wholeness symbolized by the generally circular shape of the flying saucers at the core of this modern myth.

---

[1]Archetypes are inherited *a priori* forms that represent constant, perennial factors in humanity's psychic nature. Images of archetypes arise spontaneously in every epoch the world over in dreams, mythology, and art. An archetype is projected when its image is seen as coincident with a person or an object.

According to Jung, the widespread rumors of strange objects in the sky quite probably have mythological foundations. He even suggests that they represent "*a living myth*":

> We have here a golden opportunity of seeing how a legend is formed, and how in a difficult and dark time for humanity a miraculous tale grows up of an attempted intervention by extra-terrestrial "heavenly" powers--and this at the very time when human fantasy is seriously considering the possibility of space travel and of visiting or even invading other planets. (*Flying Saucers* 323)

A "living myth" is a set of archetypal symbols and narratives with enough credibility, popular appeal, and cohesiveness to provide meaning to a mass of contemporary individuals. Also, a living myth is a myth in step with its times to such a degree as to be, for members of that group at least, an acceptable lens through which to see their lives against a larger context.

Further, the living myth *enthralls* individuals, providing a context of wonder and mystery and giving meaning to the universe and the individual's place in it. Stories of gods and goddesses, their ritual pronouncements, and their gifts to and requirements of humankind--these have performed all those services throughout the history of humanity.

A myth usually has as its essence some aspect of the quest, or the monomyth which, according to Joseph Campbell, has appeared all around the globe and in all times. The monomyth is the narrative of the hero's quest for the secret of life, for enlightenment, or for some sort of salvation.

In the nineteenth century, the *intellectual* credibility of the stories of the Bible--taken *literally*--began to decline. Since these major myths at the heart of the Christian religion were seriously undermined by the beginning of the twentieth century, Western humanity has since tended to live in a wasteland situation in which the gods are in need of rebirth. Those who *can* gain true spiritual sustenance from the Bible stories and their imagery of at least two thousand ago are the fortunate few. Yet many practice Christianity as an unconscious defense mechanism without finding in it anything to treat their deepest inner desires and fears.

Yet for many, the Christian myth is dead. In the UFO phenomenon and the subgenre of science fiction and fantasy, a rebirth of myth, at least of *some* sort, is in the process of happening. It could be argued even that many of the best values that have been a part of Christianity are in the process of translating themselves into new forms.[2] Surely, indeed, valuable aspects of Greek paganism found a place in Christianity when it was new.[3]

Campbell's comment that mythology "is psychology misread as biography, history, and cosmology" (*Hero* 256) is another way of saying that the matters of the microcosm, the individual psyche, come to be mirrored in the imaginative construct, or mythic image, of the macrocosm or universe. That is, the psychology of the individual works by projection, by way of a casting outward,

---

[2] For example, the intellectual honesty of many post-Christians such as Nietzsche--the refusal to believe that which is not true--in a ironic way, comes out of certain aspects of Christianity and the Biblical tradition. (That is, Nietzsche takes seriously such admonitions as those about not bearing false witness and Jesus' condemnation of fraud. Nietzsche searches deeply into the foundations of institutional Christianity and finds it fradulent in its history, its doctrines, and its practice. In an ironic sense, he rejects Christian on what is essentially a Christian principle.)

[3] It really is highly questionable as to whether what we might call "the mythology of Outer Space" will ever develop into an institutional religion such as Christianity. Matters are very different today from what they were then. Indeed, one of the great causes of danger in the last half of the twentieth century is the theocracy. In particular, factions in the Middle East believing in this or that institutionalized religion seem constantly to threaten world peace. Many times such groups are of the "chosen people" category, the mythic aspects of which Joseph Campbell discusses in *Myths to Live By* (184-87) and elsewhere. Of course, this is not to say that science fiction writers have not created some "cosmic religions," such as Arthur C. Clarke's "Cosmo Christers" in *Rendezvous with Rama* (1973).

as it were, of internal contents onto the screen of mythology, one element of which is an image of the cosmos.[4]

Jung admits that analyzing contemporary events involves dangers arising from the lack of a broad perspective. He notes, however, how the proliferation of stories of unidentified flying objects since the latter 1940s accords significantly with the kind of *mythological* phenomena related to the end of an era (*Flying Saucers* 311). In practically every crucial period of human history marking the end of an era, the transition to a new era, or a period of uncertainty concerning the future--"signs and portents" have arisen. The archetypal symbol of the apocalypse or *revelation* of what is new certainly is rife today as it has been in many crucial periods of the past.

Actually, in the age of UFOs and science fiction,[5] the collective unconscious is projecting certain of its contents onto the external world as collective images in the form of waking dreams and visions, rumors, and visionary literature/film about the arrival of aliens from outer space, about space travel by human beings, and about the future of humanity.

UFOs, according to Jung, fit in the same category as the collective visions of "the crusaders during the siege of Jerusalem, the troops at Mons during the first World War, the faithful followers of the pope at Fatima, Portugal." Many instances in the annuls of history and biography could be added to the list. Jung mentions his own experience at a seance when the four other people present, yet not Jung himself, saw a moon-like object floating above the medium's body

---

[4]This matter is discussed at some length in the Chapter 1.

[5]Many commentators see the genre of science fiction as having had its beginnings in classical Greece. They mention the third voyage of Swift's Gulliver (1726) and Mary Shelly's *Frankenstein* (1919) as well as other works as the beginning of the genre. Robot servant girls actually appear in Homer's *Iliad*. Yet most see these as anomalies, more or less, with science fiction beginning in earnest with later nineteenth-century figures such as Jules Verne and H.G. Wells.

(*Flying Saucers* 314). Knowing of numerous other such instances, he suggests that, "Even people who are entirely *compos mentis* and in full possession of their senses can sometimes see things that do not exist" (315). The UFOs that began to be "seen" about the end of World War II are to be related to the mass psychology involved in the so-called "War of the Worlds" incident of the apocalyptic pre-war times. Orsen Wells did a radio drama based on H.G. Wells's *The War of the Worlds*. Many failed to hear or notice the introduction explaining the dramatic nature of the broadcast and thus were frightened into thinking that Martians were invading New York. The incident caused what Jung refers to as "a regular stampede and numerous car accidents" (*Flying Saucers* 315).

Frequently, though, many of the early embodiments of the myth of the arrival of the aliens portray the aliens as essentially benign creatures watching the earth, especially watching recent technological developments such as those in atomic physics and nuclear fission, hoping to help protect humanity from itself. The naivety as to the literal aspect of some of these early renditions is seen in that the aliens are portrayed as actually concerned about the negative effect earth's weapons might have on neighboring *planets*. However, the concerns of some of these stories that humankind is in danger of self-destruction were more to the point.

In "The Day the Earth Stood Still," a 1951 popular motion picture, the benevolent alien, Klatoo, warns that human beings must stop playing with nuclear weapons or risk being burned to cinders by aliens. Ironically, such a statement is essentially true if the phrase involving aliens is omitted, in that humanity now has the ability to, in effect, burn *itself* to cinders. In the terms of Jungian psychology, in such a context, the destructive aspect of the alien may represent something within humanity itself, the dark and unknown other, the shadow side involving the monstrous courage to walk forbidden paths, involving even the abandon which could end in planetary suicide. The benevolent alien Klatoo, on the other hand, would seem to represent *one* of the voices from the shadow side whose business it is to warn.

Certainly, in many senses, events of the twentieth century sometimes seem apocalyptic ones, marking the end of an era. The 1914 war was one, and the world economic upheavals of the late twenties and early thirties, as well as World War II, certainly qualify. Yet, a more far-reaching event, which in important senses made all our "wars to end all wars" possible, had already occurred: the demise of the health of the mythic complex which had sustained the Western world for over a millennium--Christianity.

The Renaissance, with its rebirth of science, and its splitting of Christendom into "sects," was the beginning of this downfall of Christianity. In essence, humanity's rational intellect, along with the empirical method, so enthralled Europe that science, in a very crucial sense, came to be the new pseudo-religion at the heart of Western culture. Humanity began progressively to forget its depths and to deny all those things with which science could not deal quantitatively. These happen to be the deeper things, which can not be treated any better than by myth, by ritual, and by poetry.

Further, since science seemed to work so "efficiently," people became hungry for facts and statistics. They began to take Christian doctrines and the myths they are based on literally and to require this mythology to be something factual in the same sense that science is factual. At the same time, many of the beliefs they retained became hollow in regard to the meanings which had in earlier ages resided in the Christian myth.

As science advanced during the nineteenth century, the Christian God was more and more in the process of being discredited because He could not stand against the empirical criteria of science. Darwinism and the new knowledge about geology and astronomy ate away at continued general acceptance of the Christian myth as fact.[6] Of course, many subtle aspects of human psychology and of social change were involved in these changes. Nietzsche's proclamation of "God is dead" was truly prophetic in that it saw far beneath the surface of the collective Western soul.

With events in the twentieth century, the demise of living power in Christianity has become clear to many objective and balanced thinkers. Not only has the influence of scientific ideals on what is left of Christianity continued in varying degrees, but Christianity in general has lost more and more power. Despite the ranting of television evangelists insisting on belief in the "literal" reading of the Bible, both apostasy and hypocrisy are rampant.

All Western societies now have become intensely pluralistic, and much of what is believed concerning religion by many is purely superficial; many individuals are left prey to any kind of psychic infection which touches them at their depths, whether it be of benign *or* of malignant effect. Regarding the latter, the phenomenon of National Socialism which led to World War II is a prime example. Much of the original Christian myth, for example, *was* truly energized from the depths of the psyche, but much in the modern sects is more dangerous than surfacial complacency, for the projection of dark sides of the archetypes is involved.

Indeed, in the final decade of the twentieth century, America is perhaps ripe for its own "religious" Hitler. At the very least, the fundamentalists present a life-denying literalizing of Christianity in a state of radical fragmentation. Yet also these fundamentalist Christians actually threaten all the contents of Pandora's box. Clearly one of their central occupations is constantly to project outward the

---

[6]In ancient times, all myths need not be have been taken as concrete fact by every member of the population. Probably individuals have existed in all ages who took other than a consensual view of reality. Of course, regarding any living myth, in most instances in the past, the majority of the populace believe the myth literally--thus the importance of the need for myths to keep up with the generally accepted science of the time. See Campbell, "Mythological Themes."

deep psychic element which Jung calls the archetypal shadow. When they excoriate "unbelievers," "humanists," "liberals," or "communists," they are attacking their own failings projected outward. Perhaps, some of the pent-up psychic energies which *would* otherwise be released in dangerous fundamentalist religious forms such as persecution of those deemed "servants of the Devil" are instead expended on dangerous aliens, UFOs, and space fantasy.

Further, the television ministers who solemnly or gleefully warn of the apocalypse are not alone in their concern with apocalyptic themes. All manner of sources speak of the end of an age. The astrologers tell of the incipient end of the age of Pisces, or the Fishes, the beginning of the age of Aquarius. Various authorities tell of "dead-ends," of a sort being faced by various of the empirical sciences, especially physics and biology, dilemmas which seem to require some sort of "intuitive" or "quantum" leap which would go beyond all the usual techniques and ways of thinking of the scientific West. The environmentalists predict unprecedented negative changes. Some concern themselves with the probabilities for nuclear war and other ways that the entire biosphere might end.

Perhaps the most crucial symbol of the apocalyptic nature of the modern age is the mushroom cloud, representing the "gift" or "by-product" of modern physics which has given humanity the ability effectively to destroy life on this planet. Ironically, the image of the mushroom cloud suggests *what* humanity risks destroying--the natural world of spores and seeds, plants and animals, living on the dank, fecund, perennial earth, the world as well as humankind, who, despite all its intellectual pride and egotistical arrogance. This world really is dependent on "dirt."

A number of apocalyptic currents involve such phrases as "the planetization of the human race" (Thompson, *Darkness* 13 ff). Now, we live on a single globe which has increasingly shrunken during the past century. No more horizons exist for the one who lives in a truly contemporaneous sense. The whole civilized world may be reached by telephone and television almost instantaneously. Airline transport makes any portion of the globe physically accessible within a couple of days.

Indeed, if we are all that close to each other in terms of routine communication and travel, then we are strikingly closer in the sense of the possibility of disagreements with other nations. The weapons of the former Soviet Union (who*ever* has control of them now) and those of the United States, though those land masses are on opposite sides of the blue globe--as seen from space--can make the world red with total war in a matter of minutes. The missiles of one nation can reach the cities of another with incredibly devastating power in a matter of minutes.

Various poets and prophets in this century have pointed out the apocalyptic nature of this age in regard to man's psychic fragmentation and the eruption of his uncontrolled negative side in war which he seems to have more and more opportunity to begin. Well before the beginning of the contemporary age of UFOs, William Butler Yeats--in "The Second Coming" (1919)--speaks in apocalyptic tones of the loss of order and wholeness. After imagining the turning and widening gyres and wheels of the historical process, Yeats notes that the falconer and his bird have lost communication with each other. He sees things falling apart and witnesses the loss of any meaningful center--again the image of the broken mandala.[7] The ending of the poem is one of the most chillingly prophetic ones of this century of horrors. Yeats indicates his realization and asks the question: "What rough beast, its hour come round at last,/ Slouches toward Bethlehem to be born?" (121). A multitude of answers has been given and continues to be given to this day.

---

[7]The mandala, or "magic circle" in ancient Hindu iconography, is essentially a quartered circle or wheel. Jung sees the mandala as a symbol of the deep self, the archetypal center of the psyche, which provides wisdom, balance, and wholeness. Also see José and Miriam Argüelles, *Mandala*.

Yeats' allusion to the symbolic spirals of historical development constantly crossing frontier after frontier seems to be a prophetic allusion to the way history has so accelerated in the twentieth century that by just after the end of the next war, because of the atomic bomb, war itself as a way of settling disputes will have become obsolete. The poem seems to foresee a new type of humanity as emerging in these apocalyptic times, one in whom the aggressive shadow side linking us with the predatory animals may have come to predominate.

On the eve of World War II, W.H. Auden composed "September 1, 1939." He presents humanity's only means of salvation as the unification of its internal oppositions and becoming one *human* race so as to conquer its dangerous tendencies to shadow projection, moral laziness, and intellectual dishonesty--"We must love one another or die" (368). This last stanza of Auden's poem contains a kind of inverted version of the same scene with which the "Contexts" chapter begins--the night with all those bright points of light called stars. But here the night is not only the cosmic darkness of the deep spaces among the stars of heaven but also the moral darkness of the times with perhaps a reference to the black-outs of artificial lighting for the purpose of protection from attack during the World War II years. He sees the individual's vulnerability against the context of night, which may be meant not only as just the night before a battle, but also the dark night of the soul. Instead of the stars, the points of light here might represent those more integrated individuals who can see beyond shadow projection and "us-them" scenarios to planetary unity and individual human integrity, by the power of the mythological being who binds together opposites, Eros. The cosmic context invoked at the beginning of the previous chapter is indeed an alternative to the kind of world of conflict and dissolution which, increasingly, has taken a toll on life in the twentieth century. The refuge from such a world is, indeed, one in which humanity is unified against its complex problems and hopeful about the future. For Auden is able to see communication going on between and among these particular individuals who (despite all absurdities) strive for more depth and wholeness in their lives--those "ironic points of light." Like these individuals composed of dust and Eros, matter and the divine power that unifies opposites, he hopes that, despite all despair, he, too, (the poet himself) may affirm life.

Auden's ideas in this very apocalyptic poem are closely related to Campbell's idea that today our community *is* the planet, not the bounded nation (*Hero* 388). As Buckminster Fuller put it, we are all passengers on a single spaceship called earth (Campbell, *Myths* 262). In the conventional sense, all the frontiers on the planet for nations and peoples to invade and explore have been used up. Few hiding places for wonder, mystery, and newness remain, so (at the end of the twentieth century) humanity is looking also into space. In doing that, it is looking into the *terra incognita* of the human psyche. Humanity looks more and more now to space as the new frontier--"Where no man [sic] has gone before."[8] Space has become a screen onto which are projected archetypal contents. Space is sometimes seen as harboring alien beings who in visiting us remind us of what it is to be human.[9]

The mass of reports of "unidentified flying objects" began about the time that America dropped atomic bombs on two Japanese cities and ended the second world war. The UFOs are clearly parallel to the apocalyptic appearances of divine

---

[8]This is a phrase from Gene Roddenberry's original *Star Trek* series (1966-69) which was changed from "no man" to "no one" for the 1987-94 *Star Trek: The Next Generation* series. Seven *Star Trek* movies were made between 1979 and 1992. Another movie using characters from both shows is being planned for sometime after 1994. *Star Trek* is probably the most creative, hopeful, and humanistic SF project involving both television and cinema ever. It has spawned a myriad novels and comics, and even a few clubs. See also Chapter 11.

[9]Campbell (*Inner Reaches*) touches on this fascination of contemporary human beings with outer space as involving projection from within the human psyche. An excellent example of this *reminding us what it is like to be human* appears in the moving speech by the starman at the diner in Arizona near the end of that early 1980s movie (starring Jeff Bridges and Karen Allen).

beings during times of trouble. In previous ages, individuals or groups looked for redemption in such forms from situations which had become spiritually barren or corrupt.

According to Jung, "The present world situation is calculated as never before to arouse expectations of a redeeming, supernatural event" (*Flying Saucers* 328). The dangerous forces unleashed by human technology, symbolized by the atomic bomb, are clearly related to the state of the Western psyche, indeed, to the *human* psyche. The mass of humanity has lost its living mythologies. The old gods are dead. Further, modern attitudes regarding science have tended to diminish the individual's spiritual confidence as he sees himself in the immense context stretching between the vast universe of logic-defying black holes and ineffable galaxies, on the one hand, and the subatomic particles with their baffling paradoxes, on the other.

The mythology which will be able to give meaning to our new global, universal context probably will not be a revived form of one of the old ones, such as that offered by the fundamentalists or the believers in the Islamic *jihad*. As Jung says, "Desperate efforts are made for a 'repristination' of our Christian faith, but we cannot get back to that limited world view which in former times left room for metaphysical intervention" (*Flying Saucers* 328). Indeed, a scientific discovery, once made, cannot be unmade. It just is not possible for a world of computers and space shuttles to return to a world of lambs, goats, and Roman soldiers.

Most of us no longer *can* believe in purely supernatural anthropomorphic gods like Jove or Jehovah who take an interest in and intervene in human affairs, so we look for a new myth more in keeping with something we can accept. The new myth in the case of that of outer space is based to a great degree on scientific extrapolation onto future possibilities and on pseudo-science pure and simple, as well as all manner of scientific theory and scientific fantasy.

With modern humanity's acceptance of the forward-looking mood of science, for wonder and meaning and depth of experience, we must--in many basic and essential senses--*must* look to the future and to the "final frontier" of outer space and all it implies about our inner space. As Arthur C. Clarke has pointed out on numerous occasions, from a basic or primitive point of view, magic and technology are indistinguishable from one other. Modern humanity's new myths and its envisioning of the wonder and magic in the far reaches of space and time serve the same purposes as did ancient man's stories of gods and goddesses. It now provides the context, the stage on which humanity can see played out the dramas of the deep psyche.

For, as Jung points out, again and again, if an individual loses his gods, for any reason whatever, he will get other, usually more up-to-date, ones. If the people who report visitations of flying saucers are like the peasants who saw Zeus in a cornfield or Odin in a tree, then the contemporary authors of science fiction novels, short stories, and scripts are like the Homers and Virgils of earlier times.

Reports and fantasies of extraterrestrial visitations are closely related to the scientific nature--or at least to the pseudo-scientific understanding--of the modern age. However, at the same time, they contain the same sort of material to be found in the ancient myths of the gods who sometimes visited human beings. In many of the first reports of UFOs, as in visions of gods, the extraterrestrial visitors were said to claim to be watching humanity and its doings, being especially concerned with its recent dangerous toying with the atom.

According to Jung, the sightings of and the fascination with UFOs which has been so rife since the middle nineteen-forties "provides the most favorable basis for a projection, that is, for a manifestation of the unconscious background [or the unconscious context]" (*Flying Saucers* 328). Further, the UFO phenomenon involves the activation of an archetype that has always contained and expressed order, deliverance, salvation, and wholeness. It is the archetype of the self.

The usually "disk-like or spherical" shape of the unidentified flying object is analogous to a religious symbol called the *mandala* (Sanskrit for circle). This symbol, varying in form, is to be found in almost all ages and in all locations. In the far East, the subdivided circle is employed as an object of contemplation. In the West, mandalas are in some senses stylized elaborations on the Christian cross and are frequently found in cathedrals. Many European cities are ordered on the plan of the mandala-like or circular shape. Peoples, tribes, and clans all over the world with religions of all levels of complexity have employed the mandala both in sacred and utilitarian contexts. Native American tribes, for example, incorporated it in the construction of living quarters, shields, and fireplaces. The mandala appears repeatedly in the dreams of modern individuals as a symbol of the attainment of inner balance, harmony, or unity of the psyche (*Flying Saucers* 325-29).

The mandala is, in fact, a "symbolical representation of the *self*." The self includes not just the ego or the conscious mind but also both the conscious and the unconscious portions of the psyche. Jung was anticipated in this idea by the purveyors of Hermeticism during the Middle Ages. Jung says that the archetypal character of this concept "is borne out by its spontaneous recurrence in modern individuals who know nothing of any such tradition." According to Jung most everyone in the modern age is almost entirely ignorant of such ideas and traditions--"which is of course the most unsuitable vehicle for a mythological tradition" (*Flying Saucers* 326-27).

That is, people's being unaccustomed to such symbolisms prevents the ongoing of any *conscious* tradition. It does not, however, prevent their appearing as, for the most part, unrecognized symbols of the self in rumors about strange lights in the night sky or in adventurous quest stories about space explorers.

The goal of the monomyth of the hero and of the psychological process of individuation is to come to terms with this self as an internal archetype, as well as to experience and reach a rapport with other archetypes of the collective unconscious. According to Jung, these archetypes, in symbolic form, are what make up all mythologies in all times, in all places.

Jung suggests that all that is needed to understand the meaning of the UFOs is to pause and think of them as visions seen in the sky in the same sense that gods, demons, or other supernatural beings were seen in visions by humanity in earlier times. If we do that, we see them as part of a larger symbolic context of meaning--in short, the living mythology of space and the future. It is a contemporary form, however fragmented, both of the perennial and universal myth of the hero's quest and of what Jung calls the process of individuation.

Such reports are closely related to the science fiction literary sub-genre, which draws on speculations and extrapolations from the advances made in astronomy and physics in the nineteenth and twentieth centuries, as well as on technological accomplishments such as the airplane, the automobile, and the atomic bomb. Yet while being framed in contemporary scientific, or pseudo-scientific terms, such forms represent attempts of the fantasy, dream, imaginative element of the human psyche to escape from something which is a "wasteland" or "dead-end" situation in a number of respects.

After the end of World War II, the world was split into two halves by the Cold War situation which had increasingly been a concern since the war's end. The United States and the Soviet Union emerged as what later came to be called Superpowers who divided the world between themselves in influence, both in possession of the power of world destruction if their nuclear arsenals were ever used.

Further, not only was the world split in the political/ideological sense, but also the individual was (and is) split within himself, cut off from the deep collective unconscious. This deep reality used to express itself in religious experience, but religion now has become, for many, either a matter of dead ritual or of egotistically fed lunacy.

So, some myth of redemption in an apocalyptic age was inevitable. The myth of the apocalyptic arrival of extraterrestrials more advanced both spiritually and technologically is in a general sense congruent with many scientific ideas popular today. Joseph Campbell argues that any myth must agree with "the science of the time" in order to function in a living sense ("Mythological Themes" 140).

According to Jung, since World War II, life in general has become so strange and threatening that the psyche's natural "projection-creating fantasy soars beyond the realm of earthly organizations and powers into the heavens, into interstellar space, where . . . the gods, once had their abode" (*Flying Saucers* 320).

In the three major sections of his book, Jung covers manifestations of the new myth in three areas: "UFOs as Rumors," "UFOs in Dreams," and "UFOs in Modern Painting." He then discusses the "Previous History of the UFO Phenomenon." Further, he does what he calls consider UFOs "In a Non-Psychological Light" but essentially further discusses the archetypal symbolism of the UFO experience.

Jung finds no reason to doubt that in many cases of rumors of UFOs, a foundation in authentic experience definitely exists (*Flying Saucers* 413). That is, many of the individuals who claim to have seen UFOs are by no means engaging in lying or conscious fabrication. Nor does he find it necessary to assume that they were mistaken and only saw some natural object without recognizing it as such.

In regard to the "collective vision" in which a group of people report having seen a UFO, our skeptical rationalist tendencies seem to make it harder to accept the existence of a collective visionary phenomenon than to accept the hallucination of a single individual. Such tendencies would remind us of the extreme coincidence of more than one individual, especially of a large group having the same vision at the same time.

Jung speaks of "synchronicity," the meaningful coming together of inner experience with some external situation.[10] An individual's having a vision at the same time as does another person might qualify as a case of what Jung calls synchronicity. The degree of synchronicity is, of course, compounded when many individuals share the vision of an object that is not literally present. Jung held that the incidence of synchronicity indicated the play of archetypal forces in the collective unconscious of the individual/s in question.

One kind of movement of the archetypal forces likely in this age of the death of traditional religious consciousness involves the generation of a new image of divinity or of the powers standing above and beyond humanity. Unconsciously, humanity yearns for a new definition of the heroic quest for enlightenment. We want new heroic figures with more universal meanings and "relevance" than Superman or Elvis Presley and other popular heroes that, for all the functions they might serve, never leave the realm of pseudo-myth. The sightings of UFOs involve the same process as that of sightings of and meetings with deities in ancient times.

Further, in regard to collective sightings and encounters, Jung reminds us of the *Zeitgeist* phenomenon:

> the association-processes of many people often have a parallelism in time and space, with the result that different people, simultaneously and independently of one another, can produce the same new ideas, as has happened numerous times in history. (*Flying Saucers* 319)

---

[10]According to Jung,

> Since [UFOs] seem to have appeared more frequently after the second World War than before, it may be that they are synchronistic phenomena or "meaningful coincidences." The psychic situation of mankind and the UfO phenomenon as a physical reality bear no recognizable causal relationship to one another, but they seem to coincide in a meaningful manner. The meaningful connection is the product on the one hand of projection and on the other of round and cylindrical forms which embody the projected meaning and have always symbolized the union of opposites. (*Flying Saucers* 147)

Frequently, a scientific idea crops up "here, there, and everywhere" with no collusion among the various minds involved. Within two years of each other Darwin and Wallace both come up with the theory of evolution. Several physicists make the same discovery in different parts of the world without even knowing that the others are working on the same problem. In like manner, the UFO (as well as all it implies) is an image whose time has come, so to speak.

A proliferation of "sightings" of Unidentified Flying Objects commenced in just such a ubiquitous way at the end of World War II. The whole matter has grown to the point that fragments of a living mythology about aliens from outer space and their visitations to human beings are constantly current in the pulp and paperback press, on television, and in the general consciousness. This has been the case since the fifties. The literary manifestations of this mythology and variations on it range from novels and stories to biographical narratives to books proposing theories about ancient astronauts who seeded this earth with life or at some point in the long past of human evolution gave humanity a marvelous push.

In the "Epilogue" along with its "Supplement," Jung discusses, in regard to psychological/mythological symbolism, three recent works which represent the mythological function at work in literary form. In the first portion of an "Epilogue," he discusses *The Secret of the Saucers* (1955), a first-hand account of experiences with aliens and their vehicles by an airplane mechanic, Orfeo[11] M. Angelucci (418-26). He briefly discusses astronomer Fred Hoyle's 1957 novel, *The Black Cloud* (426-31).[12] In a two page "Supplement," he also comments on John Wyndham's *The Midwich Cuckoos* (1957) (431-33).[13] Jung's

---

[11]Some connection must exist here--even though it may be of a synchronistic nature--with the ancient Greek god, the dead and resurrected musician Orpheus. Yet the songs sung by the twentieth-century Orfeo are eclectic and apocalyptic in nature.

[12]See Chapter 5.

[13]See Chapter 4.

discussion of these documents points the way to the sort of informed commentary on this subject that is needed, but, in themselves, they are hurried statements on pieces Jung had just obtained and had only given an apparently rapid reading.

Jung seems not to have been a regular reader of science fiction or of the other sort of books represented by *The Secret of the Saucers*. In the text proper, he makes reference to rumors such as might appear in popular newspapers and magazines, to a small number of books on the subject, and to the *War of the Worlds* incident. Further, in the main portion of the book, he concentrates, as one might expect, on dreams of patients and on the visual symbolism of certain paintings.

Ultimately, what happens with people like Orfeo Angelucci and others who "see" UFOs and "converse with" aliens is that they project the contents of the collective unconscious outward into places appropriate to their own environment, concerns, and/or contemporary views.

Instead of having visions of angels or Jesus or the Virgin Mary, Orfeo, a 1950s believer in science and technology, sees and rides in unidentified flying objects. He converses with aliens from "out there" in the cosmos. He accepts wisdom from their lips as ancient prophets accepted the wisdom of the voice of God speaking from behind the mountain or from within the "burning bush." Orfeo is not an ancient Hebrew shepherd but a modern airplane mechanic interested in science and in such subjects as cosmic rays, methods of propulsion for vehicles in outer space, and the danger of nuclear planetary suicide.

In general, such a mythology of outer space as what is found in Orfeo's story of his experiences represents a projection onto, as it were, the screen of outer space and the new knowledge and possibilities regarding it. What is being projected onto this screen is always some portion of, or is to be seen in some relation to, the perennial myth of the hero's journey. This journey of the hero, of which the most sublime examples appear in the stories of the Christ and of the Buddha, is in turn a projection of the psychological transformation within the life of the individual, which Jung calls individuation, or the movement toward individual wholeness.

The "flying saucer" of Orfeo's experience is clearly related to the process of individuation, and in turn to the hero journey, by way of its relationship to the previously mentioned worldwide symbol of the mandala as a symbol of wholeness. Jung points out the psychological connection of the rotundum, a symbol of wholeness, and the usual round, saucer or spherical shape of the UFO. Jung says that such shapes as the rotundum and the mandala frequently show up in "situations of psychic confusion and perplexity" (*Flying Saucers* 423-24).

The message that Orfeo brings the world of 1955, obtained during his 1952-53 experiences with the saucers and their lords, takes the form of the wisdom received by the hero on his journey and spoken forth in the symbols of the process of individuation.

His imagery is that of the space age, with reference to propulsion, orbit, and things cosmic. Its specific character, however, is constituted by a combination of an ascetic version of Christianity and of a Hinduism, of the Madam Blatavsky, imported sort. That such is the case becomes clear during his first encounter with the aliens.

On a Friday night, 23 May 1952, Orfeo feels an "odd prickling sensation" while working on the night shift and while on his way home early Saturday morning from the Lockeed plant in Burbank, California. Appropriately, it is a clear night with bright stars (1). On the way home he sees a flying disk: "the fantastic thing could be one of those flying saucers I had read about" (3). After smaller "transmitter orbs" descend from the disk, a voice speaking in perfect English gives Orfeo greetings from "friends from another world" (5). Very quickly these figures take on an aura as of mythological beings. Orfeo gets thirsty, and without his mentioning the fact, the voice tells him to drink from a crystal cup on the fender of his car. The reference suggests such mythological motifs as that of the divine elixir and the Holy Grail. Indeed, after gulping down the contents of the goblet, Orfeo has "a feeling of strength and well being" (7).

The orbs then project a screen showing the heads and shoulders of two beings, seemingly a man and a woman--but with a divine touch. He sees these two as physically perfect beings having an "impressive nobility," their eyes sending forth a radiance filling Orfeo with wonder (7). Radiance is over and over throughout the world's mythologies a godly characteristic, always carrying connotations of transcendence. Orfeo goes on to say that these beings seem to have the godlike characteristic of being omniscient, of knowing everything about his past, and of being able to transmit information to him telepathically (8).

One of these "voices" tells Orfeo that he is the first human being chosen to help the people of earth become "accustomed to the idea of space visitors" (10). The voice says that the aliens have come to help Orfeo's world go through its "'growing pains'" (9). For centuries, flying disks have been recording "a detailed account of Earth's civilization and the spiritual evolution of individual persons" and permanently storing this information in "'synthetic crystal brains'" (10).

The spiritualistic nature of Orfeo's vision becomes particularly clear when he says that the voice noted that these space visitors, these "Etheric entities" do not use space ships or use "[them] only for purposes of material manifestation to men" (10-11). In other words, according to this "voice," these beings really are ultimately immaterial and merely project themselves into the *form* of physical beings who travel in flying saucers.

The myth that Orfeo is experiencing has points of reference in common with at least the popular aspects of certain modern scientific theories. For example, "Approaching the speed of light, the Time dimension, as known upon Earth, becomes non-existent; hence in this comparatively new dimension there are incredibly rapid means of space travel which are beyond man's comprehension" (11). Indeed, Einstein did so generally theorize as to such possibilities. Yet in the myth which Orfeo sees manifested, these possibilities are actualized in the case of the aliens.

One of the "facts" the aliens share with Orfeo is that "Within the Records of Light are [sic] to be found a complete history of Earth and of every entity which has incarnated on it" (11). This factor is a motif--that of what might be called the "eternal record"--has both venerable roots and modern manifestations. The Book of Revelation in the Bible makes reference to the "Lamb's Book of Life," supposedly containing the names of all those whom the blood of Jesus has saved. Orfeo's "Records of Lights" seem to be a bit more universalist, unlike the "Lamb's Book" which includes the sheep but not the goats. Indeed, like that of much of Hinduism, Orfeo's position seems to be that eventually all souls will be unified with the transcendent. Other parallels to the "Records of Light" in the modern mythology of the UFO and science fiction appear in Shirley MacLaine and Philip José Farmer.

In *Out on a Limb* (1983), Ms. MacLaine takes over the similar spiritualistic concept of the Akashic records (200) into her vision which contains reincarnation and various Eastern elements and eventually gets around to the view that extraterrestrial visitors come to this planet regularly, conveying their cosmic wisdom to certain individuals.

In the Farmer *Riverworld* series, an alien race has somehow recorded the life, the being, the blueprint of each human being from the beginning of the species until the year 2004, excluding insane people and children under the age of five, only to reincarnate all of humanity on a gigantic planet in some other star system.

Sometimes the aliens transmit to Orfeo wisdom that is like Hamlet's comment that every villain dwelling in Denmark is an arrant knave. Horatio's reply is that "There needs no ghost, my lord, come from the grave/To tell us this" (I, v, 123-29): indeed, some of the "secrets" the aliens deliver to Orfeo are ancient truisms, yet some of them seem to be relatively new and have come to be repeated many times since then.[14] Thus, Orfeo, through whatever agency, was tapping the themes of the future, as would be expected from his association with archetypal symbols. The "voice" that delivers the first lengthy oration of spiritual wisdom to Orfeo tells him that, "Man believes himself civilized, but often his thoughts are barbaric and his emotions lethal" (12). Of course, this really is quite true.

One motif appearing during this first of Orfeo's contacts with the aliens is the idea that human life on earth has evolved in such a way scientifically and technologically that now life itself on the planet is endangered. According to the voice, that is the reason the aliens have come to earth at this point in history. This view has appeared again and again ever since the UFO reports hit the newspapers in the late 1940s and early 1950s. Jung, in *Flying Saucers*, points out the special attraction that airfields and nuclear bases held then for the legendary visitors (and they still do to some extent). He notes that the conclusion must have been drawn that dangerous developments in technology such as nuclear fission had frightened neighboring planets (316). Jung himself indicates that such fears are in essence real, relating them to the way the world was split in the late fifties between the influence of the two nuclear powers, and that this split between America and the USSR mirrored all manner of splits and schisms in the psyche in the typical modern individual. Much of Jung's analysis with certain revisions fits the contexts of the UFO experience as it moves on toward the end of century.

---

[14]On the same page (12), Orteo is presented with *Star Trek*'s "prime directive" of the mid-sixties in intensly cosmic terms: the laws of the universe will not allow the inhabitants or one planet to tamper with evolution on other planets (the crew of the *Enterprise* is prohibited, nominally at least, from interfering with the life it finds in its journeys through the galaxy).

CHAPTER THREE

THE LITERATURE ON THE MYTH

Space/time fantasy is particularly important because of the apocalyptic nature of the age, which Jung discusses in *Flying Saucers: A Modern Myth of Things Seen in the Sky* Similarly, Joseph Campbell notes that the traditional mythic forms, such as Christianity, provided living myths for much of the Western world for the last two thousand years, and thus background for much of technological modern society. Yet today for many, such materials are no longer very meaningful in the fullest sense of living myth. As Jung says, even humanity in the twentieth century can not live without myth, whether the myth in question be life affirming or life negating.[1]

Now a new mythology is in the process of arising: in a very general sense, it might be called the myth of infinity. Infinite space and infinite time are now the bounds of our universe: the space of the galaxies and the space of the subatomic particles, time leading back into the infinite past and time stretching into the infinite future.

In *The Inner Reaches of Outer Space*, Campbell notes that any new mythology must encompass the new cosmological vision of the universe as one of

> unimaginable magnitude and inconceivable violence: billions upon billions . . . of roaring thermonuclear furnaces . . . our sun among them: many of them actually blowing themselves to pieces . . . new stars with circling

---

[1]Of course, Fascism and Communism, with central myths of collectivism and progress were such substitutes for a living myth. Both had many of the trappings of a religion with "saints" and "bishops" and even inquisitions.

planets are being born right now. And then . . . from . . . beyond all these . . . there come murmurs . . . echoes of the greatest cataclysmic explosion of all--namely, the Big Bang of creation. (28)

The twentieth-century idea of the creation of the physical universe, Campbell suggests, is really somewhat similar in spirit to that of the Roman poet Ovid in his *Metamorphoses*. Its worldview is in major ways removed from the spirit of most of the Judeao-Christian Bible (*Inner* 29) on which the sanctioned myths of the last two thousand years in the West have been based. Central aspects are the vastness of the modern cosmos and its all-pervading relativity. The modern cosmology in the context of which any new myth must arise is vastly changed from that out of which arose the myths at the center of Christianity. The latter context was closed, local, and limited; however, the former is open, vast, and ultimately without any limiting shape. Just as the planet Earth today hosts an essentially "global" society with all segments interrelated, so the cosmological picture is, according to the physicists, one with unseen boundaries and a center so intricately "unified" that the baby dropping a rattle out of the cradle somehow rocks the farthest star.

In an ultimate sense, as Campbell says in an essay in *Myths To Live By*: "There are now no more horizons" (263). The twentieth century is the one in which it has been concluded by many quite thoughtful, quite discerning minds, that the wall between flesh and spirit, matter and mind, is illusory. Such a conclusion arrived at by physicists like Einstein and Schrödinger has much in common with the *philosophia perennis* at the heart of Hinduism, Buddhism, and at some stage at the heart of all of the world religions, even Christianity. Yet a revival of belief in such religions themselves is unlikely.[2]

---

[2]Certain science fiction works revive elements from religions and, in that regard, give new life to them. One example regarding Hinduism is Roger Zelazny's *Lord of Light*, which is discussed by Casey Fredericks (138-41).

What is more likely is the birth of new myths,[3] in literary and cinematic form, based on the same raw material of archetype and instinct, born out of fresh artistic and religious vision, and in keeping, in a general sense at least, with the science of the modern age. Such is what, I propose, has been happening, especially since World War II, in the form of space/time literary and cinematic fantasy.

However, since the start Jung made in the analysis of such matters, a very limited amount of work of any breadth, depth, or concentration has been put forth with respect to the critical study of this mythic material. Scrutiny of *mythic* aspects of space/time fantasy by science fiction critics is generally lacking. Usually these critics ignore for the most part such matters or touch on them only briefly with very little comprehensiveness. Here and there exceptions occur, but certainly the bulk of science fiction criticism is lacking in the mythological/psychological approach.[4]

Overviews, histories of the genre, are particularly prone to give short shrift to the *mythic* aspect of such material. Histories of the genre like Kingsley Amis's *New Maps of Hell* (1959) and Brian Aldiss's *Tillion Year Spree* (1986)[5] hardly mention myth at all. When and if they do mention Jung or myth, it is frequently merely a passing or disparaging reference. The major American journals of science fiction and fantasy, *Extrapolation* and *Science Fiction Studies*, occasionally run articles using approaches to works of science fiction by way of

---

[3]Of course, any new myths contain the same archetypal themes, such as the quest or the shadow side: thus they would bear similarities to ancient or classical myths, even though it is not very likely they will spawn religions.

[4]The work of Ursula K. LeGuin frequently has been treated in regard to Jungian psychology. Occasionally, a Jungian treatment of Clarke or some other science fiction writer will appear in *Extrapolation* or in a collection of essays. However, in general such examinations are rare.

[5]A new edition of the 1961 *Billion Year Spree*.

Jungian psychology or myth on such figures as Ursula LeGuin. But these, however successful in their own right, do not represent what is possible and, I believe, much needed.

In volume 10 of *Extrapolation* there appears Thomas Clareson's transcription of a tape of the 1968 Modern Language Association forum on "Science Fiction: The New Mythology." Until the last portion of that meeting, very little is said that comes anywhere near to addressing the depth of possibility within the topic. Darko Suvin gives a very scholarly overview of the history of science fiction in Russia and the Soviet Union. Isaac Asimov then discusses the utilitarian possibilities of science fiction to serve "science as a recruiting agency" (X-81) and to serve "as a vision of the future" (X-82). While Suvin's talk seems to concern the "literary history" of science fiction, Asimov's concerns seem to be for the most part practical and almost consumer-oriented. Frederick Pohl sees science fiction as a part of the literature of social commentary (X-86). Finally, during the general comment and question period, Robert Silverberg comments "off-mike" that, "I'd like to take issue with every word that has been spoken" (X-94). Silverberg objects to the view of some of the speakers that *the* major purpose of science fiction is prediction. He says that science fiction writers "are working in images and visions and dreams" (X-95). Other voices of like mind to Silverberg's arise. According to Lester Del Rey,

> Science fiction is the myth making principal of human nature today. Previously we had back-looking myths. They always looked back to a golden age . . . . We must have myths of some kind or another. Now we have predictive myths, forward-slanting myths. That is the spirit, the soul of sf [science fiction]. (X-102)

Yet voices like those of Silverberg and Del Rey are clearly in the minority.

Jerry Freeman indicates that he thinks he understands "the Karl [sic] Gustav Jung meaning of myth, where myth is the DNA of living." Further, he thinks that in the present basically two myths operate: a myth of optimism, which he associates with the U.S.S.R. with its apocalyptic view of the classless society somewhere in the future; and a myth of nihilism which he associates with the West. He goes on--having seen the movie "2001" the previous day--to pontificate on the myth he sees embodied in it. He describes it as "a myth in which the tenets of nihilism actualize themselves and realize themselves in the annihilation of the human species by its own hand." Then he adds: "That is largely the myth, for instance, that you could interpret 2001 as an expression of" (X-109). However, he is inaccurate about what is really going on regarding myth both in Clarke's *2001: A Space Odyssey* and in the film of the same name.[6]

Darko Suvin shows an *ad hominem* sort of prejudice when he objects to "the word myth--because of Jung and his people" (X-109). He does not clarify what about Jung or Jung's followers causes myth to be in itself an objectionable word, thus leaving his comment highly suspect. Suvin hints that it is because of both his own misunderstanding of and his rejection of the theory of archetypes that he rejects the use of the term "myth": "You're born with it, you know, and it's your archetypal conscience, and all. So that's why I would not speak of myth" (X-109). "Conscience" seems to have all the wrong connotations for the way it is applied here--but, then, it is not at all clear what Suvin is really trying to say. One would need to know to what the "it"s refer.

David Ketterer's *New Worlds for Old: The Apocalyptic Imagination: Science Fiction and American Literature* (1974) centers on examples of what might be called renditions of the myth of the end of the world. As the title indicates, it focuses only on American literature; it offers a number of interesting

---

[6]See Chapter 12 for a discussion of Clarke's *2001* and *2010*, which treats the motif of the immemorial journey of the hero parallel to what Jung calls the process of individuation and to the mystical road of the *philosophia perennis*. If humanity is there symbolically annihilated, it is only the egotistical, self-destructive part that ceases to be--actually, humanity is symbolically transformed, its negative elements transcended, at least in the one example of David Bowman, the starchild.

insights, yet neither Jung nor Campbell is listed in the index; thus, Ketterer does very little at all in keeping with the approach being used in this book.

Casey Fredericks, a classicist, has published a study with the title *The Future of Eternity: Mythologies of Science Fiction and Fantasy* (1982). Yet the overly generalized nature of "mythologies *of* science fiction" is indicative of the way in which this essay carelessly uses, in many instances inaccurately, phrases like "the Jungian anima," as though the anima were some fiction of Jung's and not an element, a component which Jung merely re-discovered and formulated in the terms of modern psychology. In his concluding chapter, Fredericks refers to Jung's *Flying Saucers* as "crazy," pointing out that,

> Jung saw in the Alien a kind of 'divine midwifery,' . . . modern man feels that he has lost control of his own destiny on his own planet and that our 'salvation' must lie in more powerful beings from outer space--perhaps they will be able to save us from ourselves." (180)

Fredericks, however, is missing a major portion of the implication of what Jung is saying in the monograph. One actual "midwifery" theme which Jung discusses concerning alien invasion is clearly of negative import (*Flying Saucers* 431-33) in *The Midwich Cuckoos* (1957) which had just come to Jung's attention in time for him to write the brief commentary he includes in the two-page supplement dealing with the novel. That is, the "alien" factor in that novel is best seen as essentially a manifestation of what Jung calls the shadow. Yet Fredericks makes almost no use of any of Jung's concepts in his analyses.[7]

Here and there a writer of an essay certainly makes a comment or defends a point in the right direction regarding science fiction as myth. For example, in an article entitled "The Role of Science Fiction," novelist Ben Bova includes a section in which he gives an overview of the work of Joseph Campbell on

---

[7]Despite making points in various instances sometimes coinciding with some Jungian positions (46, 81, 169), Fredericks, in some instances, seems to go out of his way to confuse matters concerning myth and Jung's theory. See also Chapter 16.

comparative mythology, outlining the four functions of mythology and arguing briefly that science fiction serves the functions of a modern mythology (9-11). Bova's sentiments are to the point, yet they are very brief, as are the sections or passages on myth in many other books and articles.

David Hartwell's introduction to science fiction, *Age of Wonders* (1984), touches on the mythological aspect of much of science fiction in a chapter called "Worshipping at the Church of Wonder," one in which it might have been appropriate to deal at length with the oft-mentioned "sense of wonder" in so much science fiction in relation to the metaphysical and cosmological functions of mythology. Yet Hartwell hardly goes beyond this, in itself, interesting comment:

> Science fiction stories are performances, just like the Christian mystery plays of the Middle Ages. In the mystery plays, full of miracles and wonderful paradoxes (he was dead and yet he lives, a virgin has borne a child), the audience experienced in dramatic reenactment the wonders of their faith . . . So "science fiction" has come to signify . . . stories that arouse a "sense of wonder." A science fiction story clothes and enacts in narrative a wonder. (52)

Yet Hartwell makes no use of Jung's theory of archetypes either in general or in relation to discussions of particular works of science fiction.

In many instances, a critic makes a relatively accurate statement concerning myth and science fiction without explaining his meaning in enough detail or dealing with specific examples. For example, Leslie Fiedler, in an article called "The Criticism of Science Fiction," points out that the challenge of criticism is to "identify" a given writer's "mythopoeic power, his ability to evoke primordial images" (10), yet Fiedler does not go on to clarify in detail or to suggest the value of the theory of archetypes or of comparative mythology in thus approaching a work of science fiction in which that happens.

Robert Galbreath, in "Ambiguous Apocalypse," shows what seems to be a very partial understanding of Jung's theory in *Flying Saucers* when he makes reference to "'technological angels' (as Jung called flying saucers)" (55). He makes no use of any of Jung's concepts in his discussion which ranges over several works in regard to which Jung's theories would have been quite appropriate.[8]

Ultimately, then, very little has been done in the way of the application of Jung's and Campbell's theories to a broad range of science fiction literature. Jung himself published no more of any significance on the subject after *Flying Saucers* (he died in 1962), and Campbell never treated the theme at length in relation to whole works of literature. Besides the material in *The Inner Reaches of Outer Space*, he has an essay in *Myths to Live By* called "The Moon Walk--The Outward Journey." There he makes a very useful statement regarding context, the theme of this book's first chapter. With evident approval, he quotes Buckminister Fuller: "All humanity is about to be born in an entirely new relation to the universe" (242). Yet some might argue that for many, such has really already happened.

He discusses briefly the opening scenes from the film "2001," saying, quite accurately, that the "moonwatcher" ape in that sequence represents the visionary consciousness in contradistinction to social or political or utilitarian, merely mundane ways of thinking (247). By no means, though, does he deal with the mythological and archetypal symbolism of the work in its entirety.

Though it does not treat the new myth with any degree of depth or comprehensiveness, "The Moon Walk" contains a number of significant statements, perhaps the most relevant to the present discussion being the one in which Campbell sees the lunar astronauts as voyagers, questing heroes, who have "pulled the moon to the earth and sent the earth soaring to heaven." He sees the quest of the space pioneers as continuing from the earth as our mythological

---

[8]In a note to his article, Galbreath outlines Jung's exercise in science fiction commentary in *Flying Saucers* as well as mentioning certain similar appearances of the theme (177). It is not clear why he thus relegates Jung primarily to a footnote.

mother to "the deserts of Mars" and beyond into the future continuing into spaces "already present in our minds" (252). Campbell here may have reference to three concepts he touches on elsewhere. Kant held that the ideas of time and space were something like built-in perceptual components of the mind. The Newtonian laws of motion are presumably the same throughout all space (if updated by Einstein's theories). The human mind has the magical ability to imagine and creatively formulate, in artistic and mythological senses, realities that the individual may never yet have experienced or may never be able to experience in any physical sense.

Indeed, space and this "human adventure" that, according to the first "Star Trek" movie, "is just beginning"[9], is what has been entering the general cultural consciousness in the last century or so through the mythology of science fiction. The final essay in Campbell's *Myths to Live By* proclaims that the new mythology must be that "of infinite space and its light." The light of infinite space, cosmic light, is that "light of the void" referred to by the Buddhists and really present in some way in mythology ubiquitously. Campbell rightly points out that this light "is without as well as within." He sees human beings as being drawn to such light as moths are allured to a candle (275).[10]

What Campbell says here is quite true, but the "spell" that allures masses of readers and viewers is what is woven into the mythological images, narratives, images, and themes of science fiction and space/time fantasy. Campbell is very sparing in his references to modern mythic literature generally. About science fiction in particular, his commentary is all but nil; the only passage of any

---

[9]"The human adventure is just beginning" is shown on the screen at the end of the first "Star Trek" movie. This story concerns, ultimately, the unification of a human being with an already composite computer lifeform. See the novelization by Roddenberry.

[10]Campbell makes similar comments in the early part of *Inner* (28).

significance is that one reference to the film "2001" in *Myths to Live By* (247-48).[11]

Yet both Campbell and Jung make groundbreaking statements on the new myth, but leave the job of application of these ideas to literary examples for others. Indeed, neither Jung nor Campbell was primarily a literary commentator. Jung was a practicing psychiatrist and psychological theorist, and Campbell, though an academician employed by an English department,[12] was, by his own admission, a comparative mythologist. The challenge implied (perhaps unconsciously) by the seminal work of these two figures has, I believe, been risen to only fitfully. It is the purpose of this book to do something more.

---

[11]In 1982 on the "New Dimensions" radio program, Campbell was asked about UFOs as myth:

> Oh, indeed. . . . spirits from outer space were formerly located in the moon and the sun . . . And now we do have space vehicles in a way that never existed for other traditions. But they had mythological vehicles. When the chariot was invented, the gods drove chariots.
> The rockets . . . people tend, I think, to project them. But--I don't want to say yes or no on UFOs. . . . I think there's enough . . . mysterious evidence that makes one just say, "Well, I don't know what's happening." But certainly the idea is one that fits the mind's tendency to think of creators coming down.

However, he was not being asked for a "yes" or a "no" answer on UFOs. Campbell seems hardly to have considered the questions of the mythology of space in literary form (science fiction) in any direct sense.

[12]Campbell taught in the literature department of Sarah Lawrence College in Bronxville, New York, from 1934 until his retirement in the early seventies (Keen 69).

CHAPTER FOUR

VIRGIN BIRTH, SHADOW, AND TERRIBLE MOTHER: WYNDHAM'S *MIDWICH CUCKOOS* AND ARCHETYPAL SYMBOLISM

John Wyndham's *The Midwich Cuckoos* (1957) weaves together several mythic strands: a twentieth-century version of the virgin birth, the divine child motif, and the archetypes of the shadow and the terrible mother in the form of an alien invasion. In so doing, it portrays the tendency toward projection in a modern world bereft of general belief in traditional myths. The deep currents of archetypal forces are projected onto the contemporary image of an alien invasion.

At the center of Wyndham's narrative is a modern version of the virgin birth. In the modern tradition of "More is better," "woman" becomes "women," fifty-eight to be exact. In the remote English village of Midwich, every woman of childbearing age not already pregnant, suddenly becomes pregnant. This strange event occurs during a twenty-four hour period while the village is under a soporific spell cast by a UFO which has landed in the village. The novel concerns the outcome of these unusual births as well as human reactions to them. An analysis of the piece gives important insights into the psychology of the modern myth of the coming of star children to earth.

The image of collective pregnancy caused by an unknown alien force is a modern version of the trans-cultural mythic motif of the virgin birth. The birth of a divine or heroic personage to an ordinary human mother impregnated by a god concerns, as Campbell suggests, unification of the transcendent, the noumenal and unbounded reality, on the one hand, with the phenomenal world of time and space, categories, and divisions, on the other (See *Hero* 297 ff).

Here, though, the myth appears with new meanings and in a somewhat ironic inversion. The mother is still ordinary woman--or "women" in this case--though certainly not necessarily virginal in the traditional sense. The father god or progenitor, however, is certainly not the traditional Western patriarchal god in the image of the human father in hyperbolic proportions. This time, the progenitor is a kind of *deus absconditus*, a hidden, alien god, perhaps even a demon of sorts. Its purposes and productions are never even begun to be understood. We are forced to assume that He or It comes from the depths of outer space. Its children are "humanoid" but by no means human psychologically *or* physically--they have no individual egos and really fit no known racial category--yet are more intellectually advanced than ordinary human beings and seemingly in possession of inscrutable purposes having nothing in common with ordinary human interests.

Traditionally, the virgin mother is a mythic image of one aspect of that inborn image or archetype Jung calls the anima. The anima, in this sense, is closely related to the down-to-earth aspect of humanity, the earthly, the ordinary, the natural: it is related to emotion and feeling, to life-enhancing value of a mysterious but earthbound sort. Above all, the anima is the benefactress, and the hero which she bestows onto the world represents a positive value (Franz 177-188).

The women of Midwich, however, are typically modern, civilized, middle-class women exhibiting very little character of any kind and very little of the archetypically feminine element. Little rapport of the nature of what the Greeks called Eros exists between them and the men of the village and between them and the children. For the most part, the only way they are tied to the children is by the strange force eventually developed by these changelings or cuckoo children that enables them to keep their mothers from taking them and leaving Midwich.

The children are the shadow-heroes or young gods (or is it "devils"?) that these virgin births have bestowed upon the world. In his less than two page summary commenting on Wyndham's book, in the Supplement to *Flying Saucers: A Modern Myth of Things Seen in the Sky* (431-33), Jung correctly notes that their particular origin and golden-colored eyes point to their kinship with the sun deity of worldwide myth.[1] Traditionally, the sun has symbolized spirit and the transcendence of the negative aspects of life. Yet, also traditionally, the divine hero has had infused into him by his mother some degree of the feminine values of feeling, or valuation, and emotion.

Despite the speedy development of the children--at the age of nine, they have the physical maturity and intellectual capacity of children aged sixteen--they are devoid of feeling. They have no humanized emotions except perhaps those inspired by the "law of the jungle"; they *will* survive at all costs; they have no compassion whatsoever, as seemingly they intend to become the dominant species on the planet. Their use of their psycho-suggestive powers of will to punish parents and other villagers is extreme, causing individuals to do such things as to stick themselves with pins, beat themselves about the head, or run their automobiles into brick walls.

Jung correctly notes their imbalance in favor of something like a hyperbolic version of the traditionally masculine goal of advancement in conscious power and the lack of any of the feminine:

> It is obvious that the sun children, miraculously begotten, represent an unexpected capacity for a wider and higher consciousness, superseding a backward and inferior mental state. Nothing is said, however, about a

---

[1] According to Jung, the children's eyes, with their "quality like glowing gold," "looked like living, semi-precious stones". "if one could disregard the strangeness they had a singular beauty" (136). According to Maria-L. von Franz, stones, as well as the gold of "the philosopher's stone" frequently symbolize the self (205-10). She also points out the appearance of the self as youth or child (199 ff.).

higher level of feeling and morality, which would be necessary to compensate and regulate the possibilities of advanced perception and intellect. Characteristically enough, this aspect does not seem to enter the author's field of vision. (432-33)

Jung, indeed, finds "something definitely suspect about these children" (433). Yet, he does go on to say that, because their group mind status precludes individual development, "Had they been spared an early extinction, they would have founded an entirely uniform society, the deadly boredom of which would have been the very ideal of the Marxist state" (433). That Jung follows that last speculation with the statement that the "negative end of the story remains a matter for doubt" (433), however, leaves the matter uncertain as to whether he fully understands what seems to be the intent of the narrative.

For something quite definite *is* said in the narrative about the lack of such factors as developed feeling and morality. The narrator discusses the relationship between the children and their sometime mentor, home town author Gordon Zellaby, as friendly but impersonal, lacking "the dimension of feeling and sympathy" (128). In other words, the narrative clearly notes the fact that, psychologically, they are lacking in the feminine element.

Jung is clearly mistaken, also, about another question which has an important bearing on our approach to the story as a narrative containing archetypal symbolism. That is the question of the narrative's attitude--some would say the author's attitude--toward the children and the extraterrestrial evolutionary force they represent. Jung claims that

> It is sufficient for him [Wyndham] that the children have a definite advantage of some kind over contemporary man. What if the children should symbolize the germ of some higher potentiality transcending the hitherto valid form of man? In that case the story looks like a time-honored repetition of the hero's threatened childhood and his early death through treachery. (433)

Yet the children represent collectively "the hero" only in an ironic, negative sense. The positive hero archetype, as is suggested by Coomaraswamy, is finally and ultimately identical to God or to the archetypal Self, the central archetype.[2] The hero's quest represents the individual path of individuation, or the development or evolution of the individual psyche toward the ideal of wholeness. The hero is the one imbued with the ambition for wholeness, for oneness with the Father (in mythological terms) or (in psychological terms) the Self. Indeed, this quest is what is enacted in the great culture myths both Eastern and Western, whether it be in the story of the Buddha or that of the Christ.

However, as Erich Neumann points out, in an age of collapsing myths, exploding literary canons, and the forgetting of cultural standards, the "archetypal figures of the Devil and the Terrible Mother dominate the world" (24). The old myth collapses and is replaced by a new one--in some instances a recasting of the archetypal motifs in the terms of a new age. Sometimes the new myth is life-enhancing, but sometimes it is ironic and representative of the destructive and apocalyptic elements referred to by Neumann. Indeed, such is the case in countless science fiction works, *The Midwich Cuckoos* being an excellent example.

At one level, the children represent the shadow, of which the Devil is the chief Western embodiment, as having usurped the place of the hero and of the archetypal Self. These children's circumstances, in a *structural* sense, bind them to the solar hero of Western myth, as Jung points out. Yet in the turn of the events of the narrative itself, they represent the shadow side of humanity, the negative, selfish, ruthless, and empire-building side. They would sacrifice an entire species--the human, in this case--so that their plans could be carried out.

---

[2]According to Ananda K. Coomaraswamy, "In the last analysis the hero is always God, whose only idiosyncracy is being, and to whom it would be absurd to attribute individual characteristics" (*Art* 44).

Here we have the tables turned on a humanity itself already responsible for the extinction of many species, as well as on an erstwhile empire-building white race responsible for the displacement and enslavement of many traditional cultures.

Further, these children represent twentieth-century humanity's darkest fears about its own inadequacies and about the apocalyptic nature of its time, its fears about the future in the form of an invading race or species with intentions of superseding it. Indeed, these seeming sixteen-year-olds are monstrous and terrifying. Having no compunction, no heart, no feeling, they represent civilized man's long repressed, therefore very intense, fears erupting from the archetypal shadow. The blurb on the 1976 Ballantine paperback printing is quite accurate, as to actual facts, in referring to the children as "sixty unbelievable threats to the human race!"

Most definitely, these children do represent apocalyptic fears. In one sense, also, they represent the repressed predatory side of humanity, the animal side he has pretended to banish in order to be "civilized." The children, then, are cast in the role of the animal who survives and dominates by killing if necessary, and has no sense of morality except that of "the law of the jungle."

The other archetype mentioned by Neumann as being particularly prevalent in an apocalyptic age of collapsing traditions, is the Terrible Mother, a negative variation on the anima. She appears in Wyndham's text in the form of Nature as hideous and cruel Goddess as posited by Midwich's writer-sage, Gordon Zellaby: "It is because Nature is ruthless, hideous and cruel beyond belief that it was necessary to invent civilization." Zellaby finds "no conception more fallacious than the sense of coziness implied by 'Mother Nature,'" insisting that "each species must strive to survive, and that it will do by every means in its power, however foul, unless the instinct to survive is weakened by conflict with another instinct" (109). Zellaby's being a humane, kindly, civilized man certainly conflicts with his realization that the children *must* be destroyed because they threaten the *human* species. Yet utterly destroy them he does, with a strong charge of dynamite, while wearing the guise of the kindly magus, the informal and friendly schoolmaster. That he sacrifices his own life in the process points to the insoluble nature of his dilemma.

Zellaby--himself quite conscious of the dilemma-- suggests that "It makes one long for H.G.'s [H.G. Wells's] straightforward Martians" (181), adding that "no solution is morally defensible." He holds that

> "In a quandary where every course is immoral there remains the ability for the greatest good of the greatest number. Ergo, the Children *ought* to be eliminated at the least possible cost, with the least possible delay. I am sorry to have to arrive at this conclusion. In nine years I have grown rather fond of them." (181)

He then hints that he intends to sacrifice himself to destroy this threat to Midwich and the world, pointing out the dangerous decadence of modern society: "Humanitarianism will triumph over biological duty--is that probity, would you say? Or is it decadence?"

The child is an immemorial symbol of transformation, of the birth of what is new and full of potentiality.[3] The potentiality can take any direction, as all mythic symbols are capable of appearing in all manner of ambiguous aspects: not only do they have light and dark capabilities but those of every shade in between. Here the child is an apocalyptic symbol of negative import, representing the unknown and generally unacknowledged depths of the psyche. More insightful

---

[3]Jung discusses positive aspects of the divine child archetype:

> The "child" is born out of the womb of the unconscious, begotten out of the depths of human nature, or rather out of living Nature herself. It is a personification of vital forces quite outside the limited range or our conscious mind; of ways and possibilities of which our one-sided conscious mind knows nothing; a wholeness which embraces the very depths of Nature. It represents the strongest, the most ineluctable urge in every being, namely, the urge to realize itself. ("Special Phenomenology" 135-36)

The child archetype as represented in Wyndham's cuckoos is of a negative cast, but the "ineluctable urge . . . to realize" themselves is certainly there. These beings are totally determined to thrive and certainly have no qualms about wiping out any one or anything in their way.

than his neighbors in Midwich, Zellaby sees the children as, in the world of the novel, they really are--the Enemy. Zellaby has been alone in the village in realizing--from the beginning--that the children represent an invasion of another species from beyond the earth. Symbolically, that could imply "from the unconscious," "from another dimension," or even "from the future."

During a conversation with the narrator late in the story, Zellaby points out our lack of knowledge about the evolution of the human race, the inability of scientists to discover the "missing link" (176-77). He suggests the possibility that what he calls "some Outside Power" (Nature, perhaps?) may have "arranged" this planet as some kind of "testing-ground" for finding

> "whether this time he [She or It would do as well] has produced a successful tearer-to-pieces, or just another torn-to-pieces; to observe the progress . . . and see which of them have [sic] proved really competent at making life a form of hell for others." (178)

Zellaby finds his own "inventor speculations"--akin to the naturalistic and evolutionary cogitations of Shaw's Don Juan in *Man and Superman*--"uncomfortable" (178). In such a scheme, the children would have been sent to exterminate the human species. Indeed, it is clear to Colonel Westcott and to Zellaby that the children's purpose is to survive and eventually to dominate (179). In the final chapter, "Zellaby of Macedon," Gordon Zellaby employs his own shadow side in the form of the guile and the ruthlessness necessary to dispose of the children, heroically sacrificing himself in the process.

Zellaby realizes that "the sanction of power" overrides both social and legal sanctions (183). He tells his wife that they are involved in a situation to which the givens and rules of civilization do not apply. He tells his wife that she is "judging by social rules, and finding crime." She has just alluded to certain acts of the children which should *not* be condoned. Yet he is "considering an elemental struggle, and finding no crime--only grim, primeval danger" (183-84). Zellaby has reference to the situation before or outside of the organized categories called "civilization." Despite everything, he realizes that the only thing to do is to kill the children as quickly and as surely as possible, just as one would kill a threatening lion or a shark. Such is the "law of the jungle," which has no reference to morality but only to the question of one's own survival.

Yet our culture, he knows, opposes "the ruthless liquidation of unarmed minorities." Further, the children have been allowed "to shift the problem they represent to the territory of a people [the villagers] even more ill equipped to deal with it" than are the political and military leaders able to deal with it (180-81). He says that such a shifting of responsibility" is a form of evasive procrastination which lacks any moral courage at all" (181).

In a general sense, he seems to be implying that modern society is decadent and generally ineffectual. No real rapport exists between the leaders and the populace; thus, dissociation ensures that they can not be anything to each other but tacit enemies. The leaders here have no foresight, no ability to imagine how impossible it is for the people of Midwich to solve the problem of these children--a problem that will not simply go away. The people themselves are quite unlike the primitive villages (in other locations, where other such children have been born) whose religious wisdom, however crude, has worked together with their basic instincts to get rid of the children. They are unlike the Russians who have destroyed the whole town of Gizhinsk in order to be rid of *their* star children. The people of Midwich are representative of those modern masses of crushing mediocrity who, living "lives of quiet desperation," are perfectly able to ignore the obvious--here, to close their eyes to the fact that these children are alien *invaders*. The people of Midwich represent a mass humanity able to go on its merry but unconsciously troubled way, acting as though over-population, the possibility of nuclear war, or the possibility of ecological suicide simply does not exist.

Zellaby's letter to his wife written just before the courageous act in which he sacrifices himself to kill the children is glimpsed by Gayford:

". . . no bitterness, my love. We have lived so long in a garden that we have all but forgotten the true face of Nature. It has been said: *Si fueris Romae, Romani vivato* more, which was possibly sensible. It is, however, a more fundamental expression of the same sentiment to say: If you wish to keep alive in the jungle, you must live as the jungle does." (189)

Zellaby seems to have discerned in Midwich a metaphor for the general dissociation of modern man from his roots in elemental things, in the instincts, in living myth. Man has fooled himself into thinking he is now safe because of the triumphs of science and civilization. The shadow and any number of archetypal forces are still quite capable of erupting in such instances as the genocide and destruction caused by the Nazis or by the Cambodians. In earlier times, the archetypes were given natural expression in living myth. Now in the modern world, all the old myths, at least in their old forms, are dead. Humanity lives in the fool's paradise of "civilization," for the most part unable to deal with the depths of experience.

In *The Midwich Cuckoos*, John Wyndham has provided a psychologically sophisticated mythic rendition of the theme of the virgin birth, which here points to the natural and uncontrolled appropriation yet negation of the feminine by a hostile and uncanny force. Further, the seemingly alien children represent the enemy, the shadow motif, as well as being a dark ironic rendition of the divine child of transformation. The force that produced them is sometimes presented as a Nature cruel in its mystery or as a Terrible Mother. As the "hero" of the story, Zellaby represents the modern Western individual who--though perplexed with any number of ambiguities--has the insight to perceive the contradictory nature of most moral questions and to base his actions on an attempt to take a comprehensive view of experience, seeing the depths and the heights as well as the common day of mediocrity.

CHAPTER FIVE

COSMIC LIFE AND HUMAN CONSCIOUSNESS:

ALIEN VISITORS TO THE SOLAR SYSTEM

This theme of humanity's confrontation with aliens of extraterrestrial origin--as seen in Wyndham's *The Midwich Cuckoos*--is an important part of the texture of the modern myth of outer space. Rather widespread and persistent is the mythic motif of the alien as a thing of evil--the bug-eyed monster of the pulp fiction of the forties and fifties, and its descendants. In these more graphically evil embodiments, the alien is, in Jungian terms, essentially and primarily a shadow figure. He frequently represents the evil, the fearful, the bestial, the predatory. He is that which exists within humanity but which civilized humanity, at least, would like to forget about, to put behind itself as having been conquered. In other words, the repressed, rejected side of humanity is projected onto the figure of the alien, the alien thus becoming a kind of scapegoat for humanity's own demons.

This "alien as shadow" motif takes many forms. One is the theme of the arrival of aliens who are seen as wishing to take something from humankind, whether it be water, uranium, children, or the entire planet. Examples range widely. H.G. Wells' classic *War of the Worlds* has alien intelligences on Mars looking at Earth with lustful eyes. John Campbell's "Who Goes There" formed the basis for such predator movies as
"The Thing."[1]

---

[1]Stephen King discusses various alien predator movies/books in *Danse Macabre*, including "The Thing" (144 ff).

In the John Crispin's movie/novel of the early eighties, "V," seemingly humanoid aliens arrive, pretending to wish to buy water from the governments of earth while actually lusting after human flesh for food. This situation is clearly mythic in a highly traditional sense. The shadow element here is associated with the reptile. The Christian devil, has frequently been portrayed as something serpentine or dragon-like.

Such renditions of the mythic theme of the shadow, or dark side of the psyche, represent one level on which the alien motif appears in modern science fiction and fantasy. Examples are quite widespread, sometimes extremely intense, and very important culturally. These shadow figures are usually humanoid or animalistic. Other appearances of the alien theme--especially since 1950--are in important ways quite different from the basic form of the alien as shadow motif.

In such treatments, the alien is still to some extent, or at first, a shadow figure but frequently one with qualities extending beyond the usual symbolism of the shadow. For example, sometimes the alien does not take even remotely humanoid form. Or the alien may never appear on the scene, as is the case in Clarke's *2001: A Space Odyssey* and *Childhood's End*.[2] The reader sees only the alien's possessions and servants. The alien may be a machine of sorts, as in "Star Trek: The Motion Picture."[3]

Further, many such instances portray the alien as the kind of good shadow figure which represents positive aspects repressed or ignored by most of

---

[2] These novels are discussed in Chapters 12 and 9 respectively.

[3] In "Star Trek: The Motion Picture," a gigantic computer ship--a hybrid made partly of the early space probe, Voyager, and the productions of inhabitants of a robot planet--threatens Earth, while seeking its "Creator." A similar theme is involved in the fourth Star Trek movie, "The Voyage Home," in which Earth is endangered by a space probe which has been periodically coming to communicate with the whales; this time the whales do not answer, since they are extinct. Kirk and his crew thus have to bring a pair of whales through time from the twentieth century to keep the probe's insistent "hailing" from destroying the Earth.

humanity. In some instances, the alien force is an embodiment of the superior wisdom of the unconscious, in particular of that dominant, the God-archetype, which Jung calls the self.[4]

Hoyle's *The Black Cloud* and Sagan's *Contact*

Jung himself discusses Fred Hoyle's *The Black Cloud* (1957) in just over five pages (in the epilogue to *Flying Saucers*). He calls the novel "a description of fantasy-contents whose symbolical nature demonstrates their origin in the unconscious" (430). Sir Fred Hoyle is a British astrophysicist known for his championing of the steady-state theory of the universe. Also, in recent years he has helped to formulate a theory that life on earth began from genetic particles which travelled through space on meteors. Hoyle has written (or co-authored) a number of science fiction novels.[5]

In Hoyle's novel, astronomers discover a massive circular cloud of hydrogen moving toward the earth about eighteen months before it arrives. As the cloud arrives, apocalyptic events ensue. The earth's temperature is raised to the point that 7,943 species of plants and animals become extinct (104). Then warm rains fall; insects and plant life flourish fantastically. However, since the heat has, as it were, frozen man in his tracks, no advantage can be taken of the fertility of the desert soil or of the land in general. As the narrator says, "The lord of creation [the human being] was beaten to his knees by his environment, the environment that for the past fifty years he had prided himself on being able to control" (105).

---

[4]In *Psychology and Alchemy* (originally, *CW* 7, par. 44), Jung says that "the self is not only the centre but also the whole circumference which embraces both conscious and unconscious; it is the centre of this totality, just as the ego is the centre of consciousness" (*Memories* 398).

[5]His *October the First will be Too Late* is discussed in Chapter 16.

Here Hoyle sounds the immemorial mythic theme of hubris, a person's egoistic pride in ones own accomplishment and power, which the gods from time to time have to compensate for by sending adversities or adversaries of one kind or another.[6] Now in the modern world, the gods are projected onto forces from outer space, humanity's macrocosmic context. Humanity is brought low and thrown back into something like a primitive state, minus the aid derived from myth and ritual or magus and witch doctor.

The next adversity sent by this alien God in Hoyle's tale is the extinction of all light from the earth. Jung points out another such apocalyptic "black cloud" in Western mythology, in the alchemical treatise *Aurora Consurgens* ascribed to St. Thomas Aquinas: "'Beholding from afar I saw a great cloud looming black over all the earth, which had absorbed the earth and covered my soul'" (427). This motif, appearing in the Book of Exodus and in the Christian Middle Ages, takes on modern form in this science fiction "frolic" Dr. Hoyle hoped his scientific colleagues would enjoy.[7]

The next plague brings more warm rains, hurricanes, and floods, followed by extreme cold and wintery weather. The sky takes on an unnatural faint dull red caused by the heating of the cloud itself as it spreads around the sun (110). When the edge of the cloud reaches the earth's atmosphere, its outer shell is heated to "tens of thousands of degrees." A "shimmering blue" is seen at night radiating from the upper atmosphere: "Perhaps here and there some hardy northern shepherd guarding his flocks may have regarded the violet-streaked night with wonder and awe" (110).

---

[6]Note such examples in the classic Western literature as the Tower of Babel episode (Genesis 11: 1-9), Homer and the Greek dramatists, and the Anglo-Saxon *Beowulf* (c. 800-1000).

[7]Hoyle's "Preface" reads: "I hope that my scientific colleagues will enjoy this frolic. After all, there is very little here that could not conceivably happen."

The deadly beauty here reminds us in the late twentieth century of the beautiful sunsets colored by the ultimately deadly and perhaps apocalyptic pollution in the atmosphere. The example of the shepherd's wonder and awe suggests the fact that in the modern age individuals in different situations are living in different periods, or perhaps simultaneously living somewhat incompletely in more than one period of earth's history and development. Hoyle's shepherd is hardly living fully in the 1960s; in many senses, he is perhaps living in the Middle Ages or in classical Arcadia. People at the end of the twentieth century on various parts of the globe are living what is essentially a tribal existence, even though they may see a jet airplane go over every day or two and even may have access to a few items produced by twentieth-century technology. Ignorant of the apocalyptic fears which plague the astronomers or the industrialists reading their newspapers, Hoyle's shepherd may be free to feel a mystical joy regarding the colors in the heavens, perhaps even (mistakenly) to see them as portents that the bad weather is over.

However, for anyone living anything like *fully* in the twentieth century, the new contexts in which humanity in required to live now will not allow an ancient obliviousness in regard to the starry heavens and our life on this fragile blue-green globe travelling through the blackness, through the apparent emptiness of that context. Certainly, primitive man found terror in the skies as well as beauty therein, but now humanity's whole worldview is so changed that the old forms within which human beings found awe and beauty, hope and fear, as well as images of retribution, have disappeared or changed in meaning. The same archetypal themes, though, play themselves out in the new mythology--whether in the science fiction "frolic," in the space travel fantasy novel, in a television series like *Star Trek*, or in a film like *E.T.*

The temperature in Hoyle's story falls so low that about a quarter of the world's human population dies within a six-week period. Then, finally, the sun returns. The archetypal nature of the cloud is indicated by the fact that the narrator points out that all manner of religions flourish as the apocalyptic event approaches. As darkness remains over the earth, everyone becomes "pervaded in their innermost beings with the emotional complex of the old Sun-worshippers" (116). The narrator says that the undertones of this ancient religious tendency are set in motion and will never again "be damped out."

One might wish Hoyle had expanded on this theme and made what he intended here clearer. As might be expected, this novel written by a scientist in the fifties, contains very little overt condemnation of what humanity is doing to itself and to its world by the overuse and misuse of industrialism and technology. In many respects, a condemnation of sorts is *implied*, though, in the sense that the novel involves a living out of ecological catastrophe and collapse. It is, however, brought about from without--read also "within" in the symbolism of the mythology of outer space. The collective human shadow--the unconscious clustering of all the horrendous things humanity has done with science--is perhaps projected outward onto an astronomical phenomenon.

In its attack on nature, humanity has denied the divinity of nature, of the plants and animals, of the sun and the moon and the stars. The return of those "undertones" of Sun-Worship Hoyle has his narrator to hint at perhaps represents the hope for a compensatory movement away from scientific egotism back toward an enlightened version of the situation in which man realizes his place in nature as one part in a vast whole which he did not make and can not truly control and to which he owes something like reverence.

In regard to the symbolic nature of the cloud, Jung suggests that

> Whenever a confrontation of this kind occurs, there is usually an attempt at integration. This is expressed in the intention of the cloud to remain for some time near the sun, in order to feed on its energy. Psychologically it would mean that the unconscious draws strength and life from its union with the sun. The sun loses no energy, but the earth and its life, signifying man, lose a great deal. Man has to pay the price for this invasion or irruption of the unconscious: his psychic life is threatened with the gravest injury. (*Flying Saucers* 430)

Jung's comments might lead one to see the novel as allegory. The sun might stand for the self or for pure universal consciousness. The cloud might be seen to represent the shadowy unconscious. The earth would stand for the human ego or for the phenomenon of the universal consciousness embodied in psychic life. Yet this scenario is highly problematical. The part about the sun, in particular, is unworkable unless the sun is seen as one of several symbols in the story which point to the self, or universal, "Christ" consciousness. Also the coming together of humanity and the cloud (consciousness and the unconscious) might be seen, symbolically, as a movement toward the recognition of the self.

In *Fabulation and Metafiction*, Robert Scholes suggests that Jung's theory of archetypes makes "a new allegory" inevitable in modern fiction. He disagrees with Jung's insistence that "'an allegory is a paraphrase of a conscious content, whereas a symbol is the best possible expression for an unconscious content whose nature can only be guessed because still unknown'" (53). Yet to disagree with Jung's position on the subject is simply to misunderstand the meanings of the words "allegory" and "symbol."

"Allegory" is appropriate to the literature of a period of agreed upon moral and metaphysical beliefs. The allegorical figures used by a poet like Edmund Spenser stand in simple one-to-one relationship to the consciously understood qualities they represent. However, the symbolic tradition beginning with nineteenth-century romanticism involves itself with realities (or at least with understandings) which are not commonly and consciously understood by a body of believers, as was the case in Spenser's age. The symbol--which is more multifaceted and variable than the allegorical figure--embodies archetypal contents in periods when religious orthodoxies are either moribund or in clear decline, or when the archetypes are embodied in pure myth with no, or very little admixture of, intellectualizing.

Hoyle's sun, cloud, and earth are not allegorical figures but true symbols. For one thing, no simple one-to-one relationship exists. First, before anything, we have here a story. The sun is the sun, and the earth is the earth. Then, as symbolic elements, they *suggest* a number of associations and meanings--some based on things that have been associated with them since history began and some because of the plot arrangements of the particular story.

Perhaps it is sensible to point out, as Jung does not, that one association to be drawn is the fact that mythologically two basic kinds of consciousness exist as distinguished from the shadowy elements of "the unconscious." Traditionally, the sun is a symbol for the concept of what might be called undifferentiated, "divine" consciousness, *pure* consciousness. Yet such a symbol points to an unknown, a mystery showing some similarities to the image of God in the Christian Middle Ages but many differences as well in that today very little is agreed upon in regard to it. The earth would thus suggest human daylight consciousness, the world of conventional realities, the world of human technological powers--but certainly not any single agreed upon reality.

After the cloud, in the form of a gigantic disc, has paused near the earth, radio transmission stations have trouble transmitting messages because of the atmospheric ionization (119-21). Soon it is discovered that the patterns of ionization are predictable. One of the scientists theorizes correctly that "the cloud contains an intelligence," that really the cloud is a living being. Kingsley, one of the major characters, also decides correctly that the cloud came to the sun in order to refuel on light energy (134).

One of the responses Kingsley gets for his refueling theory is that "'This comes of reading science fiction'" (132). Certain aspects of science have become such matters of orthodoxy and blind faith in the form of certain opinions which most scientists refuse ever to question that, to many, such a suggestion that the cloud's activities could be intentional is to be rejected out of hand as an absurdity. Indeed, many see no value in science fiction as anything at all but escape literature, despite the fact that science fiction and the things associated with it are coming more and more to serve the purposes of a modern mythology and in general to stretch the imagination and intellectual flexibility of individuals. At one point, Professor Kingsley comments: "We're all inhibited against such thinking. The idea that the Earth is the only possible abode of life runs pretty deep in spite of all the science fiction and kid's comics" (142). Yet even as Hoyle was writing that, a change in the Zeitgeist was occurring. Science fiction was about to become respectable in the universities, the UFO legend that began in the forties was growing and becoming diversified, and by 1986 a writer could get a million-dollar advance for his account of his own abduction by little grayish-white people.[8] Many people at all levels of society now are interested in one way or another in the possibility of alien life.

The latest computer is used to set up an apparatus for communicating with the cloud. After sending a message of scientific and mathematical materials, as the best common denominator, the scientists receive a return message: "'Message received. Information slight. Send more'" (144).

The cloud learns a great deal about communicating with human beings and gives the scientists a code to use in communicating with it. It tells them a great deal, from its own point of view, about their deficiencies as a species. It refers to them as "animals with technical skills inhabiting planets which are in the nature of extreme outposts of life" (149). The cloud points out that since human beings live on the surface of a planet exposed to its gravity, their size, and therefore their "neurological activity," is limited. Since they have to have muscles for movement as well as skulls for protective armor, brain size is limited: "'By and large, one only expects intelligent life to exist in a diffuse gaseous medium, not on planets at all'" (149). The cloud says that the building of chemical foods on a large scale is impossible without starlight, thus leading to "'a tooth and claw

---

[8]Horror novel author Whitley Strieber received a $1,000,000 cash advance on *Communion* which narrates his encounters with little ash-colored creatures who, he claims, abducted him several times, both in 1985-86 and at various periods earlier in his life (Klass 21-22; Taves 90-96).

existence in which it is difficult for the first glimmerings of intellect to gain a foothold in competition with bone and muscle'" (150).

The cloud's comments suggest the whole subject of speculation concerning the possibility of various forms of intelligent life throughout the universe, a subject broached in all manner of books on the subject by scientists and philosophers. For example, in *God and the New Physics* (1983), Paul Davies comments on such possibilities as those discussed in *Life Beyond the Earth* by Gerald Feinberg and Robert Shapiro:

> They argue the case for life based on plasmas, electromagnetic field energy, magnetic domains in the vicinity of neutron stars and a variety of bizarre systems. Now consciousness and intelligence are software concepts; it is only the pattern--the organization--that counts, not the medium for its expression. (Davies 210)

Indeed, the peculiarly human tendency to which Davies alludes--of judging purely by externals--is one of the habits which makes it hard to come to terms with our own shadow projections. We project our own dark sides onto that which is unusual or different. If we cast our shadow projections onto those who are different in respect to race, to religion, or to national origin--how much more would we do so with conscious beings based physically on different molecule patterns?

One of the mythic functions of the sort of alien encounter story as this one is to play out this problem of the confrontation of the shadow on the cosmic scale. The American and the Soviet governments in this story act on common human shadow projections and thus fire nuclear weapons at the cloud. They are acting on what one of the scientists would call the view that it is "'axiomatic that any non-human intelligence must be evil'" (162). This view is an enlargement of the general shadow mechanism of distrusting anyone who is non-American, or is non-Soviet, or belongs to a different group, or is in some way alien. The cloud retaliates for the aggressive act by reversing the direction of the rockets. More than a quarter of a million people are killed. The cloud obviously has no more scruples about killing than do the superpowers. Even before this event, one of the scientists, commenting on the possibility of reprisals from the cloud, alludes to its mythological nature: "'You know in a way this is remarkably like some of the ideas of the Greeks. They thought of Jupiter as travelling in a black cloud and hurling thunderbolts'" (171). Adherents of the religions with the Roman mythology at its core believed that Jupiter exacted just revenge on those who had committed "hubris" and over-stepped the bounds of decency. In the eyes of the United States government, particularly, though,

> the hydrogen [bomb] deaths were murder, murder on a gigantic scale, perpetrated by a small group of desperate men [the scientists studying the cloud are here being blamed], who to gratify insatiable ambitions had allied themselves with the thing in the sky, men who were guilty of treason against the entire human species. (174)

In other words, the perpetrators of the aggression place the blame on another group--the politicians and the military leaders blame the scientists, who hardly seem guilty of any direct aggression. In making this totally unfounded accusation, they succumb to shadow projection or rather to failing to see their own complicity in the megadeaths but seeing it in another group.

Soon after the matter of the rockets, the cloud tells the scientists that it is about to leave the vicinity of the sun. In answer to their question as to why it has decided to leave, it begins by commenting on earthly religion. The cloud can make no sense of religions which imagine entities residing outside the universe, since by definition the universe contains *all* that exists. It holds that the concept of a "god" having invented the cosmos is "a mechanistic absurdity" indulged in by way of anthropomorphistic thinking because of the ability of human beings to make constructs (177).

Yet, says the cloud, many mysteries remain. The cloud maintains that its own intelligence is of a higher order than that of humanity, but it wonders if intelligences higher than its own exist somewhere. Though it has never found such an intelligence, it believes that "'such an intelligence does play an overwhelming part in our existence'" (177). It believes that such a superior intelligence would be necessary for any order or laws of physics to exist, for these specific laws to exist but no others.[9]

This matter of the possibility of an informing principle or pattern of order throughout the universe is related not only to the myths about gods but to Jung's ideas of the self. According to Jung, the self is the deepest aspect of the psyche, in fact the psyche's most primary informing principle, which is a "psychoid" phenomenon in some way mirroring nature at large.[10] The self has much in common with the Atman which Hinduism sees as the individual incarnation of the Brahman, or the supreme god or One of the universe.

In *The Doors of Perception*, Aldous Huxley discusses C.D. Broad's theory of a Mind at Large. According to this theory, each individual consciousness is theoretically at any moment capable of remembering all that has ever happened to the individual and of perceiving all activity everywhere in the universe. The reason the individual does not so remember and perceive thus is that one major function of the brain and nervous system, on this planet at least, is to act as a reducing valve to filter out all but what is relevant to the life of the individual (See also Hoyle 22-23ff). What the cloud describes as a higher intelligence than itself is a motif in the new mythology of space related to the Jungian idea of the self.

Another such version of the self from recent science fiction which parallels Hoyle's novel in certain ways is found in a novel by another astronomer, Carl Sagan. Sagan's *Contact* (1985) tells the story of the first contact with

---

[9]See the discussion of Sagan's novel *Contact* later in this chapter (108-11).

[10]According to Jung, in *The Structure and Dynamics of the Psyche* (originally in *CW* 8, 436), "The collective unconscious . . . represents a psyche that . . . cannot be directly perceived or 'represented,' in contrast to the perceptble psychic phenomena, and on account of its 'irrepresentable' nature I have called it 'psychoid'" (*Memories* 397).

extraterrestrial intelligence, from the point of view of a female radio astronomer, Ellie Arroway. After receiving intricate messages from a planet in the Vega system, she and other scientists are able to carry out a massive program to build an object outlined in certain directions sent to Earth by the Vegans.

The object seems to be a space craft of some kind. On the day that the object is to be functional, Ellie and four other scientists get inside the thing and close the door. From the points of view of those gathered to observe the "blast-off" nothing happens: yet the astronauts come out of the thing after a few minutes telling strange tales. Ellie and the others travel to the Vegan system through a kind of trans-dimensional tunnel. They meet Vegans in the physical form of human beings now dead yet each of whom at some time had a strong emotional connection to one of the travellers. Ellie, for example, converses with her beloved stepfather who died when she was ten. She is told that the Vegans did not build the trans-dimensional tunnels, that they merely found them. They do not know who built them, only that whoever did left the Vegans' part of the universe a very long time ago. They believe that those higher intelligences are on a level with what might be called "gods." The Vegans believe that those unknown intelligences are actually responsible for the laws that rule nature.[11] They have even hidden messages in the very structure of mathematics. Here, God seems to be a mathematician. As Ellie tells the Reverend Palmer Joss, "Whoever makes

---

[11] In a *Star Trek: The New Generation* episode (probably during the 1992-93 season), the *Enterprize* is shown on the trail of the components of a computer program somehow made up of "messages" embedded in the very DNA of organic matter spread across the galaxy. A Klingon and a Cardassian ship are in quest of the same information. When, despite various complications, the program is run, the hologram of a humanoid being of indeterminate sex appears before the warring tribes to deliver a poignant message: This species existed long ago, and a cosmic loneliness prompted it to spread its DNA across the galaxy; if its far-flung decedents have indeed found the message, then whatever differences warring branches of its decedents, the fact that some are viewing the hologram means that hope exists for unity among these intelligent descendants.

the universe hides messages in transcendental numbers so they'll be read fifteen billion years later when intelligence finally evolves" (418).

The Vegans tell Ellie that "There was a Galaxy-wide civilization that picked up and left without leaving a trace--except for the stations [of the trans-dimensional tunnel]" (365). They have no idea where these godly beings went but expect them to return someday, thus seeing themselves merely as caretakers. The impression conveyed by the Vegan is of these predecessors as having definitely had material form, at least at the time that they used the tunnels. It can be inferred that perhaps they have broken the bonds of flesh and blood and now exist on other non-physical levels.[12]

Some time after Ellie's journey across the galaxy, a computer program she has devised finds the message in the calculation of the ratio mathematical *pi*. After running and running, the program finally prints a sheet of 0s containing in the middle a circle traced by 1s. The circle is, on earth, a universal symbol for God or the self as seen in mandala icons East and West. Ellie realizes that an intelligence well beyond that even of the tunnel builders did this. Some thinking, creative entity build this message into the very structure of mathematics:

> "It's already here. It's inside everything. You don't have to leave your planet to find it. In the fabric of space and in the nature of matter, as in a great work of art, there is written small, the artist's signature. Standing over humans, gods, and demons, subsuming Caretakers and Tunnel builders, there is an intelligence that antedates the universe." (*Contact* 430)

Hoyle's cloud also alludes to the possibility of such an intelligence. The cloud says that if such an intelligence does exist, it is not limited by time or by space in any way (177). About two thousand million years ago, one of the intelligent clouds claimed to have answers to questions about such a supreme

---

[12]See Chapters 9 and 12 for discussions of works by Arthur C. Clarke which touch on the evolution of beings beyond the realm of "flesh and blood."

intelligence. In the time between broadcasting the claim that it had a solution and the time that this cloud would have sent the answer, this cloud simply vanished. The same thing occurred again about four hundred million years ago, and has now happened for a third time. Hoyle's cloud now is going to the area where this last event occurred in order to investigate.

The cloud says that some clouds have thought that the said cloud with the message committed suicide. Suicides of clouds caused by abnormal neurological conditions have at times occurred in the form of vast nuclear explosions. Yet in the two previous instances of a cloud's disappearing after claiming an understanding of higher intelligence, no traces of such a nuclear suicide were found. The present cloud hopes to settle all arguments as to what actually happened.

Two possibilities come to mind. Of course, it could be argued that the three clouds came to such a nihilistic realization that they despaired and thus committed suicide. On the other hand, it could be that the clouds in question reached a realization that precipitated them into another level of reality. Perhaps these clouds, like questing heros, are to be seen as experiencing a kind of transformation--one in which matter is converted into pure energy. Perhaps the same thing happened to them that happened to the tunnel builders here in Sagan's novel. Perhaps, it transmuted them into a totally non-corporeal form. At any rate, the motif is left open-ended.

Most communication has been one way, information from the human beings flowing to the cloud. Concerning the possibility of the cloud's giving anymore information to human beings than what it already has given, the cloud is hesitant:

> "there may be inherent limitations . . . to the type of information that can be exchanged between intelligences. . . . It seems as if any intelligence that attempts to pass on such information [regarding "the deep problems"] gets itself swallowed up in space, that is, space closes about it in such a

> fashion that no communication of any sort with other individuals of a similar hierarchy is possible." (*Black Cloud* 179)

The scientists are eager for all the information the cloud can give to them and thus to humanity. This is a motif similar to that later appearing in Sagan's novel. Hoyle's scientists arrange an apparatus in the nature of a "teaching machine" which the cloud describes for them. Two volunteers in succession are driven into delirium by wearing this "thinking cap" device. It seems that these men are killed by the contradiction between their old ways of thought and the new ways, the new circuits that are established alongside the old in order for them to receive the cloud's direct information. Jung's conclusion, in *Flying Saucers*, is that

> Nothing is learnt of the contents from the other side. The encounter with the unconscious ends bootlessly. Our knowledge is not enriched; on this point we remain where we were before the catastrophe. The only thing is that we are at least half a world poorer. The scientific pioneers, the spokesmen of the *avant-garde*, prove too weak or too immature to receive the message from the unconscious. (431)

In important respects, Jung is excessively pessimistic. Surely, the experience as a whole is likely to have a maturing effect on the species ultimately. Jung really is a bit hard on the scientists. He might have spoken more to the point if he had said that the specialization and differentiation of their consciousness may have been what caused their problems. Indeed, as some characters realize, the effect might have been quite different if the unlettered worker Joe Stoddard, instead of the highly trained scientists, had been set up to receive the cloud's knowledge.

Jung sees the cloud's visit rather too allegorically when he sees it as "equivalent to a general catastrophe, such as we have experienced in National Socialism and are still experiencing in the Communist inundation" (430). Yet it is better to see the cloud symbolically, instead of allegorically. Indeed, in some respects it symbolizes the shadow, the dark side as was at work in the Nazis. However, by no means is it to be seen as that alone. The cloud is not engaged in projecting its shadow as was the case with the Nazis in regard to the Jews and the

Slavs. The human species projects its own shadow onto the cloud and exhibits familiar paranoia in the incident of the missiles. Though the cloud does send the missiles back, in important respects the cloud represents those aspects of the shadow related to that which is merely unknown but not *necessarily* evil, perhaps even to the darkness which precedes the discovery of the self.

In the epilogue to *The Black Cloud*, John Blythe, the confidant of the narrator (one of the scientists, John McNeil), speaking in the year 2021, says he is the only one with remaining copies of the code used to communicate with the cloud. He wonders whether he should distribute copies of the code to enable humanity perhaps some day to re-establish communication with such a cloud: "'Do we want to remain big people in a tiny world or to become a little people in a vaster world?'" (191). Indeed, making the second choice leads to, or is made possible by, a diminution of egotism. In general, the desire to meet with higher intelligence is just that, a desire--perhaps unconscious--to go beyond the ego into the realms Jung mapped out as the process of individuation. That road has been walked by heroes in all ages and lands in their journeys toward coming to terms with the ultimate God.

Arthur C. Clarke's *Rendezvous with Rama*

Arthur C. Clarke's *Rendezvous with Rama* (1973) is an alien encounter novel concerning human exploration of a giant cylindrical space ship or cosmic ark as it passes through the solar system in the second half of the twenty-first century. Like the cloud in Hoyle's novel, "Rama" comes into the solar system and to our sun to refuel, a fact not known until after the exploration of the gigantic object named after the Hindu deity.

Ironically, Rama remains in many important respects a mystery even to the point of its taking no notice of humanity, its missiles, or its civilization. The irony of the situation emerges strongly when the comment at the end of Clarke's third chapter is seen in retrospect: "The long-hoped-for, long-feared encounter had come at last. Humankind was about to receive the first visitor from the stars" (12). For the visitor passes through the solar system, in important respects, never met, never understood. In many important respects, the Ramans, though never met, are here symbolic of deity of a sort, particularly a *deus absconditus* of mysterious origin and unknown purpose.

When the space probe *Endeavour* has docked with Rama, Commander Norton and a crew member find, on the flat surface of one of the ends of the cylindrical object that is Rama, what looks like a spokeless wheel perhaps meant as an instrument for opening a door to the interior: "Then he noticed, with growing excitement, that there were deeper recesses at the ends of the spokes nicely shaped to accept a clutching hand (Claw? Tentacle?)" (20-21). Norton is here indulging in the old shadow projection of regarding the alien being as bug-eyed monster, the intuition that the alien must be something prehuman and bestial. Yet it is indicated that this attitude is not particularly strong among the astronauts. Norton and his crewman soon try turning the "door knob" clockwise to open and find it will not budge. Then they realize that no reason exists for clocks and corkscrews on Rama to turn in the same direction as those on earth. Indeed, their thoughtfulness has results, and the door is opened for the exploration of Rama.

The interior of Rama is fifty kilometers long and sixteen kilometers wide. If the place where the astronauts enter is considered the top, then down toward the bottom, clinging to the wall of the cylinder, is what the astronauts dub "the cylindrical sea." Inside, Rama is a world, a world these astronauts have only a few weeks to explore. Rama seems to be a "space ark," a worldlet fashioned to transport alien beings, and their descendants, over long interstellar distances. Conrad Tsiolkovsky and J.D. Bernal predicted such possibilities early in the twentieth century (41). The centrifugal force of Rama's spin gives it its own gravity.

It is calculated that more than two hundred thousand years have gone by since Rama passed near any star. It is no wonder that Commander Norton feels like an Egyptologist entering the tomb of a long dead Pharoah: Yet "Tutankhamen had been buried only yesterday--not four thousand years ago; Rama might be older than humankind" (33). Norton's first view of Rama's gigantic interior is one lighted by flashlights.

In the myth of science fiction, the wonder that humankind has found in the ancient or immemorial past is projected onto a new screen, that of vast space and unimaginably long time. About the mysterious Ramans the astronauts wonder, "who were they, *and what went wrong?*" (40) on seeing no life within Rama. They marvel as such artifacts appear as the "huge spike, kilometers long, jutting along the axis, with six smaller ones around it" (39). The question of the meaning or use of such objects is as unanswerable as is the one as to the exact destination of Rama. It is realized that Rama's journey has lasted at least two hundred thousand years and perhaps above a million (44). One of the scientists on the "Rama committee" speculates that they may have been "fleeing some disaster--but they miscalculated" (44). Despite the haunting mysteries of Rama and his being totally convinced that the Ramans are dead, Norton still finds the coming of Rama as fortunate: "We are not alone. The stars will never again be the same to us" (45).

Mythologically and psychologically speaking, such an event as the coming of Rama would have unprecedented effects. It would be on an order with the confirmation of Copernicus's heliocentric theory. It would change humankind's whole relationship to everything. Even the contemplation of such an idea in science fiction and speculative literature can be seen as embodying already a new myth, one more in keeping with the point of view of the perennial philosophy which holds that all life is, in the mystical and occult sense, One. According to the new myth, life is spread everywhere throughout the entire universe. Further, such a myth inherently contrasts with most of the egoistical and patriarchal social stances of Western civilization.

Clarke even gives examples of the already existing new mores perhaps related to the anticipation of such discoveries. These involve matters of sexual orientation and conjugal arrangements. Two of *Endeavour*'s officers are bisexuals. Mercer and Calvert have had "an apparently stable liaison" for years. For the past five years, they have shared a wife on Earth, a wife who has borne each of them a child. Commander Norton has two wives and two families on both Earth and Mars. This arrangement seems to be relatively common. The wives know about each other and exchange seasonal greetings, though they have not had the chance to meet. Even if such situations involve only a small percentage of the population, Clarke seems to be portraying a future in which society is seemingly moving away from such phenomena as homophobia and sexual jealousy. Such toleration would seem to accompany the probable cosmopolitan attitudes of a planetary state such as Earth, now that has begun to colonize the solar system.

Yet some of humankind's immemorial problems are still here. The Hermians, descendants of the first settlers of the Mercurian moon, are--if one is to judge from their ambassador on the "Raman committee"--quite paranoid about Rama:

> "Even if there are no life forms aboard, it [Rama] may be directed by robot mechanisms, programmed to carry out some mission--perhaps one highly disadvantageous to us. Unpalatable though it may be, we must consider the question of self-defence." (109)

These seemingly calm considerations actually veil an intense paranoia evident when the stance of the ambassador is seen in the context of the rest of the Rama Committee. Such tendencies indicate the psychology that makes people project their own repressed fears, insecurities, and moral darknesses onto any being seen as alien. What would in earlier centuries have been seen in another race or nationality is now seen in another species from another star system and even from another time.

Those indigenous to Mercury are forever exiled from earth because of the gravity there three times that on earth. Thus, according to Clarke, "inevitably, they claimed that they did not want to" visit Earth (221). Furthermore, "they affected a rather swaggering toughness that did not bear a moment's serious examination" (221). Yet, in many ways they really are "tough," a rather Spartan crew of pioneers. Forever on guard to protect themselves from the nearby sun and the Mercurian environment, they react to the approach of the alien craft with fear and aggressiveness as do both Americans and Russians in the Hoyle novel. Given the Hermians's shadow projection and aggression, it is significant that Clarke points out that "To most people, Mercury was a fairly good approximation of Hell; at least, it would do until something else came along" (111). The Hermians try to do something about what they see as a threat.

Their missile does not reach Rama. It is likely that if it did, Rama would show itself as capable of protecting itself as is Hoyle's cloud. The missile is rendered harmless by Lieutenant Boris Rodrigo, who approaches the missile in a small vessel called a scooter and disarms the bomb. Boris has a special reason for volunteering for this risky mission. Boris, the only overtly religious person Clarke here introduces, is a member of the Fifth Church of Christ, Cosmonaut (61). The "Cosmo Christers" base their Christian theology on the view that Jesus was a visitor from outer space.

Such a projecting of the Christ myth rather than some totally new image of the archetypal self onto the canvass of space is one more way that the new cosmic context interacts with the collective unconscious. Boris sees Rama as an unoccupied cosmic Ark sent for those worthy of salvation. He says that it may not be the "Second Coming" but surely must be the "Second Judgment." We never hear where the sheep separated from the goats are to be taken. Nor do we hear what Boris's response is to the fact that his theological theory turns out to be in error.

Much more exists of a mythological function in Rama than the episode concerning Cosmo-Christianity, though. For instance, here is the motif of mystery and wonder and the certain knowledge of a vast and godlike intelligence unimaginably older than humanity associated with Rama. This is a reliving of the drama of the self, the archetype behind all mythological Father gods of power and grandeur. The self, according to Jung, is the center of the wonder that is the psyche, yet in some strange sense it is also the center of the entire cosmos. The self archetype is here projected onto the wondrous but never actually visible Ramans.

One of the attributes which the Ramans as *deus absconditi* take on is that of creators of vast foresight, vast power, and vast age. If 200,000 years have passed since Rama passed any star, as is suggested, then it is truly ancient by all human measure. Even though it is thought at one point that Rama represents a project that somehow went wrong, at the end of the novel we realize that such is probably not the case. Rama is on a journey and has entered the solar system in order to draw fuel from our sun.

While the crew of the *Endeavour* explores the interior of Rama, they observe an image of the creation and evolution of life on a microcosmic scale. When they enter this vast world, all that exists is utter darkness. Then, as Rama moves closer to the sun, three artificial suns spread light throughout Rama. The image is that of the instantaneous command of a deity to "let there be light," and, suddenly, light indeed exists.

The internal temperature of Rama is so low that the sea at the far end of the cylinder is frozen. Soon, this sea thaws and becomes what Surgeon Commander Ernst calls "an organic soup" (126). All the building blocks of life are there. The transformation of the water from blue to pea green takes such a short time that one of the officers comments: "In a couple of days! It took millions of years on Earth" (126). Says Laura Ernst, "Rama's Shot through the anaerobic stage and has got to photosynthetic plants--in about forty-eight hours" (127). The intelligent beings who built Rama had the ability to create, like a mythological deity, about as quickly as presented even in the version starring the Hebrew God.

As the explorers go about their business, toward the end of their time in Rama various "animals" begin to appear: some are vaguely similar to such animals as crabs, starfish, and sharks. Others are of stranger configuration. One spiderlike animal with three eyes and three long stiltlike legs is dissected by Dr. Ernst, who gets the shock of her life when she cuts into it (204). As it turns out, the animal is mostly a kind of battery (208). It shares characteristics with electric eels and rays on earth. Yet this animal neither breathes nor eats; in fact, it is like a kind of mobile eye. Dr. Ernst does not think such a creature could have evolved naturally but was *designed* for a specific purpose. In fact, it is implied that such is the case with all the "animals" which have been appearing. The explorers decide that these "animals" are part of the crew (209). The machine-animals are presumed to have definite functions; they are dubbed "biots" (214).

One of the features of the interior of Rama is the appearance of clusters of structures that give the appearance of cities made up of what seem to be buildings without windows or doors. They also involve strange "interlocking spheres and crisscrossed tubes" (77, 84). While some of the crew are examining one of these cities, one crewman remarks that perhaps it is not a city at all but a "factory for making . . . Ramans" (137). This turns out to be a likely hypothesis.

Just before the explorers leave Rama, they cut into one of the "buildings" in one of these "cities." Inside, they find "hundreds of vertical crystalline columns, about a meter wide and stretching from floor to ceiling" (249). One officer realizes that from certain angles of view, the columns are perfectly transparent yet not under all illuminations: "As one walked around them, objects would suddenly flash into view, apparently embedded in their depths like flies in amber, and would then disappear again" (250).

It is decided that these are catalogues of a sort, containing the blueprints for things which could be synthesized from "patterns stored somewhere" (251):

> Hand tools (though for huge and peculiar hands), containers, small machines with keyboards that appeared to have been made for more than five fingers, scientific instruments, startlingly conventional domestic utensils, including knives and plates that apart from their size would not have attracted a second glance on any terrestrial table: they were all there, with hundreds of less identifiable objects, often jumbled up together in the same pillar. (251)

Commander Norton realizes that this may be a kind of catalogue in three dimensional images. It is assumed that the objects shown would, like the biots, be actualized at the appropriate time. The explorers find their only evidence of the physical characteristics of the intelligent beings who built this world. They find the pattern for "an elaborate harness, of uniform," obviously made for a creature rather taller than a man and seeming to have three arms and three legs (252-53).

As soon as this discovery is made, a call from a crewman outside the "building" informs the explorers that Rama's lights are going out. Soon a high-pitched whistle and light signals summon all the biots into the cylindrical sea, and as they dive in, they are torn to pieces by the shark-like biots, presumably created just for that purpose. It seems that after their job is done, the biots are to be reabsorbed into the primordial sea which gave them birth. Rama's cylindrical sea, like the great Mother Goddess of the old mythologies, is associated with both birth and death, both creation and destruction.

As the *Endeavour* leaves Rama, the giant world gains speed as it heads toward the sun. It taps the sun's energy presumably to refuel itself (270). Ironically, despite the dangers feared by the Hermians and the Terran "Pandora Party," Rama "had given a final, almost contemptuous proof of its total lack of interest in all the worlds whose peace of mind it had so rudely disturbed" (270). Like a *deus absconditus*, Rama leaves the solar system, the details of its purpose and destination unknown: "Though that, surely, could not be its ultimate goal, it was aimed squarely at the Greater Magellanic Cloud, and the lonely gulfs beyond the Milky Way" (270).

After the completion of the Rama mission, Commander Norton contemplates his success *and* his failure. He knows that the mission has provided scientists with questions to keep them busy for decades. Yet he realizes that "he had also failed":

> One might speculate endlessly, but the nature and the purpose of the Ramans was still utterly unknown. They had used the solar system as a refueling stop, a booster station--call it what you will; and then had spurned it completely, on their way to more important business. They would probably never even know that the human race existed. Such monumental indifference was worse than any deliberate insult. (273)

This response to the aspect of Rama that relates to the qualities of the vastness and the indifference of the universe is reminiscent of the eighteenth-century poet Alexander Pope's comment that if we can not have love, we prefer hate even to indifference. The same views are in evidence in the modern pseudo-mythology of naturalism. Though naturalistic writer Thomas Hardy sees the universe as blind and indifferent, he indicates his hatred of this fact in such poems as "Hap" in which he says that he would actually be happier if he *could* attribute his pains to the *hatred* to some deity other than "Crass Casualty," blind chance. Likewise, Stephen Crane concerns himself with the same theme when he has the man in the poem protest to the universe, "I exist." The universe replies: "That fact creates in me no sense of obligation."

In some senses, the mythology of the *deus absconditus* and the vastness of the universe is capable of advocating nihilism and despair. Yet in other senses it is quite positive. Certainly, it is thus here in Clarke's novel. Not only does Rama represent in one sense the insignificance of humanity in the context of the vast universe; it also contains the recapitulation of several familiar themes from the history of human mythology, themes such as those of death and rebirth, and of life's preference for order and continuation. Also, as Norton is bemoaning his inability ever to know more of Rama's mysteries, Clarke points out that one of the scientists on the Rama committee awakens on Earth with the intuition that, "The Ramans do everything in threes" (274). The principle of triple redundancy has been found to be rife throughout Rama: the Ramans have three artificial suns; they seem to be themselves creatures with three arms and three legs. The concept of three-ness here is related to a natural organic situation rather than being related to mythological meanings such as those represented in trinities or triune gods. Dr. Perera realizes that human beings will probably have other chances to explore Raman generation ships, the other two members of a trinity of such.

The Jungian archetype most closely related to Clarke's Raman adventure is that of the Self, God, the unifying reality which constitutes the center of experience. In *Rama*, both traditional and modern mythological motifs concerning the God image are presented. The creative and destructive ordering aspects of the interior of Rama are parallel to the vast history of Earth's mythologies. The indifference of the Ramans to humanity might be associated with the modern idealogy of naturalism, which in turn is related to earlier mythologies having at their centers the unknown god or *deus absconditus*. All of these aspects, ancient and modern, are included in Jung's concept of the self projected onto space and the future. The self is that mysterious, never to be fully known, center of the psyche and of the universe, which creates and destroys and provides both order and meaning.

CHAPTER SIX

THE SHADOW IN SPACE

Good versus evil has been an emphatic problem in the West ever since the episode in the Garden of Eden. Groups are constantly fighting "evil" in the form of their neighbors, and committing "evil" against their neighbors, against other tribes, against other nations. Indeed, the distinction between good and evil is sometimes thought of as the driving force behind all of history.

The modern age has been thought by many to be one bereft of living myth, and of mythological narratives dealing in any meaningful or worthwhile way with the theme of evil versus good. However, the dark side of experience, the demonic, and the subject of evil versus good, do get symbolic treatment in science fiction narratives. I would suggest that these narratives actually have a *mythological* quality and come as close as anything else to a contemporary living mythology. Much of science fiction serves some of the same functions in contemporary society that myth did in traditional societies. The motif of the journey to or from outer space (and all it suggests and implies) provides a context similar enough to the "Once upon a Time" world of myth that living, creative spirits are able to body forth in many works of science fiction the same good versus evil theme as in myths recurring throughout the aeons.

Consciousness took a major evolutionary step when a distinction came to be made between pairs of opposites. In Western traditional mythology that leap is portrayed in the Garden of Eden episode of Genesis. The conscious ego developed out of the collective unconscious by beginning to make such distinctions as good and evil, self and other.

The Jungian ideal of the process of individuation has as its goal the coming to a realization of the self or superior personality in the individual and of the wholeness of the psyche. Various warring elements of the psyche are integrated and/or accepted, affirmed. For example, in the process of individuation, the ego and the dark side are to be integrated. Furthermore, the ego, with its highly dualistic view of experience, is to be depotentiated. The self, with its affirmative, polaristic attitude, becomes more dominant. Mythologically, the atonement of the hero, his at-one-ment with the Father, the divine principle represents this psychological process of coming to selfhood (Campbell, *Hero*).

Yet before the completion represented in individuation, before the redemption and apotheosis of the hero, certain stages must be completed, one of which is the coming to terms with the dark side of the psyche or the shadow. According to Jung, the meeting with this dark brother is the essential first step toward psychic growth. In the same way, Christ had to confront Satan before he could continue to the road to the cross of sacrificial redemption. Until the individuation symbolized by such redemption, the human soul is at the mercy of the diabolic shadow side, this "enemy within." However, after the individual has come to terms with the devil within himself, he can then move on toward the stage of unification with the self, God, the transcendental ego: the son can be reunited with the Father.

The twentieth century is perhaps the first period when humanity has tried living without a traditional mythology. To the extent that such is true, the psychological drama that would have taken the form of myth must then play itself out on the stage of history. Sometimes this process is inadequate and dangerous.

In time, humanity dreams of going to the stars in vehicles fashioned by his intellectual power, yet humanity has refused to come to terms with his immense shadow side, insisting rather on repressing the dark side, the evil within, and pretending that it is not there or that it has been superseded by evolution. Yet in many other ways, life on this planet is in jeopardy because of humanity's inability to control itself or to control the Devil within, to use mythological terminology; or, to use "secular humanist terminology," to control its desires, lusts, and greeds.

Fear and desire--these are the poles of the unredeemed ego, which Ananda K. Coomaraswamy calls the Devil Himself, humanity's worse enemy: "Satan," to use the terminology of the traditional myth. Our fear of our shadow side, our instincts, and our unacknowledged failings, are one source of repression. Related to that cause are our civilized and social ideals which insist on repression, denial, and even hypocrisy. Our desires, both idealistic and otherwise, cause us to repress the consciousness of wholes--or example, the effect of our actions on the ecosystem and of our waste of natural resources.

The evil engendering nature of the human ego can only be fully escaped by transformation to a consciousness beyond the constant dilemma between fear and desire. Joseph Campbell tells the story of how, during World War II, a New York newspaper showed a photograph of one of two giant somewhat terrifying temple guardians standing on either side of the gate of a Japanese temple. Under the newspaper picture was the statement: "The Japanese worship gods like this."

Campbell was struck by the irony of the statement; it's author had it all backwards. The Buddhists do not stop with these door guardians but go on inside to the presence of the image of the solar Buddha seated under the tree of immortal life. It was the Buddha, a type of the self-conquering hero who sits under the Bo tree and withstands the demons of fear and desire, regaining the paradise lost because of the splitting apart of the opposites ("Mythological Themes" 156-57).[1]

---

[1] The same would shine forth from the other great sister world religion (Christianity), if it could be seen that the lost paradise Jesus regains on the cross is really a paradise within, as Milton says. For seminal statements on the atonement and the equivalency of these religions, see Campbell (*Power* 107).

In the Christian tradition, the paradise of the wholeness of the self is lost when Adam and Eve succumb to the temptation of the serpent who is later termed the devil. Adam and Eve eat of the fruit of the knowledge of good and evil, which the serpent has claimed will make them to be as gods (i.e., to develop the ego and social control). This evolution seems to be necessary because what consciousness wants--what life itself wants--is more of itself, in more and more life forms living life with more and more intensity.

In the West, the devil, the shadow side, has been more of a problem than it ever has in the East. In the orthodox Christian tradition, humanity is thrown out of the Garden and may not re-enter it until after death. Mythologically, the way is shown blocked by the awful cherubim at the garden gate. These cherubim parallel the door guardians at the Japanese temple, beyond which Buddhist worshippers pass every time they come to worship (*Power* 107). Further, the Buddha lives on after he has vanquished the dualities of the ego. The Christ does not, except for one or two episodes where he appears as one returned temporarily from death.

The Western world today most especially has had a great deal of trouble coming to terms with its shadow problems, since it has based too much on external, objective ideals. Today our Faustian rush for *more*, our pact with the devil of our own fears and desires, has led us to the brink of disaster.

Yet the phenomenon of science fiction peoples the cosmos with life amid timeless conflicts, adventures, and meanings. Further, science fiction utilizes all the major themes of the world's mythologies--"stories of gods and heroes"--playing them out so that the essential gods and goddesses appear again, not in the "dream time of the past," but in the future. One prominent theme there too in science fiction is the shadow side of human experience and its relationship to humanity's nature and destiny.

Dostoyevsky's "The Dream of a Ridiculous Man"

Though not usually mentioned in histories of science fiction or space/time travel fantasy, this 1881 story focuses on a journey to another planet, albeit in the form of a dream vision of a journey to another earth, much like this one except innocent and uncorrupted by the sins and failures of humanity.[2] This theme of suffering and evil, the shadow side of existence, is central to the story. The narrator dreams he is carried, after his own (contemplated) suicide, to this "unfallen" planet by "some dark mysterious creature" (213) where he marvels at the absence of evil and suffering but then proceeds to corrupt the inhabitants of that world.[3]

The ridiculous man has all his life been laughed at and thought ridiculous by everyone else as well as by himself. Yet somehow he never has been willing to admit his knowledge of his own inadequacies to anyone else. A very lonely individual who seems to be jobless, an insomniac, he has decided that nothing at matters in the least (205). Deciding to commit suicide, for a while, he procrastinates. Then one gloomy night, he notices a star, and for some unknown

---

[2] In thus placing his space journey in the form of a dream or vision, Dostoyevsky anticipates the method used by Olaf Stapledon in his *Star Maker* (1937). Furthermore, the cosmic voyager in Stapledon's story makes one of his first stops on a planet known as "the other earth."

[3] The motif of the space traveller from earth having a corruptive influence on the innocence of beings on other planets was brought to a certain prominence starting in the 1930s by C.S. Lewis, both in his fantasy trilogy--*Out of Silent Planet*, *Perelandra*, and *That Hideous Strength*--and in Lewis's own debates with Arthur C. Clarke and others. Lewis opposed all thought of actual space travel. A Christian, he believed that humanity would follow a prime directive no better than Adam and Eve did the first "Thou shalt not!" in Genesis. Chapter 8 contains an evaluation of some aspects of Lewis's vision. Also regarding this motif of the "unfallen" planet, certain "Star Trek" episodes concern encounters with "unfallen" races, for example, "The Apple" and "A Private Little War" (Ehrlich 201-20; Roddenberry and others 345-73).

reason, reminds himself of his earlier desire to kill himself. He realizes, though, that even that is a matter of extreme indifference to him (206). Perhaps noticing the star is an important part of the impetus propelling him into the specific dream journey he undertakes in the unconscious.

After seeing the star, he is accosted in the street by an eight-year-old girl who seems to have been separated from her mother by some violent encounter. The child is in a state of extreme anguish, and he feels sympathy for her, yet his feelings and reactions are very complicated. In the end, he fails really to help her and even finally chases her away (207). He realizes, though, that he has felt the same pity for her he would have felt had he not determined to kill himself (209).[4]

Ivan Karamazov, in Dostoyevsky's *The Brothers Karamazov*, gives as his most telling reason for rejecting the Christian cosmos, the fact of the suffering of children. Ivan has a dream of a visit by the shadow, a rather shabby, nineteenth-century version of the devil, and later contracts "brain fever" and goes into a coma. The somewhat similar ridiculous man has a dream in which he commits suicide instead.

According to his earlier conclusions about the nothingness of all existence, he tells us, he should not have cared what happened to the child at all. Yet he does care. He reasons that his intention shortly to kill himself should prevent him from feeling any pity at all for the child or any shame at his harshness toward her, since in his solipsistic view, his death will cause everything else to cease existing as well. He tries to convince himself fully of his solipsistic proposition, to force himself to believe that "as my consciousness sputtered out, the whole world would vanish like a phantom." He has decided that every object or reality in the world is really just a part of himself (210).

---

[4]The child, a female, embodies the anima, or feeling side of the psyche, for the ridiculous man.

Negation and denial are associated with the Christian devil, perhaps the most prominent of Western mythological representations of the shadow. The narrator's suicide plan and his solipsism represent--a compensation from the shadow side--one questionable attempt of the unconscious to solve the problem of extreme self-consciousness and feeling of ridiculousness. Since he is viewed as nothing by society, his compulsion towards solipicism arising from the shadow side negates the world in saying that the world's existence depends upon his own ego, that of a "ridiculous man." His attitude of negation, which denies existence except as a dream play of the individual consciousness, is elsewhere clearly associated with mythological representations of the shadow. In Göethe's *Faust: Part I*, Mephistopheles (the devil) is "the Spirit that constantly denies! That demon also proclaims that, quite appropriately, all that comes into being deserves to come to be no longer. His devil's point of view has it that it would have been better if nothing had existed in the first place (1339-44). Thus, nihilism--belief in nothingness--is intimately related to the shadow side of life, to corruption and sin. Both the ridiculous man's negative act concerning the child and his nihilism are, in a complicated sense, compensatory reactions of the shadow to his conscious situation.

After his proclamation of radical solipicism, the ridiculous man keeps thinking for a long time, and "quite new and unexpected considerations" enter his consciousness (210). He speculates about how it might effect him if he were living "on the moon or Mars" and were to commit some intensely shameful act and then were to be permanently transported to the earth. He wonders if he would feel the shame again every time the looked at the moon (210). He is so embroiled in attempts to solve the mental dilemmas that the girl has incited that he drops off to sleep without getting around to killing himself (210).

The ridiculous man dreams that he shoots himself, in the heart and not the head as he has intended,[5] and is buried. He is conscious in his grave and accuses God of taking revenge on him in the form of consciousness after death for what he now calls his "unreasonable suicide." Reminiscent of several literary Satans, he tells God to "'Be sure that no suffering inflicted upon me can equal the silent contempt that will be in me throughout millions of years of martyrdom!'" (213). As though in response to this challenge, his grave opens, and "some dark, mysterious creature" seizes him and leaps with him into space.

He has a journey through space without a space ship and presumably with no need of life-support systems: "It was dark all around, darker than I'd ever seen before! We were moving through space at a fantastic speed and were already quite far from Earth" (213). The creature transporting him through space is clearly a shadow representation. It bears "a human resemblance," yet he feels "a deep aversion for it" (213). This being is his own shadow side which carries him into a new world in order to undo his life-negating solipicism.

They approach a star shining in the distance, which the shadow creature tells him is the star he saw just before finding the little girl (213). They journey deep into the stellar distances. They traverse through deep space, going beyond where they can see any familiar constellations (214). They come to a planet which at first seems a duplicate of the earth, with the same continental outlines.[6] The ridiculous man is stricken with an extreme love for the earth, reminiscent of that of Dostoyevsky himself and of Dimetri in *The Brothers Karamazov*. He wonders

---

[5]Mythologically, the heart signifies the feelings, the feminine, the earth--while the head is related to intellect, to masculinity, and to the abstract.

[6]This motif is not unknown in space travel fantasy since Dostoyevsky's time. For example, in the first season of the original *Star Trek* the episode "Miri" has the starship *Enterprise* visiting such a planet, one on which a planet-wide plague has caused the earth-like planet to become a planet only of children. The similarity to our earth is seen rather clearly in the television version (See Spies 251-76).

if suffering exists on this other earth, thinking that on the old earth, "we can truly love only with suffering and through suffering" (215).[7]

The shadowy creature deposits him on a paradisal island in the Greek archipelago or somewhere near mainland Greece on this parallel earth (215). It is as though he is on the old earth except for certain pervasive Edenic qualities. A festive air pervades the place, a feeling of triumph. A delightful sea inspires him with feelings of love. The beautiful plants there inspire him with a sense of love and welcome (215). He finds the inhabitants to be joyful, fulfilled, tranquil, beautiful, and intelligent. He concludes that this earth has not been desecrated by "the Fall of Man."

According to the narrator, these people do not *strive for* meaning, for their lives already contain meaning (216). These people live in harmony with the universe and with all beings, knowing the language of plants and even having some intuitive communion with stars (217). Unlike the situation in the mythic Eden, sex, reproduction, and death do exist on this planet. Yet neither does "*cruel* sensuality," quarrels, nor jealously exist. Death is peaceful, rapturous even, and these people have a belief in eternal life with a sense of absolute certainty. They have no religion in the ordinary sense, no temples or ceremonies, but have, rather, "a sort of tangible, live, and constant communion with the universal Whole" (218)

Evil enters in the form of the visitor, this "ridiculous man," who, despite his admiration for these people, causes their fall from innocence: "The truth is that--well, that I ended up by corrupting them all" (220) His memory of the dream is not clear enough for him to be able to recall just how he did it: "My

---

[7]This idea is a favorite theme of Dostoyevsky's. He has the ridiculous man go on to say that "We don't know how to love otherwise; we don't know any other love. I want to suffer so that I may love" (215). Though Dostoyevsky does have characters, like Dimetri, Raskolnikov, and Sonia, who do learn to love seemingly only through experiencing intense suffering, he sometimes seems to think such suffering is *necessary* for any love to be possible.

dream flashed through eons, leaving in me only a general impression of the whole" (220). He compares himself to "a sinister trichina, like a plague germ contaminating whole kingdoms" (220).[8]

In the process of their corruption, these people progress through untruth to voluptuousness to jealousy to cruelty (220-21). They experience suffering and come to love it and even to declare that suffering is the only way to truth (221). Then they develop science. They proceed to worship their own longings. Ideas and disputations become paramount, and religions appear worshipping non-being and self-annihilation (223). The ridiculous man comes to love "their degraded earth even more than I had loved it when it was a Garden of Eden" (223). Finally, he is so saddened by their plight that he asks them to crucify him, even explaining to them how to construct a cross. They only laugh at him and take him for a fool, threatening to put him in a madhouse (223-24).

He awakens from his dream in a state of love for everyone. He has now an intense thirst for life and desire to preach a gospel of love. He now refuses to believe that wickedness is the normal state of man: that "if everyone wanted it [harmony, universal love], everything could be arranged immediately" (226).

The ridiculous man begins in a state of depression, of alienation and rootlessness typical of many nineteenth-century and twentieth-century intellectuals. He has so repressed the shadow side as to have it erupt in the form of denial of the independent existence of things, solipsism. His conscious reaction to such feelings (and to his image of himself as a "ridiculous man") brings on the desire for suicide. The shadowy figure in his dream then transports him to the other earth where eventually he corrupts an innocent humanity, in compensation

---

[8]Dostoyevsky uses the same metaphor in the epilogue of *Crime and Punishment* in which Raskolnikov dreams that the minds of all humanity are infected by parasites which engender *ideas* setting people at odds with each other. This image of evil as a germ or a parasite is also used in Colin Wilson's *The Mind Parasites* (1967), discussed in Chapter 7.

for which his life acquires a new meaning. He is now required to preach the doctrine of love in the hope of undoing the "fall of Man."

In some respects the pattern is similar to that of the journey of the ancient mariner in Coleridge's poem. He journeys into a world in which he sees the living out of his own dark side, and when he returns home, he (or that self within him) requires himself to preach the gospel of what he thinks he has learned on his journey, no matter how it may dismay his listeners.

The ridiculous man may now thought to be crazy because of his fanatical devotion to a single idea, but the compensation caused by his journey to the other earth has at least taken away the danger of suicide. It is as though the unconscious, in his case at least, has found it necessary to adhere to the belief that "where there is life, there is hope." Certainly, ideas like the stars, the cosmos, and the other earth are employed in symbolic ways to play out a paradigm of revival, even if it is of a somewhat ironic sort. Besides anticipating a number of themes of later science fiction and space fantasy, Dostoyevsky's story appears as one of the first stories containing the space travel element to embody the shadow motif.

Guy de Maupassant's "The Horla"

Another such story is Guy de Maupassant's "The Horla" (1989). This story is presented in the form of journal entries. Early in the series of entries presented, the narrator notes his concern with those "mysterious influences" that turn "happiness into gloom" (314). What at first seems to be only musings concerning "the mystery of the Invisible" (314) becomes a definite case of paranoia (317). He also has questionings concerning the possibility that unknown animals have existed on the earth since time immemorial with humanity generally having no knowledge of them. Some of his questionings are reminiscent of the twentieth-century cult of the "abominable snowman" or "sasquatch" (319). He proceeds to have dreams of some sort of succubus or even of a doppelgänger

(320-21) and speculates about the possibility that modern psychology may provide some of the keys to the problems that have arisen in his mind (331).

Finally, one night, he looks up at the sky. He wonders what sort of sentient beings might live on those worlds in the darkness of infinite space. He wonders what other life, plant or animal, might exist out there and what knowledge might be possessed on other worlds yet unknown here on earth. He wonders whether or not at some future time some creature from outer space might come to earth to conquer it (335).

Such speculation is practically identical with the question behind much of the "bug-eyed monsters" pulp fiction of the early twentieth century in which an alien encounter is cast in the terms of invasion from outer space. The prototypical literary example is, of course, H.G. Wells' *The War of the Worlds* (1898), in which the invading aliens represent an extraterrestrial version of humanity's own aggressive capacities.

He decides that an alien creature he calls the Horla may indeed have already invaded the earth (336-38). This creature, he believes, will subjugate humanity.

He also wonders if some new creature as yet unknown to man might exist, some mysterious creature made of different elements from those known to humanity. His speculations are quite fantastical and, in certain ways, anticipate future science fiction stories of the journey of the shadowy aliens from world to world. He imagines a butterfly as large as many planets moving from star to star to give each of them perfume. He imagines the beings of the universe watching it go by with great joy. Then he wonders what is wrong with him, deciding that he is being haunted by the Horla himself. It is the Horla that fills his head with such mad ideas: "He is in me; he is taking possession of my soul; I shall kill him!" (339-40).

He has suddenly realized the wandering of his fantasy into this benevolent butterfly fantasy, suddenly accusing the Horla of muddling his mind. It seems that the Horla is for him the alter ego or shadow side in the unconscious, embodying his fears, uncertainties, and, in general, the opposite side of his belief in the certainty of science and progress.

The horla is, in an important sense, the dark face of progress. Humanity has, by the end of the nineteenth century, discovered many facts about nature which make life easier, but along with those discoveries and those developing technologies have come all manner of fears related to man's Promethean nature. A part of man fears that he has stolen fire from the gods, as it were, in making the advances he has made, and that he will somehow have to pay for these thefts.

Of course, the narrator in Maupassant's story has gone quite insane. His deep, dark fears both about himself and man's status in the world, which have developed into his fantasy of the invasion by the alien horla, constitute a possession by the shadow. The narrator has lost all control and finally thinks that he can lock the horla in the house and kill it. He sets fire to the house and flees, only to realize that he has sacrificed the lives of his servants whom he has locked inside with "the horla" (342-43).

The narrator is indeed beside himself in his final utterances: He sees homo sapiens as being succeeded by the Horla. A human being may die at any undetermined time through any chance event. Such is not true of the horla for he has reached "the limit of his existence." He decides that the horla is not that dead after all and that he will thus have to kill himself (344).

The distinction made here between the two kinds of being--humanity, on the one hand, and the alien horla, on the other--anticipates existentialist themes in the twentieth century. Also, the narrator's prediction of his own suicide is reminiscent of the prevalence of the theme of suicide in late nineteenth-century literature.[9] He seems to intuit the true case that the horla is in his own breast, the

---

[9] The theme had already begun to be exhibited in the nineteenth century in such works as Dostoyevski's "Dream of a Ridiculous Man" and *The Possessed*.

shadow within, yet he decides that, by a twisted logic, all will somehow be well if he kills himself.

In important respects, Maupassant's Horla appears as a nineteenth-century anticipation of all manner of "bug-eyed monsters from outer space" and "horrors from beyond" in the pulp literature of the first half of the twentieth century. One of the best known of the writers of such later stories was H.P. Lovecraft who, in stories such as "The Color Out of Space," treated the theme of the alien visitant as a psychological phenomenon.[10] In particular, he sometimes has the alien presence to take over the mentality of human beings; this motif appears in work of a number of other writers, such as in Jack Finny's *Invasion of the Body Snatchers* (King 5, 131).

Philip José Farmer's "My Sister's Brother"[11]

Philip José Farmer's "My Sister's Brother" (1960) treats the theme of the shadow in depth, portraying the experiences of an explorer on Mars. After being left on the ship while his companions go out exploring, Lane eventually decides he must go in search of them. He finds an alien superficially similar to a Terran woman who carries coiled about her neck and shoulders a wormlike creature

---

[10]Sometimes Lovecraft portrays the shadowy alien as a superior race which intends to take over the planet from the weakly human race after it has reached an evolutionary dead end. Cf. Colin Wilson's preface to *The Philosopher's Stone*. Also Cf. discussions of Wilson's *The Mind Parasites* in Chapter 7 and of Arthur C. Clarke's *Childhood's End* in Chapter 9.

[11]The title of the story in the anthology from which I am quoting, *The Classic Philip José Farmer: 1952-64*, is "My Sister's Brother," in some ways seems a more relevant title than the original: "Open to Me, My Sister."

(176). He observes her vomiting into a bowl to feed the worm, a fact that at first he finds alarming; yet her obviously feminine characteristics also attract him.[12]

As the alien Lane refers to repeatedly as "the biped" is cutting up a spider-like animal for food, he discovers that her name is "Mahreesya," or "Martia" as he settles upon calling her. He joins her in partaking of a seeming religious communion of sorts in which they eat pieces of "wine-moistened bread" mixed together after having first been put into each of their mouths.

He understands that she views the act as both profane *and* sacred; it shows her oneness with the deity that she worships. The ritual symbolizes the nonduality of creator and created, of human and alien, of male and female. Lane finds this ritual and its presumed meaning interesting, exciting; he finds no problem with the transcendental force pervading the universe being given many different names by the beings on different planets (181-82). Indeed, Lane seems to be open to a sort of comparative mythology of the starry heavens.

Thus this alien seems to hail from a culture which adheres to a philosophy involving a faith in the ultimate one-ness of all things. In some respects Martia is reminiscent of the people of the other earth in the dream of the ridiculous man.[13]

Lane soon finds that Martia is really quite dissimilar to a human woman in the absence in her of anything like human female sexual organs. He eventually

---

[12] She has the hips and legs of a woman, with minor differences in the hands and feet; a muscled chest but no breasts, navel, or vagina; an "extraordinary" feminine voice, "husky but honied [sic] at the same time" (177-78).

[13] Cf. the religion of Michael Valentine Smith which has been taught to him by his Martian tutors in Heinlein's *Stranger in a Strange Land* in Chapter 14. Farmer goes on to discuss Lane's own religious experience. He believes in "a personal god" and in what he sees as the fact that "a redeemer" has been sent to earth and that other worlds who need or needed redeemers will get or have gotten them (182). These points become ironic in regard to Lane's eventual treatment of Martia.

learns, from examining a children's picture book of hers he finds that she hails from a star system near the center of the galaxy. Life had evolved there in many ways similarly to the manner it evolved on earth. Martia's species is warm-blooded but not mammalian, obviously with major anatomical differences. Its history, unlike the case with the history of Earth, contains very little warfare (194). On this world, technology presumably has advanced much further than it has on earth yet without the stimulation of war. Beings from this planet can travel at nearly the speed of light, perhaps even faster, and they do travel interstellar distances (194).

Lane finds photographs of earth in the book accompanied by an emblem showing "a shadowy figure, half ape, half dragon" (194). This symbol quite graphically represents man's precarious situation split as he is between the primitive and the civilized. The part of the picture representing civilization is an ape--an ape only, not even a true human being--to signify the view that even human civilized ideals somehow lack a great deal. The dragon, of course, represents the dark shadow side in the unconscious which even (perhaps, especially) "civilized" humanity persists in projecting onto its enemies. Thus, earth has signified to Martia's people a place too dangerous to touch (194) because it is in the grips of a rather crude civilization, frequently at the mercy of the unruly and aggressive shadow side signified by the dragon. Lane realizes that if Martia's species were to contact earth, human beings would "steal your secrets" and that, then, "We'd infest all of space" (194).

Thus, Lane's position is similar of that of C.S. Lewis, who thought that humankind was so corrupted, so vicious that it would ruin any planet with which it came into contact. Also, and like the Dostoyevsky story too, where the space traveller does corrupt the planet he visits, Lane seems at first to hold the view that humankind's dark shadow self is so aggressive, selfish, and greedy that it should be given no tether.

However, almost immediately, Lane has an afterthought that, after all, perhaps humanity is showing some signs of progress, that no wars or revolutions have broken out recently. He remembers that the United Nations is settling many disputes that formerly would have led to war (195). Thus, Lane concludes, human groups have moved toward coming to terms with their shadow sides, away from projecting their own dark sides onto other groups they perceive as "enemies."

Yet after Martia tells Lane that her people have a base on Ganymede (one of the moons of Jupiter), he begins to second guess her--his paranoia takes over, and he projects his own shadow side onto her. He decides that she would never have told him what she has but for what he suspects as her plan to allow him to be used as some kind of scientific specimen by her people. Thus he sees it as his clear duty to overcome his feelings for her (200). He decides to bind her and carry her and some evidences of her civilization with him back to earth. It is typical of the work of the repressed shadow side that his decision violates his "personal feelings" toward her.

Frequently, those in the grips of the shadow, suffer great pain and conflict because the urges of the repressed shadow, an archetype and portion of the objective psyche, militate against the attitudes of the ego. Indeed, it makes him "sick," as he tries to smile while trying to bind her. He gets ill indeed, at first suspecting that either the alien food he has eaten has not agreed with him or that Martia has caused his condition by use of hypnosis.

Later that day, Martia, having said nothing to him about his attempt with the rope, spoon feeds him some "zoogloea soup." He finds qualities "so feminine and tender" in her attempts to help that he allows it. He seems temporarily to abandon his previous obedience to the shadow impulses. He thinks that he was perhaps wrong, that it is possible "good will and rapport" can exist between human and alien (202).

While going to sleep, he has fantasies of Martia and himself bringing about peace between whole worlds. He remembers that both are civilized, peaceful, and religious. He hopes for the possibility of the brotherhood of all sentient life throughout the universe (203).

On the way to the toilet, he passes by the sleeping Martia and notices "a flash of light like a gleaming jewel in her mouth"; then, recoiling "in horror," he sees "a head" rising "from between her teeth" (203). It turns out to be the head of that same worm that she sometimes carries coiled around her neck and shoulders (176).

Lane is sickened at the sight of Martia breathing easily *through* the worm. He thinks of this worm as a "monster," a "symbiote," or a "parasite": "He thought of vampires, of worms creeping into one's sleeping body and there sucking blood" (204). Lane desires an explanation, and Martia gives him one on five sheets of paper filled with drawings. He finds that the worm is in some sense at the same time larva, phallus, and offspring; yet it is not of her own genes: "She had given birth to it, but she was not its mother" (205). He acknowledges that her species, the Eeltau, obviously have a method of reproduction totally different from that of humanity and that he need not be upset. Yet he is clearly bothered, especially when he realizes that the worm, or larva, is "doomed to stay in its present form until it died of old age . . . unless Martia found another adult of the Eeltau" for whom she feels affection and who feels affection for her (206).

Lane then discovers, through Martia's drawings, the involved alien process by which new members of the Eeltau race are born and brought to mature "humanoid" form (206-07). Their reproductive methods are so foreign to Lane that he "raised his arms in despair" (208). He falls into what Jung calls shadow projection in seeing Martia's people as sub-human monsters. He says that beings of the Eeltau and Terran species would be unable to co-exist amicably, that human beings would treat the Eeltau as "disgusting vermin." The "deepest prejudices" in the human psyche would start operating; the "strongest taboos" would be involved (208). Lane seems to refer to something of the depths of the psyche in the collective unconscious in the form of the shadow. Jung sees the shadow as the cause of most of human prejudice--such as racial hatred and hatred of beings who are different. The same would seem to carry over here to the unthinking prejudgment of another species different from one's own.

Thinking himself immune to such projection of his deepest fears onto those who are different, he tries to reassure her by suggesting that acceptance and respect between the two species could begin as affection on the individual level--as with Lane and Martia--of each individual for the other, that then it could grow in regard to the mass, which is a combination of individuals (208).

Then, as he is drifting off to sleep, he speaks to himself words expressing sentiments closer to what he expressed earlier about humanity's "infesting" space. He calls it "fine noble talk" lacking any meaning. He realizes that when earth ships are able to travel interstellar distances, a state of war will exist between earth and these aliens. He finds it quite reasonable that either side might want to make a pre-emptive strike against the other (209).

In this passage, Lane speaks out of the paranoia which frequently accompanies shadow projection. The one who projects the shadow onto and hates the other being tends to fear that the other has the same designs on him. Even as he has these thoughts about her species, Lane also has kind and admiring thoughts about Martia, her friendly and attractive nature.

Then, despite his ambivalent feelings for Martia--uttering a fierce "'For Earth!'"--he hits her on the side of the neck, knocking her out. Lane then brutally kills and mutilates the larva, the worm-like creature Martia has nurtured, by using it as a whip to crack and stamping its head with his heel. One can hardly help recalling the book of Genesis here. Lane's particularly vicious aversion to this creature is likely related to its similarities to the Terran snakes and worms that have been for so long associated with the Christian devil (along with his dwelling-place, hell), chief mythological embodiment of the shadow in the Western world. The pettiness of Lane's soul at this point, his degradation, is graphically illustrated by his comment to Martia as he gags her after she comes to her senses.

He calls her a "'bitch'" and suggests that his action is the first blow in a war between the two species which the Terrans will win. He accuses her of like attitudes toward him, saying the she and her "'monster'" deserve only violent death (210).

As Lane is preparing to carry Martia captive back to his ship, two Eeltau arrive. Though they take him prisoner, they and the others who arrive later treat him with basic kindness. One female (who knows English) tells him that Martia wonders why he killed "'her . . . baby,'" and Lane says that he cannot answer. Almost immediately he relents, saying that "'it was in the nature of the beast'" (213). That is an explanation based on an intuitive realization of what Jung calls the shadow. Then he gives another answer appropriate to one having no understanding of the shadow and the way it twists human attitudes. He brags that he is no "vicious beast," that he did what he had to do in order to remain a man. The interpreter tells him that Martia will pray that he be forgiven for the murder, that someday he will change; that Martia forgives him and hopes he will come to regard her as a sister and that she thinks that he has some good in him (213).

The final image the author presents through Lane is similar to that of the "mind parasites" Colin Wilson uses in his 1968 novel[14]: "He felt as if something had been planted in him and had broken its shell and was growing into something like a worm. It was eating him" (213). Of course, the entity that has been "planted in" Lane's psyche since birth is the archetypal human shadow which, again and again, has been symbolized as a snake or as vermin. Lane has struggled with the shadow, indeed, yet is still in its grips and has by no means yet fully come to terms with it.

---

[14]See Chapter 7.

Star Trek: "The Enemy Within"

The "Star Trek" episode "The Enemy Within" was written by Richard Matheson and aired on NBC during fall of the first season (1966) of the three seasons the series ran in primetime. This episode is a classic treatment of the shadow theme. As Captain Kirk is beaming up from a planet which the *Enterprize* is orbiting, a transporter malfunction occurs, causing him to be split into two Kirks.

The first Captain Kirk appearing in the transporter room is Kirk minus the shadow side in the unconscious. He is represented as dazed looking and dizzy, his legs almost buckling under him. This portrayal represents the "airy" quality of the purely conscious, or purely intellectual, mind--the mind lacking a connection with the dark and earthy side in the unconscious.

In a little while, another Kirk appears on the transporter deck. He is "a perfect double" of the first Kirk: "Except for its eyes. They were those of a rabid animal just released from a cage." After this Kirk looks around, "tense, as though expecting attack," the transporter chief asks if he is all right. This Kirk's reply is "a hoarse growl" (Matheson 103).

This shadow version of the captain displays characteristics of the animals from whom humanity has descended and something which everyone carries about ever and always in the collective unconscious; yet another way to describe the relationship is to say that even a human being in the twenty-third century still shares certain "shadowy" levels of the collective unconscious with the animals.[15]

Another relevant fact concerning the shadow is that it represents those parts of the psyche which the ego wants to suppress or repress in the interests of the image (or persona) it has chosen to wear before civilized society. Of course, those repressed parts, for the starship captain in the twenty-third century, would

---

[15] Jung defines the collective unconscious as being "common to all men, and perhaps even to all animals" (*Portable* 38).

include such traits as undisciplined recklessness, bestial self-indulgence, and disregard of the rights or needs of others. Indeed, the shadow Kirk barges into sick-bay, ruthlessly demanding brandy. Likened to "a wild man" by Dr. McCoy, Kirk, after drinking all the alcohol he can get in sensuous and voluptuous pleasure makes extremely rude sexual advances toward Yeoman Janice Rand.

Chief Engineer Scott discovers that something like what has happened to Kirk has also happened to a dog-like creature from the planet below on being sent up on the transporter beam. The animal is split also. One doppleganger is calm domestic-seeming, as-it-were-civilized, animal, while the other is a frothing, barking, charging brute of a beast.

Suddenly, the civilized Kirk, on having the situation of the animal revealed to him, realizes what has happened. He realizes that the other Kirk running loose through the ship is his own brutish side, his version of that dark aspect of humanity each person carries within: in a sense it is a part of Kirk out on a murderous rampage for vengeance to appease the sense of loss he feels after "years of denial--the years it had spend as a prisoner of conscience, of duty, of responsibility" (111). What this passage rather clearly describes is Kirk's shadow, the side that he has repressed since early childhood. Spock notices that, without his negative side, the captain loses a certain psychological coherence. He realizes that the captain's words are "disjointed, disorganized": "This Kirk was not the integrated, decisive Kirk he knew" (112). Indeed, the individual who has persisted in ignoring his shadow side to the point that it is split off is living in a dangerous state of non-integration.[16]

---

[16]Perhaps the classic case of non-integration of shadow elements is that documented concerning one "Eve" in *The Three Faces of Eve*. One split-off set of shadow aspects becomes autonomous, calling itself "Eve Black," in obvious contradistinction to the ego, "Eve White."

As Karin Blair notes, in *Meaning in Star Trek*, Spock plays "a crucial role in this episode" (102).[17] Kirk's naive ego, divorced from his shadow side, jumps to the conclusion that he should "make an announcement to the entire crew--tell them what's happened as well as I can. It's a good crew--they deserve to be told." Spock, however, objects, maintaining the political value of the persona. As captain, he can not allow the crew to see him as vulnerable in any way. He must maintain the persona of the perfect authority, the Captain (42). Spock's position prevails.

After Kirk's "Cain" has been captured, Spock alludes his own situation in regard to Kirk's malady when he makes the ironic comment, "'If I seem emotionally insensitive to the agony of your ordeal, Captain, please understand. It's the way I am'" (118). The meaning of "It" in this utterance is ambiguous. It could mean, "Emotionally insensitive is the way I am." Or it could mean, "Split--like you are--is the way I also am." Spock is a cross between a Terran woman with all the inevitable human emotions and a father from the planet Vulcan, where everyone takes pride in ignoring and denying the emotions.[18]

When the shadow-Kirk is finally captured and restrained, he is stricken with an overpowering fear. Being no longer free to exercise its qualities of aggression and desire, being in a condition of arrested will, the dark Kirk has nowhere left to turn. It is only from the encouraging words of the ego-Kirk that the shadow gains solace, representing the world of imagination, of the ability to

---

[17]Blair's book is a valuable study, saying something about just about every episode, and is, in major respects, a Jungian treatment. Yet in the two and a half page commentary on "The Enemy Within" (101-04), even though she quotes Jungian psychotherapist Erich Neumann and talks generally about the shadow *concept* in this episode, she never once mentions the term "shadow."

[18]The war within Spock between his chosen Vulcan persona and the shadow side or his human side capable of affection and emotion is seen in several episodes, including "Amok Time" (Sturgeon 115-28) and "This Side of Paradise" (Fontana 555-70)

see beyond a single time in a single enclosed situation of imprisonment. A poet is more likely to be able to endure imprisonment than is a laborer because of his greater ability to imagine a world outside the prison or the possibility of escape or release. It is as though the ego-Kirk is able to draw strength from the shadow which at present the shadow is unable to use, judging from the language of written story: "Some strength rose up from unknown depths in Kirk" (121). Or, in another sense, it is as though ego-Kirk has one of those experiences referred to as *deja vu,* "already seen," which serves to reassure him that he is doing the correct thing and to insure his doing it with all confidence: "It was as though he had lived through just such a scene before. The words that came to him seemed familiar" (121). This element again smacks of the ego drawing upon the shadow side and perhaps can be seen to represent the beginning of the reintegration process.

The ego-Kirk realizes that he must be reintegrated with the shadow Kirk before his normal life can go on: "I must take him back--into myself. I don't want to . . . a brutish, mindless wolf in human shape" (121). Spock notes that "We are all part wolf and part lamb. We need both parts. Compassion is reconciliation between them. It is human to be both lamb and wolf" (51).[19]

Dr. McCoy goes on to explain that perhaps Kirk is not himself fully without his wolflike side, that even Spock is correct that Kirk probably would not

---

[19]Indeed, as Jung points out in *Answer to Job,* the lamb is symbolic of the Christ, though the apocalyptic Christ possessed by the shadow side is seen, by Jung, as a "wrathful lamb," wrath being the deadly sin in the middle ages which was frequently symbolized by the lion (Cf. Marlowe's *Doctor Faustus*). Commonly, a voracious animal is used to symbolize the shadow side. The tiger in Blake's poem of that name clearly represents the unbridled shadow side, the instincts, the secret life "burning bright/In the forests of the night." This side of the psyche is put to naught when penned up and kept from either the natural discharging of its instinct and will or from the integration of the shadow with the ego.

be able to command the ship, as likewise without the lamb in him his manner of discipline would be too harsh and cruel (51).

It is decided that the transporter is operating well enough to risk sending the two Kirks through it and back and again in the hope of reintegrating them. That process already has been tried on the dog-like animal's two halves, and the dog has returned as one body, though dead (122-24). The conclusion is reached that "the shock of reabsorption" killed the creature as "the consequence of instinctive fear" (123). Spock and Kirk believe that between them, the two Kirks have enough of both reason, will, and imagination to combat such shock.

However, as ego-Kirk is retrieving his double from sickbay, shadow-Kirk overpowers him, rushes to the bridge and takes over. It gives the order to leave orbit, an uncharacteristic order for the normal, integrated Kirk, in that crew members are still trapped on the planet's surface due to the transporter malfunction. The harsh shadow, when these men are mentioned, says, "*They can't be saved. They're dead now*" (127). Seeing Spock and ego-Kirk leave the elevator, it shouts, "There's the imposter. . . . Grab him!" (127). When ego-Kirk calmly says, "You are the imposter," the shadow Kirk hysterically shrieks, "Don't believe him. . . . Take them both! Grab them!" (127). Kirk moves slowly toward his shadow side, compassionately reaching out his hand. The shadow screams:

> "You want me dead, don't you? You want this ship all to yourself! But it's *mine*! . . . I am Captain Kirk, you ship of pigs! All right, let the liar destroy you all! . . . I run this ship! I own it. I own you--all of you. (127)

The positive Kirk stuns the negative with a phaser gun. The two go through the transporter and return transformed as one Kirk. This joining represents the integration of the shadow back into the total personality. In effect, the ego must embrace the shadow, just as Kirk embraces his negative side as the two go into the transporter beam. Kirk, unlike Coleridge's ancient mariner, after his experience feels sadder but *less* wise (128). This admission may indicate that he has not yet fully internalized the wisdom of the shadow, the realization that everyone has a dark as well as a light side. An indication of hope can be seen in the fact the Mr. Spock and Yeoman Rand agree that the "imposter" had some "interesting qualities" (129). Another is that McCoy tells Kirk to join the human race, perhaps indicating that he realizes something of the fact of the universal shadow, the beast within everyone (128).

Star Trek: "Wolf in the Fold"

In an episode written by Robert Bloch and first aired during the second season,[20] the Enterprize meets the devil himself--in twenty-third century guise--or at least the contemporary version of something which takes various forms in different eras whether the form be Lucifer, Jack the Ripper, or Adolf Hitler. In "Wolf in the Fold," crew members are visiting the planet Argelius, a popular Venusberg,[21] for rest and relaxation. A belly dancer is killed mysteriously while alone with Commander Scott. Scotty does not remember anything after a certain point before she was killed until after her death.

During attempts by Kirk, Spock, and Argelian officials to find out what happened, two more women are killed. In each case, death is caused by multiple stab wounds, the victim screaming in great fear before her death. One of these women is Sybo, the wife of the Argelian prefect. She is killed in a dark room while she and a number of people, sitting around a table, seance fashion, are trying to divine the name of the murderer. Sybo is one of the few Argelian women who yet possess what Spock refers to as "the Argelian empathic contact." One of the ancient "ways of finding the truth in such matters," it has generally

---

[20]1967-68.

[21]From what is shown of it, a Venusberg is a kind of Playboy club of the stars--that is, literally. Here, as is frequent in the *Star Trek* series, things are still seen primarily a masculine point of view, one of the few respects in which the show was not terribly ahead of its time.

been discarded by Argelians since their "great awakening hundreds of years ago" (Bloch 153) which presumably made these ways unnecessary. Indeed, Argelius is portrayed as a place where everyone is open and honest, presumably in all matters, not just sexual matters, as the opening scene might indicate.

This civilization is the ideal of popular Freudianism. Jealousy is viewed as the worst of transgressions, sexual inhibition as a disease. The openness, gentleness, and honesty of this society is so intense that the kind of person needed to serve in administrative posts requiring shrewdness or slyness is rather hard to find. Since Argelius is such a planet of sheep, the people necessary to serve in such posts are usually recruited from other planets. The person single-handedly investigating the murders is one Chief City Administrator Hengist, a "pudgy, round-faced man" from Rigel IV with a self-assured and somewhat pompous nature. Hengist pretends to be shocked and appears to believe that any conclusion other than that Scott is the killer is inconceivable (150-51).

Though she does not live long enough to complete her reading, Sybo does--though somewhat cryptically--proclaim the nature of the murderer, as well as some of his (its) many names. She goes into a trance state, speaking in "a much older voice, deeper, resonant":

> "Yes, there is something here in this room . . . terrible--out of the past. I feel its presence--fear, rage, hatred. . . . There is evil here--monstrous, demonic. . . . A consuming hunger that never dies--hatred of life, of woman . . . an ancient hunger that feeds on terror. . . . It has been named--boratis--kesla--redjac." (Bloch 160)

Just before Sybo screams and is found to be dead, Kirk hears "a rushing sound like the flapping of great wings" (160) reminiscent of those of Lucifer.[22]

---

[22] A detail the television episode would not allow, this one points to the mythological inspiration of this episode. The Christian devil, Satan, is a "fallen angel," and angels are traditionally portrayed as winged.

Another traditional trait of the Christian devil is involved when Scott later--on board the *Enterprise*--testifies that, just after the death-scream of the first victim, he felt "something." Kirk asks if he does not mean "someone." Scotty insists that it was "Some--thing. Cold--it was cold like a stinking draft out of a slaughterhouse. But it wasn't really there" (164).

Thus, the evil being responsible for the murders is associated--in the various suggestions made so far--with fear, with hatred, with wings, and with cold--all items traditionally associated with the Christian devil. Fallen angels would perhaps still have wings. Cold is associated with the devil in the tales of witchcraft in the Middle Ages and Renaissance.[23] Hatred of all life and creation, especially of woman as the symbol of life, is also a traditional characteristic of the devil.[24] Because of this hatred of mankind, the Evil one would inspire fear. Traditionally, the devil promotes death, hence the reference to "a slaughterhouse."

In the court investigation, now on board the *Enterprise*, Mr. Spock uses the computer to find that all three names Sybo gave refer to mass murderers of women: "Red Jack," or "Jack the Ripper," on earth (132); "Kesla" on Deneb II; and "Boratis" on Rigel IV. None of the murderers was ever apprehended. In fact, a string of other such unsolved cases could be documented between earth of the nineteenth century and Argelius of the twenty-third (167-68).

---

[23]This association of *cold* with the Prince of Darkness appears in more than one place, whether it be in Dante's *Inferno* or in the "The Exorcist" (1973) This might seem to conflict with image of the *fires* of hell, but these opposing symbols make different points about evil, or at least about the Christian personification of evil. To put it simply, cold implies lack of life, the negation of life and creation, while fire represents (for one thing) the passion for destruction--primarily, evil's attempt to negate the good. The primary symbolism is that of the self-ignited and consuming hatred of the fallen angels.

[24]Cf. Satan's approach to *Eve* first as the eventual vessel of life.

127

Spock and McCoy postulate that all the murders could have been committed by a single entity, a being practically immortal, and deriving its sustenance from terror. Spock says that such a postulated entity would exist without form in the usual sense, assuming whatever physical form fits its purpose. The computer cites a precedent for the existence of such an entity in the "cloud creature" on Alpha Majoris I (169).

McCoy and Kirk suddenly remember that Mr. Hengist, the city administrator, is from Rigel IV. Spock uses the computer to find that the knife from the first murder originated on Rigel IV. Seeing the circumstantial evidence pile up against him, Hengist runs for the door. As Kirk knocks him out, the lights fade, the room is filled with the sound of great wings flapping (171), as though the entity were leaving the body of Hengist.

When the lights come back on, it is found that Hengist is dead. The evil entity has fled to the computer, from which it screams in "obscene merriment" its erstwhile name, "Red Jack." A "scene" containing many of the commonplaces related to the traditional Christian idea of hell appears on the computer screen as

> a riot of changing colors. . . . Serpents writhed . . . Naked women . . . [riding] shaggy . . . goats. Horned beasts pranced with toads. . . . Above them, . . . fiery winds . . . snow. Up from the glacial landscape rose a towering three-headed shape, its mouths agape with gusts of silent laughter. . . . A cross, upturned . . . an unspeakable travesty of the crucifixion . . . vast, leathery wings unfolded. (171-71)[25]

---

[25]This scene does not appear in the television show except as moving colors on *Enterprise*'s viewing screen. Presumably, television editors required the cutting of mythological/theological content of this nature. The prose passage is full of diabolic imagery: the extremes of heat and cold, animals such as frog and serpent, punishment of human beings, blasphemy regarding the central Christian symbol, and Dionysian sexual imagery related to the devil's role as tempter of Christians to "sin" and as bearer of the role of the earlier sexual deities, as well as the Miltonic "leathery wings." (Dante's *Inferno*, which in important respects, represents Catholic ideas on hell in the Middle Ages, contains ice and a triune demon at the pit's bottom. Cf note 23.) Russell mentions the metaphor of cold and says that "Jung himself used this imagery" (232).

This scene clearly indicates that this Red Jack entity is indeed an embodiment of the Christian devil existing in the twenty-third century.

Kirk and McCoy decide to administer a heavy sedative to everyone on the ship. They realize that the entity will try to terrorize everyone before killing them all. Thus, the entity flees the computer[26] and enters the body of Jarvis the Prefect, who starts an "insane howl" of "Kill! Kill you all! Suffer, suffer! Die!" Spock puts an end to that song with the Vulcan nerve pinch, and now Hengist comes alive again (176). Somehow, Kirk and the others are able to carry Hengist to the transporter room, and they beam Hengist and the entity within him into "Deep space--widest angle of dispersion" (177). "But it can't die!" says Dr. McCoy. Spock takes the rationalist point of view: "Indeed, its consciousness may survive for some time, but only in the form of billions of particles, separate bits of energy, forever drifting in space--powerless, shapeless, and without sustenance" (177).

So, symbolically speaking, the verdict here is that evil is not really an ultimate force which is indestructible. Yet here evil is not portrayed as the human shadow, the dark side of consciousness needing to be re-integrated with the ego.

The entity in this story does not carry the double meaning that the Christian devil does. The Christian devil is, in one sense, the personification of the human shadow. Yet, also, it seems to be a symbol of evil, primal and eternal, as an absolute principle existing outside of humanity. The entity appearing in this episode is like "the devil himself," in important respects not a particular individual's shadow side, yet it is given a purely naturalistic interpretation by the major voices of the story. Thus, "Wolf in the Fold," like so much of science fiction and fantasy, represents the presentation of mythological symbols in space age guise.

---

[26]Again, in the printed form, the flapping of great wings is heard.

Indeed, these are but a few of the examples of the theme of evil and of the dark side of the human psyche mythologized onto the new projection screen of outer space and the future. The shadow also plays an important role in all of the next three chapters, each of which is a treatment of the mythic elements in a single science fiction novel.

CHAPTER SEVEN

COLIN WILSON'S *THE MIND PARASITES*:

SHADOW, SELF, AND PSYCHOLOGICAL EVOLUTION

In *The Mind Parasites* (1967), Colin Wilson shows the strong influence of the more visionary elements of Bernard Shaw in his ideas on Creative Evolution. Wilson combines such concepts with mythic space age versions of what Jung would call the confrontation with the shadow and individuation or the journey toward the self.

In the preface to *Back to Methuselah: A Metabiological Pentateuch* (1921), Shaw refers to that piece and to *Man and Superman* (1902) as "legends" or "fables" of what he calls "Creative Evolution" (71-72), as "unmistakably the religion of the twentieth century" (64). Calling *Methuselah* his "beginning of a Bible for Creative Evolution," he hopes that it will soon be left "far behind" by a hundred "apter and more elegant fables by younger hands" (72). "Creative Evolution" is hardly *the* myth of the century as Shaw saw it, but it *is* related to Jung's idea of the individual's psychological journey paralleling the hero's journey in myth.

Shaw was correct in his prediction as to "apter," if perhaps not "more elegant," fabling--at lease regarding what is presented in Colin Wilson's work. *The Mind Parasites* Wilson's first novel of ideas--is a science fiction tale whose opening is set in the last decade of the twentieth century. It presents a picture of human evolution and the problems of the modern era which gains from but in important ways surpasses that of Shaw. It avoids the vagueness of Shaw's ideas on "Creative Evolution" but profits from containing psychological insights paralleling those of Jung.

Further, it Wilson's novel qualifies as mythic in that, despite the fantastical nature of the story, many of its ideas are believable, as extrapolations on the science of the time. That its depth gains a great deal from being seen from the point of view of Jung's psychology of the collective unconscious is related to Wilson's psychologically valid central literary (and essentially mythic) symbol of the "mind parasites."

Shaw's realization of the prime importance of the mythic element--or at least of what legend or fable represents--is, in itself, quite valid. However, the productions of this "professional legend maker" (62), as Shaw calls himself, are not themselves very vital examples of myth in literary form. They are in one sense not realistic enough and, in another sense, not fantastical enough to really "live" as myths. As Joseph Campbell points out, in "Mythological Themes in Creative Literature and Art," myth (in one of its functions) renders a cosmological image of the universe "in keeping with the science of its time" (140). Shaw's fables are quite weak on the scientific element.

Further, Shaw's vision *is* essentially humanistic and social, rather than being in any major ways cosmic and psychological and open to the unknown and to the mysterious. His stories (parts of his dramatic pentateuch) taking place in 2170 ("The Thing Happens" 155-), in 3000 ("Tragedy of an Elderly Gentleman" 199-), and in 31,920 ("As Far as Thought Can Reach" 261-)--ignore, for the most part, the probability of much technological change. Shaw's contemporary H.G. Wells, by comparison, despite his sometimes very Victorian-all-too-Victorian elements, does present pictures of the future that are to *some* extent in keeping with realistic expectations extrapolating on the science of his time. Shaw, though, almost totally ignores one of the major preoccupations of the twentieth century--technological change. This omission, in a work dealing with the future, leaves it somewhat insipid.

133

Very little of *Back to Methuselah* is really fantastical or visionary or symbolical in the sense of many of the greatest myths. As through a transparency, what we see always is Shaw the moralist and social critic, the enemy of hypocrisy and of any sort of "mental shabbiness." Here he is, trying to translate his long-held frustrations with society and politics into this vague fable on the Life Force. His ideas of emergent deity and creative evolution generally parallel concepts of various contemporaries, including William James, Henri Bergson, and C.E.M. Joad. Yet the way Shaw presents it, the idea has very little of life about it, very little of the mystery and "mad vision" of the best mythological works of science fiction.

According to Franklyn Barnabus, in *Back to Methuselah*, evolution is the "pursuit of omnipotence and omniscience," of "greater power and greater knowledge" (141-42). It is that "and nothing else," he says. His brother Conrad, partner in the preaching of evolution, makes the point that "The Eternal Life persists; only It wears out Its bodies and minds and gets new ones like new clothes" (141).

Interestingly, the above passage is a loose paraphrase of the Hindu *Bhagavad Gita*'s proclamation concerning the mind-stuff of the universe, the cosmic self that embodies itself in all existence yet pre-eminently in life and in consciousness (50). The self, in the perennial myth, though, is not "struggling" or "pursuing" but rather playing, hiding from itself in myriad forms of existing reality (Coomaraswamy, *Hinduism* 6-7). It certainly is not searching or struggling for more power and knowledge in the sense of a being in need, as Shaw's Life Force seems to be. This cosmic self is frequently termed "God," "Brahman," or the "Tao," and is certainly is related to what Jung calls the self, which is transpersonal and by no means the same reality as the ego.

It is, of course, possible that Shaw means something close to the above ideas in at least some of the statements of his mouthpiece characters, yet such is somewhat questionable. Shaw has his evolutionary philosopher Don Juan, in *Man and Superman*, speak of the primacy of contemplation to the life of the new man, the Superman, who is essentially a philosopher. Yet what he means is not very clear. It is very likely that this "contemplation" has in it very little of the mystical and psychological depths involved in the perennial mythic image of the sage, as in Hinduism, Buddhism, Taoism, and native cultures all over the world.

Though some of his statements have a certain mythological import if one is free to interpret them in any way he pleases, such is a bit impractical in that very little clear support resides in the text for such interpretations. Shaw is an attractive writer, and we can put up with his fuzziness sometimes. More importantly, in this matter of the mythic consciousness in literature, he presents at least a crude conception of the mythic needs of our era and the concept of evolution--despite his flaws.

Shaw's writings found a worshipper of sorts in Colin Wilson, despite the fact that Wilson has again and again concerned himself with themes and techniques quite beyond Shaw's rationalistic social concerns. Mesmerized by Shaw during his teen years, Wilson later wrote a highly laudatory critical volume called *Bernard Shaw: A Reassessment*. In the "postscript" to that book, he mentions his contribution to the "parables of creative evolution" by younger hands as "a rather bulky novel," *The Philosopher's Stone* (1968), strangely ignoring *The Mind Parasites* of the previous year (279). But that novel surely qualifies, too.

In *The Mind Parasites*, Wilson strives for realism of a sort. His vision of the future of the late 1990s and touching on the first two decades of the twenty-first century contains space travel, which is not totally outside of the realm of realistic expectations, and goes far enough into the fantasies of our day as to include the motif of contact with extraterrestrials. On the other hand, the novel's central symbol of "mind parasites" is clearly of mythological import in the best

Jungian sense.[1] The myth has very modern, very psychologically relevant meanings.

When archeologist Dr. Gilbert Austin becomes executor of the scientific papers of his deceased friend, psychologist Karel Weissmann, he enters a voyage of "creative evolution" in the psyche through the confrontation and overcoming of the mind parasites. These strange entities function as the dark cherubim guarding the hero's road to enlightenment (See Campbell, *Hero* 71-73, 77 ff.), as embodiments of what Jung calls the shadow ("Archetypes" 20-23). According to Jung, the shadow archetype stored within the collective psyche is manifested in the Christian devil, the nay-sayer, Göethe's spirit of negation (Jung, *Psychological Aspects* 348).

Weissman's suicide, Austin discovers, was caused by an attack by the mind parasites, which have been attacking man's psyche, sapping his vitality, replacing it with negativism and despair since about the time of the French Revolution. Beginning to read of Weissmann's amazing theory in the scientific notes that he left, Austin comments on the idea in historical context. Austin reads Weissmann's comment that he has for some months thought that the human species has been in the process of being attacked by a kind of "mind cancer."

Austin sees this "mind cancer" as the "neurosis" or "spiritual malaise of the twentieth century." He mentions such elements as rising suicide rate, incidence of child murder in the modern family, danger of nuclear conflict, and drug addiction (55-56). Certainly, such elements represent negatives in human experience, cases in which the darker impulses get humanity by the throat, so to speak.

The splitting off of the shadow side to the point that it takes over in certain instances is certainly one definition of the neurosis mentioned by Austin. Austin finds other passages which closely parallel descriptions of what Jung calls

---

[1]See Chapter 6 for other discussion of this motif.

the shadow embodied in the objective correlative of the "mind parasites." Austin claims that for over two hundred years the human psyche has been constantly preyed on by the energy vampires. In some instances they were able to completely take over a human mind for their own use (65). He gives the example of De Sade and later mentions the probability that Hitler was such a soul possessed (67).

Austin undergoes an attack of the mind parasites throwing him into a state of mind replicating the bleak house of materialistic determinism, absurdity, and insignificance which has plagued the twentieth century:

> All at once, my thoughts took a gloomy turn. I felt totally insignificant, meaningless, standing there. My life was the tiniest ripple on the sea of time. I felt . . . the indifference of the universe, and a kind of wonder at the absurd persistency of human beings whose delusions of grandeur are incurable. Suddenly it seemed that life was no more than a dream. For human beings it never became a reality. (30; Also cf. 109).

Austin is able to bring himself out of this slough of despondency by realizing his humanity, his status as a conscious entity. He realizes that his mind contains great depths, that "Whether it is an illusion or not" his mind "contains knowledge of all the ages" (31-32).

The mind parasites are a modern mythological embodiment of the archetypal shadow emerging from the collective psyche. The other great mythological embodiment in the novel is Austin's imaginative vision of the human mind, an image clearly parallel to the collective unconscious with what Jung calls the self as the center of creative self-renewal, transformation, evolution. Austin envisions the psyche in its wholeness as a world of never-ending creativity:

> If space is infinite, how about the space *inside* man? Blake said that eternity opens from the centre of an atom. My former terror vanished. Now I saw that I was mistaken in thinking of myself as an object in a dead landscape. I had been assuming that man is limited because his brain is limited . . . . But the spaces of the mind are *a new dimension*. The body is a mere wall between two infinities. Space extends to infinity outwards; the mind stretches to infinity inwards. (31-32)

He does not fear the parasites, the spirits of negation, when he is empowered by such thoughts.

Certainly, Austin's thoughts are akin to those of the Tantric Buddhist, Lama Anagarika Govinda, quoted with approval by the contemporary atomic physicist, Fritjof Capra:

> The external world and [the Buddhist's] inner world are for him only two sides of the same fabric, in which the threads of all forces and all events, of all forms of consciousness and of their objects, are woven into an inseparable net of endless, mutually conditioned relations. (143)

Jung also notes the startling parallel between the outer, the universe, the world of atoms of matter, and the inner, the world of the psyche, when in a discussion of the archetypes, he says that, "If on the basis of its observations psychology assumes the existence of certain irrepresentable psychoid factors, it is doing the same thing in principle as physics does when the physicist constructs an atomic model" ("Nature" 124). He goes on to note the parallelism between the two necessarily negative terms, unconscious and atom, a term meaning "indivisible" (not divisible). Austin's reflections here in Wilson's science fiction fantasy are in keeping with the speculations and observational images of twentieth-century psychologists and physicists.

While on a fruitless archaeological expedition which later turns out to have been engineered by the devious mind parasites, Austin and his scientific partner Reich discuss directly Jung's concept that "human minds are not separate islands, but are all part of some great continent of mind" (39). They speak also of Aldous Huxley's having come to similar conclusions.

Huxley saw the mind as a kind of infinity within every human being. He sees the human psyche as its own world, a planet having its various kinds of terrain and animals (40). Huxley, in *Heaven and Hell*, in such a metaphorical manner, is clearly being metaphorical, speaking in a "mythological" fashion, as is Jung when he speaks of the elements of the collective unconscious which are embodied in the human figures pictured in the symbols of myth and dream. Jung, for example, sometimes uses personal pronouns, speaking of the anima as "she," and alludes to such personages as "the old wise man." Though having no form and not being human in the ordinary sense, these beings within the human psyche contain such creative power that they have embodied themselves as the *dramatis personae* of the myths, religions, and dreams of mankind since time immemorial.

The characters in Wilson's novel confront the parasites as real beings which have invaded mankind, as such creatures do in Raskolnikov's dream near the end of Dostoyevsky's *Crime and Punishment* (1866). Yet, such is the way with myth, whether ancient or modern. Acteon sees Diana as the goddess, a beautiful woman with superhuman powers, but we may examine the myth and realize that Diana is the anima, the feminine portion of the male psyche with which the heartless dandy has never come to terms (*Primitive Mythology* 62-64).

In some of the key portions of the story, the mind parasites function very much as Jung says the repressed archetypal shadow does. These parasites stir up racial hatred between militant Blacks in South Africa and Neo-Nazi's in Western Europe. The conflict comes close to precipitating nuclear war, which might mean the absolute end of all evolution (and life) for the human species. But disaster is averted through the now highly evolved will, the psycho-kinetic and contemplative powers, of Austin, Reich, and their colleagues. In using the concentrated will to defeat the enemy within, they gain great inner powers.

The shadow, an actual component of the psyche symbolically embodied in the mind parasites, is described in connection with the intense scene on the space ship where Austin and his allies engage in the last symbolic battle with the mind parasites. Austin says that

> Something infinitely evil and slimy was pushing its way from inside me. They were one; they were 'It,' something I can only compare to an immense, jelly-like octopus whose tentacles are separated from its body and can move about like individuals. It was incredibly nasty . . . like . . . finding that some great carnivorous slug has eaten its way halfway into your body. (177-78)

It is significant that the moon is driven away from the earth out into space in the process of their ridding the earth of the mind parasites. Man evolves beyond the state of enthrallment by the shadow (which is so frequently associated with the moon). The speculation about the parasites having travelled from the moon to earth in the distant past is essentially a piece of scaffolding for the real story perhaps lacking much deeper meaning.

Austin and Riech come to realize, through their own experience and through the writings of the late Dr. Weissmann, that the overcoming of the mind parasites by the human race will precipitate a giant leap in the psychological evolution of humanity. Coming to terms with the shadow, according to Jung, is a major step toward "individuation," "selfhood," the evolution of the individual psyche. Here the overcoming of the parasites is actually possible only after one has looked deep within to the point of recognizing and developing the powers of the deep psyche which emanate from what Jung calls the self, the transpersonal core of the individual; or what Austin refers to as "a secret life source in the depths of [humanity's] being"--as "this deep source to man's conscious being" (181).

In evolving thus creatively--through the use of conscious will as well as acquiescence to the deep unconscious self--the life force beyond the ego--Austin and his friends, and ultimately the human race, may now reach out beyond--to the sentient, but perhaps not by any means always human, universe. Out there, this aspect of evolution is seen in the contact and meeting with extraterrestrials from Proxima Centauri by Austin and Reich. Having made psychic contact with the alien beings, they get themselves chosen for an archaeological mission to Pluto. Later, their ship, the *Pallas*, is discovered to have been abandoned. Austin and Reich have left on earth a contingent of individuals to try to teach humanity the new way of perceiving reality which they have evolved. Having been at the center of the advanced guard of evolution, Austin feels he has "lost contact" (220) with most of the rest of humanity.

One of Austin's last recorded statements is highly reminiscent of Wilson's mentor, Shaw: "The human race could go back to school. And why not, since it was largely composed of schoolboys?" (222). Also reminiscent of Shaw is Austin's suggestion that in this new stage of evolution, "men will live for centuries instead of dying out of boredom and defeat at the age of eighty" (217). Yet, indeed, Wilson's fable contains most of Shaw's major insights but with much more intensity and clarity in a tale that is more far-reaching in its mythic form and psychological import.

CHAPTER EIGHT

SHADOW/SELF AND THE DILEMMAS OF THE IDEAL--
CHRISTIAN OR TECHNOLOGICAL

That Hideous Strength (1946), the third novel of C.S. Lewis's "space trilogy," is set against the background of space travel and civilization's technical advances in the middle of the twentieth century. It portrays an anti-life conspiracy mounted by petty individuals mesmerized by the ideal of "progress through science," which Lewis had attacked in non-fiction prose form in *The Abolition of Man* (1943). These individuals are possessed by what Jung calls the archetypal shadow representing the worst repressed portion of civilized humanity, the underside of Western Christian consciousness (223 ff., 298 ff.). In several respects--especially in the using of the mythical magus Merlin as Christian antagonist to these forces--Lewis unwittingly undercuts his own attempt at Christian polemic and participates in a new myth.

The Nazi's--Lewis's contemporaries at the time he was writing the novel--were, like Lewis's scientists also possessed by the archetypal shadow, possessed by their desire to conquer and subdue the non-Aryan world. They were also possessed with the images of themselves as representing the "master race" which would "clean the planet" (Cf. *Hideous* 172) of other "inferior races" which life had so indiscriminately produced. They were, they believed, the embodiments of godhood in human form, using the imagery of the Nordic pantheon to enhance this image.

Lewis's fictional history of the last days of the National Institute of Co-ordinated Experiments (ironically, N.I.C.E.) is portrayed as taking place "vaguely 'after the war'" (7). In many of the essentials, this company is much like the Nazis, though portrayed as emerging in the England. The philosophy Lewis thinks he is portraying as being at the heart of the organization is the vitalism of figures like Bernard Shaw, Henri Bergson, and C.E.M. Joad. However, Lewis makes his proponents of vitalism to be cold-hearted monsters who devalue organic life in their desire to supersede it.

These individuals and the organization they use as their instrument are portrayed as being shadow-possessed in several ways. Lewis is quite correct in his portrayal of the smoldering and bumbling and uncoordinated nature of evil, and of the shadow-possession of these essentially bureaucratic types. However, his choice to attack the vitalistic philosophy he thought he knew and knew he hated in Shaw, *et al*, was a mistake in that Lewis is not able really to portray any form of vitalism but that of a caricature in such figures as Frost and Filostrato.

Despite the fact that Lewis had the opportunity to be acquainted with a number of versions of the new evolutionary myth of humanity's future after leaving his earthly cradle, he is unable to do anything but malign it in a most provincial manner.

The N.I.C.E. plans ultimately and totally to conquer the feminine, the earth, other human beings, other planets and species out there in space, even to conquer death--at least in regard to certain individuals. Its members plan ultimately to realize--but in the wrong way, as emissaries of Satan or Lewis's dark eldil--what the Christian Lewis thinks were God's original intentions for humanity--the metamorphosis to godhood.

The N.I.C.E. people fall into two categories in regard to their shadow-possession. Some--like Wither, Lord Feverstone (Dick Devine), and Jules--are egomaniacal, petty individuals who are hollow at the core and, in that sense, possessed by the shadow side of being, by the evil of non-being masquerading as being. Such evil is, like Conrad's Kurtz, open to the use of no one knows how many active forces of evil. Thus, these bureaucrats and functionaries, whose language is pure verbiage, are the facade, mirror, and instrument of the other category of N.I.C.E. members, whom they ape.

The other N.I.C.E. men--like Frost, Filostrato, and Straik--are scientific and philosophical visionaries utterly possessed by the shadow. Egoistically, they are possessed by the malign aspect of the God-image, in theological terms--or by the dark side of the father-image, in secular (or Freudian) terms. Possessed by the hatred of the feminine and by their intellectual, masculine hubris, they wish to destroy everything they believe drags them down and to become gods. So, in one sense, they are possessed by the shadow side, the malign aspect of the very technological civilization which they purport to represent as humanity's only hope. Actually, they are possessed by the lust for destruction, the destruction of the feminine, of all of life which is not deemed the direct servant of humanity in its new role as god.

Lewis, in another manner, associates the people of N.I.C.E. with the shadow. In his introduction, he calls his book "a 'tall story' about deviltry" (7). Jung suggests that, in the West, the archetypal shadow or dark side of the psyche finds its deepest mythological embodiment in the Christian myth of the devil, Satan or Lucifer (181). In Lewis's novel, the collective human shadow, which is parallel to the devil, takes the form of the macrobe (or dark eldil) of the planet Thulcandra (earth), a figure who never actually appears directly in the story.

Charles Moorman, in *Arthurian Triptych* (1960), speaks of Lewis's "silent planet myth" as central to the meaning of the space trilogy. By "silent planet myth" he means the pattern emerging in *Out of the Silent Planet* (1943), first novel of the space trilogy that culminates in *That Hideous Strength*. There "Eldils" *stands for* "Angels"; "Maleldil the Elder" stands for the Christian "God"; "Maleldil the Young" stands for "Christ"; and "the bent eldil" stands for the fallen angel or "Lucifer." "Thulcandra" (earth) is silent because Maledil has quarantined it to prevent its corruption from spreading to other planets.

This one-to-one relationship of Christian theology to figures in the space trilogy even goes to the point of having Maleldil forbid the king and queen on the virgin water planet "Perelandra" (Venus) to sleep on the single fixed island (*Perelandra*). Like Adam and Eve in the "Garden of Eden," who can eat of any of the plants but one--these beings may sleep on any of the floating islands, no reason having been given as to why they must not sleep on the stationary one but that it is the command of Maleldil.

Clearly, what Moorman here calls "myth" is actually "allegory." His terminology is simply incorrect; myth is one thing, allegory another. In the space trilogy, Lewis has used an allegorical method in fashioning this so-called "silent planet myth." Further, he has also used "mythic materials," in a somewhat profligate manner, in *That Hideous Strength*, in the form of elements from the Arthurian tales of the Christian Middle Ages.

In *Out of the Silent Planet* Cambridge philologist Elwin Ransom travels to Malacandra (Mars), there learning about Maleldil, eldils, the silent planet, and so forth. Later, after his return to earth, he is taken by eldils to Perelandra (Venus), in the novel of that name, to become a savior there. He convinces the Green Queen there (the "Eve" of Venus, or "Perelandra") not to disobey Maleldil, not to cause Perelandra to fall and become like Thulcandra, the fallen, or "silent," planet. During his mission on Perelandra, Ransom kills Weston, the scientist who forced him to go to Malacandra in the first place. Weston has been trying to convince the Green Lady to disobey Maleldil and in the heat of his "devilish" arguments has become truly possessed by the bent eldil of Thulcandra. At this point, Ransom is, as it were, [or as someone like Lewis might say] empowered by the Holy Ghost to kills Weston.

We meet Ransom again in *That Hideous Strength* living as Director, or Head, of the household of Christians at St. Anne's. He is now "Mr. Fisher-King." A wound he incurred in the fight with Weston has never healed and will never heal, like the wound of Anfortas of the Grail legend or like humanity's wound in the form of Original Sin (one might add). Further, he has taken on the office of Pendragon, descendent of King Arthur. He, as well as his spiritual ancestor Arthur, has been lifted onto a level parallel to that of the Christ.

Lewis portrays Ransom and his associates as individuals who (appropriately, he thinks) accept the existence of the world as it really is, as what Lewis might call a union of mind, body, soul, and spirit. They see themselves as the earth's last chance against the forces represented by N.I.C.E. As Ransom is the "Head" of the St. Anne group, so (ironically) the real "Head" of N.I.C.E. is one of its monstrous experiments. The eunuch scientist Filostrato has somehow revived and kept alive the head of a decapitated criminal. Yet the head is in constant misery, and when it does speak it conveys messages from the "bent eldil" (Satan).

Actually, the head has essentially a symbolic meaning to the few N.I.C.E. members who seem to know about it. With it they associate the idea of evolution, in one sense the human race's moving on to other planets and eventually to the stars, as had been envisioned by their martyr, the fallen scientist Weston. Also, they envision humanity's evolution--with the help of technology--beyond even the organic state. N.I.C.E. masterminds like Filostrato are possessed by the shadow side in their hatred of the body, the hatred of all organic life. They are possessed by their egoistical conceptions by their own intellectual capacities and by their malignant version of a scientific and evolutionary ideal which would produce immortality. Thus, Filostrato:

> In us organic life has produced mind. . . . We do not want the world any longer furred over with organic life . . . all sprouting and budding and breeding and decaying. . . . [We want to] learn to make our brains live with less . . . body . . . to build our bodies directly with chemicals, no longer have to stuff them full of dead brutes and weeds . . . to reproduce ourselves without copulation. (173)

This is, of course, a kind of self-contradictory point of view. From the point of view of Ransom, and probably also of Lewis himself, the success of the technique with which N.I.C.E. is experimenting would be "the beginning of what is really a new species--the Chosen Heads who never die. They will call it the next step in evolution" (197). Ransom fears that the other kind of humanity will become "its slaves--or perhaps its food" (197).

The philosophical idea Lewis here portrays as utterly diabolical in the context of his allegorizing of Christian and Arthurian materials is not necessarily negative in all its forms. Evolution beyond the organic is treated more objectively in much recent science fiction, one excellent example being in the work of Arthur C. Clarke, especially works like *2001: A Space Odyssey*, *2010: Odyssey Two*, and *Childhood's End*.[1] In fact, humanity's journey to the stars and into the future and into other forms of being is admitted even by some academic commentators to be, in effect, a living myth (Scholes, Rabkin 43-47). Indeed, it is perhaps part of *the* new myth of the twentieth century. Lewis's space trilogy participates in this new myth by default when Lewis undercuts his own attempt at Christian polemic.

An important element in *That Hideous Strength* from the very beginning is the figure of the magus Merlin. The hope of resurrecting him to be on their side is behind the desire of the N.I.C.E. to buy Bragdon Wood where Merlin is reputed to have been buried. The Christian group, of course, is fearful when they learn of that plot; they think it quite likely that if Merlin in resurrected, he will gravitate to the side of the evil scientists. However, they are wrong, as Merlin is only too happy to assist the Christians. The Christians have tended to see the general plan of the scientists as another attempt to scale heaven and reach godhood, as in the story of Babel: however, Merlin confounds their language at a banquet, starting with the speaker, and then others who try to speak to him; finally they are all babbling about, not understanding each other, becoming first emotional, then violent, and ultimately fighting and killing one another (343-58).

---

[1] See Chapters 12 and 9.

For Lewis to have Merlin become the agent of Ransom, a Christian and a savior figure, and to be so extreme, militates against any Christian polemical intentions--unless the Christianity to be promulgated is of a particularly bloodthirsty kind. The violent apocalypse of babble and blood which destroys the N.I.C.E. is engineered by Merlin--who is supposed to be a Christian acting in the interest of the St. Anne's household and in the interests of humanity. As Robert Plank points out, "the conflict that *That Hideous Strength* is about is solved by a peerless massacre" (35). Thomas Howard makes an unsuccessful attempt at exonerating Lewis's and Merlin's methods:

> The irony here, of course, is that all this pale and vitiated cerebralism at Belbury drives straight towards such phenomena as torture, vivisection, the unnatural preservation of the Head, and the final apocalypse when the whole thing explodes in blood and entrails. It is as though there were some judgement devised by some great dramatist, in which the punishment not only fits the crime, but in which the punishment is simply the crime itself turned back on the perpetrator. (150-51)

Yet such is not the case. The punishment is enacted by Merlin, the St. Anne's group, and the animals they release on purpose. Robert Plank is closer to a truly Christian position when he says:

> Would not Christian virtue shine brighter if the evil scheme were frustrated but the evil-doers were redeemed? . . . Lewis has not been an author to shrink from such a tour de force [redemption of the sinful]. Here, however, he piles body on body, bloody deed on bloody deed, climaxing it with the apocalyptic scene of the beasts invading the banquet. ("Lewis's Trilogy" 35)

Howard, on the other hand, is simply extreme in his attempt to legitimize what Plank's last statement mentions. He holds that:

> If you will reject and violate Nature--Nature in all of its manifestations, from plain trust between two people to kindness to animals to true sexuality and even to anatomy itself, then Nature will spring back upon you and destroy you, which is what happens with the unleashing of the animals to Belbury. (151)

Howard is less than accurate because this deed is one which is actually carried out by the "good" side and is just as "hideous" as the deeds which are, for the most part, only contemplated by the "evil" N.I.C.E. Such righteous indignation carried to the point of naked violence is an eruption of the shadow side of Christianity, just as are the cruel methods of behaviorism contemplated a part of the shadow side of modern technology.

It is ironic that this apocalyptic deed has Merlin at its center. Peter H. Goodrich alludes to Merlin as a prototype of the Faustian figure, the mad scientist figure which is most definitely related to the hubris of technology (109). In the portrayal of the N.I.C.E., we witness the modern mind in such a state of hubris as to bring forth its shadow side from the unconscious in the form of the lust for pure destruction in the quest for pure spirit.

Despite Thomas Howard's views on Lewis's insistence on "Charity" and on the innocent "dumpiness" of the Dimbles of the St. Anne's household--these "Christians" have just as dark a shadow do as the technocrats. The fact that the Christians stoop to the same methods as the scientists indicates that Lewis's theological position is extremely weak from any but an Old Testament, "vengeance is mine" point of view.

Lewis' ethical assumptions simply cannot be trusted. Despite his attempts at Christian allegory--improperly termed "myth" by Moorman--Lewis unwittingly participates in the proclamation of a new myth. It is the myth of space, of humanity's future both in time and space. The vistas of space travel and the possibilities of evolution are not negated just because Lewis associates them here with such weak vessels as Weston and Filostrato.[2]

---

[2]One is somewhat surprised to notice that Lavery's *Late for the Sky* (1992) never mentions this novel. Lewis's position in this novel in general, at least superficially, would seem to have much in common with what Lavery seems to be advancing. Could the reason possibly be the shameful way in which Lewis brings the novel to a conclusion?

Merlin stands as an amoral magus whose actions for the "good" side and his legendary characteristics point up the unacknowledged presence of the dark sides of both the Christian and of the scientist. As Peter H. Goodrich suggests, Merlin is, historically, a significant forerunner of all the mad scientists of the modern science fiction tradition. Merlin represents the hope of fulfilling one's egoistical wishes, "to shape the phenomenal world to our wills" (112).

By placing Merlin in the position of instrument of Logres, the godly land, a spiritual land contrasting to the earthly Britain, Lewis portrays his protagonists as being no better ethically than his antagonists. He thus leaves the field of the future open for a new kind of humanity identical neither to the Filostratos nor to the Dimbles.

The very presence in *That Hideous Strength* of the motif of the evolutionary advancement of humanity beyond the organic level places Lewis's work within that plethora of material of the middle to late twentieth century which constitutes a new myth. It is the myth of humanity's future in time, of its quest leading into the depths of space and perhaps even beyond matter, as exemplified in the works of a multitude of works of "science fiction."

CHAPTER NINE

SELF, OVERMIND, AND EVOLUTION:

ARTHUR C. CLARKE'S *CHILDHOOD'S END*[1]

Critics agree that Arthur C. Clarke's *Childhood's End* is a science fiction classic (Huntington 211; Samuelson 196). First published in 1953, in 1980 it went into its forty-second printing. One reason the novel has been as popular as it has been is that in a symbolic, mythic manner it treats some of the most engaging topics and pressing anxieties of our times. Though critics have noted a number of mythic parallels, they have tended to emphasize the scientific and speculative aspects of the theme of the evolution of humanity into Overmind. However, one point of view has been too much neglected--the one seeing the novel as symbolic in C.G. Jung's sense of symbols pointing to the archetypes.[2]

C.G. Jung called the symbol of aliens arriving from another world a living myth (*Flying Saucers* 314-29). Such an unprecedented event early in *Childhood's End* takes modern humanity's attention away from the cold war and the space race. The "Overlords" provide humanity with something like technological perfection, minus the tension concomitant with the human lack of the inner power and self control needed in the face of such productions of technology as the

---

[1] This essay first appeared in *Publications of the Mississippi Philological Association* (1984): 134-52. It reappears here with the kind permission of the Mississippi Philological Association.

[2] Jung saw the symbol as a multidimensional expression--having much in common with myth and pointing to archetypal realities residing in the collective unconscious--of the process of individuation in the individual psyche, also an evolution.

atomic bomb.[3] Ironically, these aliens from the heavens who save humanity from its warring instincts, its greed, and its violence are in the form of the medieval Christian devil, a major mythic symbol of what Jung calls the shadow, archetype of the dark, frequently non-utilized portion of the psyche.

The Overlords bring a paradise, a technological, modernized version of the Golden Age of myth parallel to the Biblical eschaton in which conflict is at an end, and "the wolf also shall dwell with the lamb" (Isaiah 11:6). Then comes apotheosis, the end of humanity as we know it and its transformation, redemption, through unification with the Overmind, a mysterious transcendent entity of pure spirit. The transformation, the unification with the Overmind of the last generation of children into pure spirit after they spontaneously develop paranormal psychic powers is parallel to the Christian myth of the apocalypse of redemption coming at the end of the world and ending all conflicts such as those between good and evil, God and the devil. Indeed, frequently in myth the child is symbolic of renewal and unification. Jung points out that the combination of the size of the child with the motif of invincibility--as is the case by the end of this novel--"is bound up in Hindu speculation with the nature of the atman which corresponds to the 'smaller than small yet bigger than big' motif. As an individual phenomenon, the Self," the non-egoic center of the psyche symbolized by the atman, is "'smaller than small'; as the equivalent of the cosmos, it is 'bigger than big'" ("Special" 136). The Hindu atman is another symbol parallel to Clarke's Overmind. Clarke's choice of the children as the bearers of the evolutionary leap is appropriate as is the image of the starchild at the end of *2001: A Space*

---

[3]Cf. Jung:

> It is not that present-day man is capable of greater evil than man of antiquity or the primitive. He merely has incomparably more effective means with which to realize his propensity to evil. As his ["rational"] consciousness has broadened and differentiated, so his moral nature has lagged behind. That is the great problem before us today. *Reason alone no longer suffices.* (*Undiscovered Self* 298)

Odyssey,[4] another story whose opening is set in a world split by conflicts based on egotism, greed, and power.

In the brief "Prologue"--set in the late 1970s, according to Eric S. Rabkin (22)--Clarke sketches a picture which is just as true today as it was to the 1950s--the cold war, the space race, technological and political rivalry between the superpowers. While in no way employing the psychology of the archetypes, Eugene Tanzy notes the fact that the spiritual environment of the opening of the novel is the same as that described by Jung five years later in *Flying Saucers: A Modern Myth of Things Seen in the Sky*--a world dominated by modern humanity's "tension-distraught, fragment-torn psyche" (Tanzy 185). Jung speaks of the way our schizoid world is divided between West and East, obsessed with political ideas, ideals, "isms" which have taken the place of deep spiritual experience. Jung makes the point that all such external tensions and conflicts along with the ideological issues that fuel them are emblematic of an excessive "rationalism" and the narrowly compartmentalized and dissociated state of the modern "civilized" psyche (*Undiscovered Self* 259, 262, 278). Clarke portrays humanity on the verge of space travel, perhaps soon to be powered by the energy of the atom, symbol of the apocalyptical nature of the age, reminder that humanity's technological abilities seem now, in the second half of the twentieth century, to have disastrously exceeded his self-knowledge and comprehensive morality.

The prologue centers on the two scientists who head the American and Russian space programs, Reinhold Hoffmann and Konrad Schneider, respectively. These fellow Germans last saw each other in 1945 when, after the fall of Hitler, "Konrad chose the road to Moscow" (8) and Reinhold went with the Americans. "The Russians are nearly level with us," a colonel tells Reinhold as the American spaceship is being readied for launch: "They've some kind of atomic drive--it

---

[4]See Chapter 12.

may even be more efficient than ours, and they're building a ship on the shores of Lake Baikal" (9). A little later, the colonel remarks that "We'll show them that Democracy can get to the moon first" (9). This antipathy--which one critic calls a "rather cliched rivalry" (Howes 151)--is a dangerously petty stance, actually a sort of reactionary provincialism, a nationalistic attitude of such a narrow and chaotic consciousness as to prevent one from seeing or truly valuing the totality, the mother earth which is being threatened by the squabbling superpowers with their weapons set up to defend "to the death," to recall an appropriate cliche, "our way of life."

Indeed, the precariousness of humankind's situation previous to the arrival of the Overlords is clarified at more than one point in the novel. Jan Rodericks, the adventurous would-be space explorer who stows away in the model whale on the Overlords' ship, admits the probability "that we would have destroyed ourselves with cobalt bombs and the other global weapons the twentieth century was developing" (123).[5]

Further, Karellen, the master overlord, tells the BBC that, "When we arrived, you were on the point of destroying yourselves with the powers that science had rashly given you. Without our intervention, the Earth today would be a radioactive wilderness" (136). Such an effect would have been caused by humanity's inability to take the long view, the holistic view which looks at much more than questions of national "security," which values the individual and the species and sees them against the backdrop of a universe of divine mystery.

The symbolic arrival of the aliens involves, potentially, a realization of humanity's unity as a species and with the planet, the whole earth reality, as seen against the perspective of the voids and distances of the universe. Presumably, only the few, like Rikki Storgren, Secretary-General of the United Nations, are

---

[5]Jan is speaking at a time at least fifty years after the arrival of the Overlords.

flexible minded and cosmopolitan enough in spirit to have experienced such a realization on the coming of the alien ships.

Some of humanity's negative propensities still have to be controlled by the force of the Overlords' technical power. Through Stormgren, Karellen--at the only time he ever seems to be angry--delivers the threat, "You may kill one another, if you wish, and that is a matter between you and your own laws. But if you slay, except for food or self-defense, the beasts that share your world with you--then you may be answerable to me" (44).

The threat is carried out at the next bullfight in Madrid, where the first wounding of a bull is felt, for one telling moment, by every spectator, every human participant present. Bullfighting becomes, on humanity's own initiative, at this point, as antiquated as the atomic bombs the overlords took away from him. The Overlords cause the cessation of political oppression of the (white) minority in South Africa by showing how effectively the sun can be extinguished at noon in that land (19-20).

Shortsighted opposition to the Overlords in the form of a "Freedom League" demands "Freedom to control our own lives, under God's guidance," and offers other such loaded cliches as "Man does not live by bread alone" (16). These ideologues have the narrow egotisms of limited consciousness at heart, as can be deduced from the statement of their leader, Wainwright: "Many of our leaders are blind; they have been corrupted by the Overlords. When they realize the danger, it may be too late. Humanity will have lost its initiative and become a subject race" (16). The word "America" or perhaps even "White America" or "the capitalist West" could be substituted for "humanity" to show the sentiment's formal similarity to the petty nationalisms of the cold war portrayed in miniature in the novel's first pages and even the race hatred acted out in the America of the 1960s.

In *The Undiscovered Self: Past and Present*, in which he treats the psychological climate of the cold war years, Jung points out that "all division and all antagonism are due to the splitting of opposites in the psyche" (113). However, he says that "We can recognize our prejudices and illusions only when, from a broader psychological knowledge of ourselves and others, we are prepared to doubt the absolute rightness of our assumptions and compare them carefully and conscientiously with the objective facts" (115). In this novel, the latter conditions are symbolized by the entrance of the cosmic perspective via the Overlords and humanity's evolution toward Overmind. The Overlords force the seeds of humility and honesty onto humankind.

Ruled by fear and suspicion, the opponents of the Overlords project their own negative sides--what Jung calls the shadow--onto the Overlords, who rule humanity, as it were, by remote control, not showing their physical appearance. The petty, shortsighted attitudes of the Freedom League are epitomized by a newspaper report they inspire. The headline reads, "IS MAN RULED BY MONSTERS": "The explanation for the Overlords behavior is quite simple. Their physical form is so alien and so repulsive that they dare not show themselves to humanity" (29).

The Overlords do continue to hide their appearance for at least fifty years, twice what God, in the Hebrew myth, decreed through Moses that the children of Israel must wait before entering the promised land (54). Yet that policy is not so absolute as to be without exception. Like the mythical hero Moses, who is not allowed to enter into the promised land, Stormgren receives a substitute boon.

Karellen permits Stormgren to glimpse his form from behind as though by accident--just as Jehovah lets Moses see his "hinderparts" (Exodus 33:23).[6]: "Yes, Karellen had trusted him, and had not wished him to go down the long evening of his life haunted by a mystery he could never solve" (64).

Yet the mass of human beings are not ready to confront the Overlords. Their views are still too narrow; the individual is still too much ruled by the fear

---

[6] Cf. Rabkin, "Genre Criticism" 100.

that causes him to look at anyone who is different, somehow unknown, or more subtle than the norm as a likely source of all the evil that actually exists within his own heart.

However, when the Overlords finally do show themselves, humanity has matured enough that only a few people in the crowd faint when the longlived Karellen steps down out of his ship revealing his appearance to be that of Satan. In an ironic sense, the suspicious members of the Freedom League were right: the Overlords did hide themselves because of their appearances, because to human beings of immature and limited consciousness, they would seem repulsive, their form signalling evil, the ancient fear of the unknown, fear of that which is not understood:

> The leathery wings, the little horns, the barbed tail--all were there. The most terrible of all legends had come to life, out of the unknown past. Yet now it stood smiling, in ebon majesty, . . . with a human child resting trustfully on either arm. (68)

In Jungian terms, the time has arrived when humanity can face without overwhelming fear the darkness within experience and within the individual soul without shrinking. The individual's coming to terms with the shadow, with his unknown face, is a very important step toward his evolution toward maturity, psychic wholeness, individuation--in the same way that the Overlords are here the midwives in the birth of humanity's transcendence of his limited evolutionary stage reached in the *cul de sac* of the twentieth century.

Karellen as fatherly God/devil holding two innocent children as he stands outside the ship, is a symbol with deep mythological connotations concerning the relationships between opposites. One is reminded of the coming to rapport of the wolf and the lamb in the eschatological writings of the Hebrew prophets. Another somewhat parallel image involving the theme of apparent conflict harmonized is the image of the Hindu Black Goddess Kali as described by Joseph Campbell:

> She brandishes the sword of death, i.e., spiritual discipline. The blood-dripping human head tells the devotee that he that loseth his life for her sake shall find it. The gestures of "fear not" and "bestowing boons" teach that she protects her children, that the pairs of opposites of the universal agony are not what they seem, and that for one centered in eternity the phantasmagoria of temporal "goods" and "evils" is but a reflex of the mind. (*Hero* 170n)

Campbell's description implies the mystical doctrine of the one mind-stuff, the consciousness of the cosmos. The Overlords represent the imminence of humanity's translation to Overmind. That event symbolically parallels to the mystic's movement from finite ego-consciousness to superconsciousness, and the individual's movement--in what Jung calls the process of individuation--from the state of limited consciousness bound by the ego to consciousness of the self, which unifies all pairs of opposites.

Human beings and Overlords for some time live in peace and harmony, though human beings continues to speculate on various mysteries the Overlords still see fit to conceal. Human beings assume that medieval representations of "the devil" were based on memories of some time in the distant past when the Overlords visited the earth with unpleasant and fearful results. But near the end of the novel, the Overlord Rasheverak tells Jan Rodericks that this theory was on the right track but in the wrong direction. He says that "premonition," not "memory," is the correct word, that the minds of artists and people of religion had gone beyond time and space and picked up an image of the dark, the unknown, the fear-inspiring, of what was to appear, "not at the dawn of history, *but at its very end*" (207).

Jung terms such events occurrences of "synchronicity," made possible by an aspect of certain levels of consciousness which stand outside of time and space. He sees instances of synchronicity as being involved frequently in aspects of psychic growth, transformation, and the process of individuation. In many important respects, Clarke's story of the transformation of human being to

159

Overmind is parallel to the process by which ordinary, limited consciousness in the individual is transformed into psychic wholeness, in which the various levels of consciousness are unified and the individual is able to view experience from a broader perspective.

Humanity's final approach to the apotheosis of transformation into Overmind begins at a party attended by the future mother of the first two children to experience what the Overlords call Total Breakthrough (175). Some of the guests meet the Overlord Rasheverak, who is studying Rupert Boyce's collection of books on parapsychology (81). George Greggson is surprised that a presumably technical-minded Overlord should be interested in such matters. Rupert Boyce replies that "Nonsense or not, they're interested in human psychology" (86).

In the hands of Greggson and Jean Morrell a "ouiji board" gives several nominally correct but not particularly impressive answers to yes/no questions. Yet to the question, "Who are you?" the board answers with "IAMALL" (98). It answers the question as to the home of the Overlords with the correct identification number of their star system--an event which informs the Overlords that Jean Morrell is an important link in the imminent evolution of the human species.

A few years later, the son born to Jean and George, begins to show "psychic" powers--precognition and the ability, as monitored by Karellen and Rasheverak, to explore places light years away in dreams. Soon, Jeff's sister, Poppet, develops amazing powers of telekinesis. When Greggson goes to Rasheverak to discuss the children's "problem," he is told about "Total Breakthrough," and that even back at the "ouiji board" party before their marriage, Jeff, though not yet born, was communicating thought the mind of his mother-to-be. Rasheverak comments that "Time is very much stranger than you think" (175)--a sentiment parallel to Jung's ideas on "synchronicity."

Rasheverak says that all human attempts at explanation of the psychic transcendence of time and space have been "rubbish" except for those using the "suggestive and helpful" (175) analogy which "sees every man's mind as an island surrounded by ocean. Each seems isolated, but in reality all are linked by the bedrock from which they sprang" (176). Aldous Huxley calls this view the *perennial philosophy* and finds it woven throughout human history. In *The Doors of Perception*, Huxley presents Broad's support of Bergson's theory concerning the *eliminative* function of the brain and nervous system:

> According to such a theory, each one of us is potentially Mind at Large. . . . To make biological survival possible, Mind at Large has to be funneled through the reducing valve of the brain and nervous system. What comes out at the other end is a measly trickle of the kind of consciousness which will help us to stay alive on the surface of this particular planet. (22-23)

The transformation which occurs in *Childhood's End*, considered on one level, involves a transmutation in which the "reducing valve" is in effect abolished and the mind of the human race, through the children, is opened to the universal mind, to what the Overlords call Overmind. Humanity is unified with, or is able to realize its oneness with, a force symbolic of the reality the *perennial philosophy* calls such names as the One, the Oversoul, the whole intelligent being of the universe itself.

Clarke's Overmind can be seen, then, as the condition involving the evolution of humanity from the *cul de sac* of the petty egotism and short-sightedness of the cold war period to a state beyond humanity as we know it in which such problems are not an issue because such conflicts based on the limited consciousness of the ego have--by the widening of consciousness--been abolished.

Thus, another way to see these events is as being parallel to the evolution of the individual psyche from the childhood or perhaps adolescence of egotism to selfhood, the broader state of consciousness toward which the process of individuation leads. According to Jung, the self is an entity beyond the ego which unifies such opposites as consciousness and the unconscious in a totality:

"According to this definition the self is a quantity that is supraordinate to the conscious ego" ("Relations" 177). Individuation is parallel to the religious concepts of redemption, of spiritual renewal, of a reformation in which "the original state of oneness with the God-image is restored. It brings about an integration, a bridging of the split in the personality caused by the instincts striving apart in different and mutually contradictory directions" ("Christ" 38).

Jung's self is to be associated with Clarke's concept of Overmind, as are God- or totality- concepts generally, East and West. The ancient Hebrew clause indicative of "God"--"I am that I am"--is parallel to the "IAMALL" the Overmind communicates through Jean Morrell. The same applies to the Hindu concept of the Atman-Brahman, as to Emerson's Oversoul and to the contemporary physicists' view of the combination of "matter" and "energy" we call the "universe" as being more like a gigantic thought than like an object (Talbot, *Mysticism* 175-77).

After the rest of the adult human species has perished, Jan Rodericks, the last human being, witnesses the apocalypse, humanity's apotheosis, his unification with, absorption into Overmind. Aspects of the final scene parallel the mystical experience alluded to by proponents of the perennial philosophy.

Jan watches the earth's atmosphere disappear and its mass become transparent as the children leave matter behind and integrate the energies of the planet into their being. Light is a central aspect of Jan's experience, light which is a perennial symbol of both godhead and consciousness, as well as a principle which modern physics holds to be a kind of absolute. Jan is engulfed by a feeling which is neither joy nor sorrow but a sense of fulfillment:

> Everything we ever achieved has gone up there into the stars. Perhaps that's what the old religions were trying to say. But they got it all wrong: they thought mankind was so important, yet we're only one race in--do you know how many? (217)

Indeed, the aspect of "the old religions" Jan faults is the element which could not go beyond egotism, whether egotism regarding the separate individual, the nation, the social group, or the species.

Like any symbolic work, *Childhood's End* is rich enough to be capable of being read on more than one level. As speculative fiction, it concerns the idea of an unprecedented evolutionary leap. As a psychological and symbolic novel, it represents the individuation process as individual consciousness evolves beyond egoistic limitations. Further, Clarke's novel tells an intriguing story concerning human emotions and conflicts. He humanizes the aliens, especially in the character of Karellen and in the sorrow expressed by Rasheverak for George Greggson, the first human being to know of the arrival of "childhood's end" in his son. Despite some tendencies toward some of the usual inadequacies of the science fiction genre, the novel is very meaningful on the psychological, mythic, metahistorical, and literary levels and deserves its classic status.

CHAPTER TEN

LOVE, PSYCHE, AND TRANSFORMATIONS:

THE ANIMA AND FARMER'S *THE LOVERS*

Jung's psychology sees mythological and fantasy worlds as projections of the archetypal contents of the collective unconscious. Applying that perspective to Philip José Farmer's *The Lovers* (1961) is valuable for seeing how myth sometimes functions in modern science fiction literature as regards sexual love and psychology.

Hal Yarrow, Farmer's protagonist, like the archetypal hero in Joseph Campbell's *The Hero with a Thousand Faces*, enters a magical world: Ozagen, a planet circling Alpha Centauri. There the main sentient life form, the amiable and intuitive insect/humanoid "wog," contrasts sharply with the cruelly ordered human being of the earth future in which the novel is set.

Hal grows psychologically through beginning to come to terms with what Jung calls the anima, the feminine side (*Reflections* 114-15) of his male psyche. Campbell chronicles the same experience as those discussed in Campbell's "The Meeting With the Goddess," in which the hero is able to learn of the world in the fullness of its nature through the feminine (*Hero* 109-20).

On his native planet earth, Hal is a "joat," a "jack of all trades" employed by the Sturch (or state-and-church) of the Hai-jac Union. It governs half the world of 3050 in ways similar to those of Big Brother in Orwell's *1984*. The governing terrorist philosophy is the chauvinistic religious system of "the Forerunner," Isaac Sigmen. Some of this prophet's writings are based closely on ancient Judaism; others are elaborations on such sources as the twentieth-century works of J.W. Dunn on the metaphysics of time.

Ironically, "the Israelites," followers of the "Backrunner" are the union's worst enemies--yet the Sturch deifies obedience of a Law as strict and singleminded as that of Moses. Each person is watched by a "gapt," who assigns an "M R" or Morality Rating. A low M R can prevent a promotion, cause the loss of a job, or even make one a candidate for "H." Society is one dimensional, human beings having no freedom, their thoughts being controlled by the Sturch's "prophecy" and propaganda, their psychological and social experience so limited as to be almost robot-like.

Hal is filled with longings transcending the ideal of obedience to the Sturch. The book begins with his muttering in a dream, "I've got to get out . . . There must be a way out" (1). His situation is seen poignantly in the scenes with his wife, Mary. Mary is a chaste and dutiful servant of the Sturch and reports Hal to the local gapt for cursing or being a bad husband according to Sturch standards which demand children yet devalue sex. Mary, though, glories in the strictures and formulae of the Sturch.

Hal's life is particularly incomplete as regards his relationship with the feminine. The fact that marriage is extremely codified and formalistic takes all the true life out of his marriage to Mary from his point of view, all the mystery, all the romance and psychological depth which, according to Jung, are the particular province of the anima, archetype of the feminine.

Indeed, all indications are that the Hai-jac Sturch has sapped the lives of its citizens in general of the aspects of experience related to the anima. The anima is the unconscious, inborn pattern representing the feminine aspects and potentialities of a man's psyche. The world of the unconscious in general for the typical male is feminine in character, for it contains all those aspects and possibilities he has repressed or rejected in the name of living up to the masculine sexual and occupational demands of his society.

Hal's being chosen as the linguist on an all-male expedition on a sleeper ship to the distant planet Ozagen is a lucky break for Hal. Thus, he escapes from Mary in whom the most soul-killing and irritatingly boring aspects of life under the Sturch have found human, personal embodiment. The ruthless, totally unfeeling purpose of the expedition is to learn enough about the Wogs, or Wogglebugs, who rule the planet to exterminate them and settle their planet.

The Terran discoverer, on seeing the planet, had exclaimed "Oz-again!" (75), it is reported, because it was like another Oz, a magical realm like that of Frank L. Baum's fantasy. Indeed, in an important sense, the land, for Hal at least, is like that realm beyond that of the world of everyday consciousness which Joseph Campbell says the traditional hero enters during his prototypical journey (30). Campbell's paradigm of the hero journey--constructed out of the cross-cultural facts of myth and ritual--parallels what Jung calls the process of individuation ("Relations" 122, 127). The magical zone represents the unexplored world of compensations and complementary adventure in what Jung called the personal and collective unconscious.

These "Wogs," while walking erect and being basically the size of human beings, are reminiscent of insects--hence "wogglebugs." In important respects they represent the Jungian shadow archetype which involves the aspects and potentialities of experience repressed, rejected, or ignored by the conscious attitude (*Reflections* 242, 243, 248). The Wogs place great importance on the role of feeling, something essentially denied by the Hai-jac Union. In fact, Fobo, the wise wog who becomes Hal's best friend, is a psychotherapist, known specifically as an "empathist," that is, one who enters into the feelings and thoughts of others. The society from which Hal comes has tended to make any sort of human empathetic contact impossible or at least very difficult. For example, no one would want another to know of his inner world for fear of detection by the "gapts" or watchers of public morality.

Another aspect of consciousness repressed by the Hal's conditioning by the Sturch is that of sensation which is of course involved in the experiences he undergoes when he and Fobo visit the city of Siddo's night world of lowlife taverns, music, intoxication, and fights.

Yet Hal's deepest compensatory experience on Ozagen is his love affair with a female, Jeannette. This experience parallels the "Meeting with the Goddess" stage of the hero-journey. It represents as well the confrontation with the anima, the archetype representing the repressed feminine side. Hal meets Jeannette while exploring ruins once inhabited by humanoids who are now all but extinct on Ozagen.

While walking in the moonlit ruins with Jeannette, to all intents a beautiful woman who has sought Hal out while the others slept, the linguistic joat finds that her language, which he is able to understand only with great difficulty, is a degraded version of Terran French. The last Terran speaker of French died centuries ago, but Jeannette is supposedly a descendent of a French expedition which left earth secretly. Of course, Farmer's having the representative of the feminine principle and the world of sexual romance be a speaker of French is definitely calculated, but a campish tone and a string of humorous ironies run through the whole novel, so perhaps it is artistically appropriate.

Jeannette energizes Hal's life, causing him to grow psychologically. As Farmer puts it, "She was what he needed to spark his guts, make him step onto a path that could not be retraced" (87). He volunteers for the gruelling 'Meter' initiation, to raise his status to that of one of "the chosen" of the Sturch so that he may move into his own apartment outside of the gaze of a gapt and, therefore, be able to keep Jeannette hidden there. He becomes a lover to her, something he could never really be with his wife back on earth. She becomes the factor that allows him to develop self-respect and strength of will, qualities discouraged by his extremely repressive and one-sided rearing by the Sturch: "Without her, he was nothing, a resentful but scared rabbit. A few hours with her had enabled him to overcome many years of rigid discipline" (101).

Jeannette is thus already exhibiting the characteristics of the individual who embodies for the man what Jung calls the anima, the archetypal image of the repressed, feminine side of experience. In particular, she represents that side of Hal's potentiality for experience--depth of feeling, height of sexual energy--that the extremely parochial, patriarchal Sturch has ruthlessly repressed.

Yet soon after she has moved into Hal's apartment she reveals a negative characteristic--alcoholism. Of course, an archetype such as the anima, which Hal projects onto Jeannette, contains both negative and positive potentialities, sometimes ambiguities. Jung makes the following point:

> Because the anima wants life, she wants both good and bad. These categories do not exist in the elfin realm. Bodily life as well as psychic life have the impudence to get along much better without conventional morality, and they often remain the healthier for it. ("Archetypes" 28)

Indeed, Jeannette's love and her need for alcohol force Hal ever further beyond the realm of the conventional morality he is sworn to uphold as one of the chosen ones. He and his wog friend Fobo go into the night district of Siddo's taverns and dives to obtain liquor, and, because of a set of complicated circumstances, Hal cooperates in the death of his former gapt or morality watcher, Pornsen.

Being in love with Jeannette, the individual onto whom he has projected his anima image, along with other aspects of his experience on Ozagen precipitate a number of gradual changes in Hal that cause him to begin to be a more psychologically whole individual. One example is his forming a true friendship with the alien Fobo.

Hal makes an honest mistake but one which could have been avoided if he and Jeannette had been more open with each other. He secretly mixes gradually more and more of the drug Easyglow with her alcohol in the hope of curing her of her alcoholism. Jeannette begins to show symptoms of pregnancy and to become very ill. Hal finally reveals to her his secret administration of the Easyglow, and Jeannette is very much alarmed. Hal takes her to Fobo, as Jeannette has told him that Fobo and some other wogs had at one time held her captive and run some medical tests on her. Fobo tells Hal that she has a chance for life if "her eggs" can be cut out before the they hatch and if she can be given a certain serum in time. As it turns out, Jeannette only looks human, being actually a *lalitha*, a being having important internal similarities to the insect.

While wog physicians struggle to save Jeannette's life, two of Hal's religious and governmental superiors arrest him for various infidelities against the Sturch, especially his affair with Jeannette. Their abuse points up the extremely patriarchal, anti-feminine, and repressive nature of the Sturch. Macneff calls him an "unspeakable degenerate" and "the worst pervert, traitor, and--and!" at which point he drools, unable to find words. He then proclaims that "You have lusted for and lain with an insect!" The strong Judaic component of the Sturch is evident: "With a thing that is even lower than a beast of the field! What even Moses did not think of when he forbade union between human being and beast, what even the Forerunner could not have guessed when he reaffirmed the law and set the utmost penalty for it" (183). That is what Hal is charged with. Macneff takes this extreme attitude, despite the fact that Jeannette is of a sentient species at least as highly developed as the human.

While all await the results of the operation, Fobo discusses the *lalitha*, "the highest form of mimetic parasitism known . . . nature's most amazing experiment in . . . parallel evolution" (185, 186). After human beings had originally arrived on the planet, the *lalitha* had found it necessary to disguise themselves as human women (186). Tribal mythic lore grew up about them, frequently portraying them as "witches, demons, or worse" (187). When the *lalitha* discovered that alcohol would keep them sterile, they were saved from the problem of reverting to their original form when pregnant. "At the same time, barring accident, disease, or murder," says Fobo, it made them immortal" (187).

Indeed, the *lalitha* is the very image of the archetypal anima as it has embodied itself in myth and legend down through the centuries. On the negative side, she is like the medieval succubus, a demon, or a witch. "Lalitha" is reminiscent of the dark primordial feminine Lilth of Jewish lore. On the positive side, she is like the goddess, or wise woman: "The *lalitha*, of course, became the repositories of wisdom, wealth, and power" (187).

Jung speaks of the anima as "the chaotic urge to life" but says that "something meaningful clings to her, a secret knowledge or hidden wisdom." He points out the nineteenth-century fantasy examples of Benoit's Queen of Atlantis, who "has an excellent library that even contains a lost book of Plato" and Rider Haggard's "She" or "Wisdom's Daughter" ("Archetypes" 30). At one point, Fobo suggests that "In the *lalitha*, Nature wrought the perfect female" (187). In Jungian terms, she is the anima in the flesh.

The news comes that the physicians have not been able to save Jeannette, but that the larvae are healthy and already resemble their father. Macneff exults in his hatred of life and the feminine principle:

> "You have begat larvae! Monsters of an unholy unreal union! Insect children!" (191).

The irony is that the "humanity" of the "alien" Jeannette far exceeds that of the life-hating officials of the Sturch.

As the officials are starting to carry Hal to be incarcerated, he and Fobo, in a desperate move, overpower them. Soon a very loud noise is heard--the wise wogs have set off a gigantic explosion under the Hai-jac spaceship, killing everyone on board. The wogs have known all along of the Terran's dastardly secret plans to conquer the planet.

Now Hal's keepers are all either dead or under the control of the benevolent wogs. Yet, though he has the freedom he has always longed for, he is now without Jeannette and her love. Fobo reminds him of his daughters and the fact that other beings of their kind are scattered about the planet. Of course, he also has a consummate friend in the wog empathist himself. Yet Hal's moan, which ends the novel, is "Jeannette! Jeannette! If you had only loved me enough to tell me" (200). Of course, if *he* had "only loved *her* enough" to tell her of his feelings about her alcoholism, to confront the problem instead of practicing secretive subversion, she might have been enabled to tell him.

Though by no means fully mature and serene, Hal has grown psychologically through confronting some aspects of the anima in his love for Jeannette. Within the confines of science fiction, Farmer projects beautifully into the far future this aspect of the age-old hero quest for wholeness through the deepening of consciousness. He deftly makes "out there," "where no one has gone before" another playing ground for the hero's struggle.

CHAPTER ELEVEN

THE OCCIDENTAL HERO

IN TRANSFORMATION:

STAR TREK--"THE NEEDS OF THE MANY"/

"THE NEEDS OF THE ONE"

Captain/Admiral James T. Kirk--in the *Star Trek* series on television (1966-69) and seven feature length films--represents the egotistical compulsive masculine figure bordering on hubris and having an inflated ego-persona.[1] Though such a hero easily claims our respect and admiration (in the West), at the same time, he really is a very insecure and problematical individual. Kirk develops psychologically over the span especially of the films "The Wrath of Khan" and "The Search for Spock" through confrontations with death, imperfection, and the necessity of sacrifice.

In the television episodes first shown between 1966 and 1969 and since syndicated repeatedly, Kirk is the traditional Western hero, similar to Homer's Odysseus, who was described as being, "resourceful" and "never at a loss" (Homer 25). Yet he is extremely egotistical, almost fanatical concerning his

---

[1]Jung discusses the problem of ego-inflation and "god-almightiness" in "On the Relations Between the Ego and the Unconscious" (88 ff). Karin Blair, in her Jungian study of the *Star Trek* television series, seems entirely to miss the point of Kirk's problematic character (83 ff).

responsibilities, his "duty," and always ready to risk his own life for "the ship," ever a cherished anima symbol.[2]

In his relations with flesh-and-blood women, however, Kirk is the typical occidental male of the "love 'um and leave 'um" type; indeed, according to certain references, the captain might come close to being a philanderer. In a number of the television episodes, when Kirk almost loses control of himself, as he does on several occasions, it is always because someone has taken over *his* ship, *his* captaincy--in Jungian terms, his cherished anima which gives meaning to his persona.[3] Kirk is the Western male who will not be denied. He takes great risks, holds great responsibilities; but he has difficulty dropping his egotistical stance, even when it gets in the way of the ongoing of life and relationship.

One feels that, though Kirk willing risks his life in the name of duty--when on the bridge of the *Enterprise*--he never gives up hope, never admits defeat. Indeed, he is actually *afraid* to face the possibility of failure. Rather than lose, he uses his Odyssean ingenuity to trick his adversaries. A classic example is in the grand first-season episode, "The Corbomite Maneuver." Ballok, a childlike but advanced alien, is "testing" the enterprize, to see of what mettle Starfleet people are constructed. When he threatens to destroy the ship, Kirk fabricates the bluff of the "corbomite" device which has the desired effect of saving the *Enterprise*. After threatening the alien with destruction, Kirk tells him:

---

[2]Blair is correct to note the connection of the shape of the *Enterprise* to the mandala, a symbol of wholeness (34 ff.). The *Enterprise* is also a symbol of the inspiring feminine factor within the man, in the same way any ship or airplane can be. The *Enterprise* is always "she."

[3]According to Jungian psychology, the persona is the mask the ego wears before itself and the world; the persona is frequently related to one's profession, occupation, duties, and responsibilities.

"Death has little meaning for us. If it has none for you, then attack us now. We grow annoyed at your foolishness" (Stohl 88).[4]

Kirk's comment about death is highly significant in an ironic way. As long as he is wedded to the *Enterprise*, he can face the risk of death in his stoic, masculine, occidental-heroic way. Yet in the early scenes of the movie "Star Trek: The Wrath of Khan," Kirk is in a state of despair. He has accepted a ground assignment and is essentially paralyzed in spirit, as though lost, cast out of his element. Further, the film opens on Kirk's birthday, which, it seems, reminds him of death.

Downcast because he has taken a ground assignment, away from the stars, away from the beloved *Enterprise*, away from the Odyssean journey "where no man has gone before"--Kirk still displays his egotistical, and optimistically heroic attributes. "The Wrath of Khan" opens with the trainee examination sequence and the brave attempt of Trainee Saviik to save the "Kobayashi Maru," the ship which (in the simulation) is supposed to be in trouble. The trainees are trapped by Klingon cruisers, and the teachers Spock and McCoy, as well as several of the trainees, have been "killed" or "injured," when Admiral Kirk appears, looking on, (according to the stage directions) *silhouetted in light*. He exudes the grace, authority, power, and godliness of the accomplished hero. Light is mythologically symbolic of that for which the hero strives, for ultimate at-one-ment with his deity. Here (for Kirk) the deity, or the ideal, is power in the ultimate, most masculine, and egotistical of senses. Kirk is the hero, but the hero who has withdrawn from the trek, the journey in the star ship, the speed-of-light *Enterprise*, feminine embodiment of his god.

---

[1]Also, a scene just before this one shows the contrasting positions of Spock and Kirk. Spock says that in chess when one is outmatched, he is checkmated, and the game ends. Kirk explodes: "Is that your best recommendation? Accept it?" Kirk, the Odyssean hero, ever resourceful, never gives up, never admits defeat (Stohl 86).

Kirk is a perfectionist--an individual who thinks he depends only on himself, on his own resources of physical stamina, physical strength, courage, will, ingenuity, all those characteristics of the Superman, the popular hero of the Western world. (Mr.) Saviik, the female Vulcan-Romulan aspirant to captaincy, looks to Kirk for insight and wisdom. Saviik is perturbed that she could not "pass" the test and save the Kobayashi Maru. She too is something of a perfectionist. Yet Kirk tells Saviik that no one wins, that the simulator game is "a test of character": "How we deal with death is at least as important as how we deal with life" (Cf. McIntyre, *Wrath* 179-80).

Kirk now has a chance to face death again on the teaching voyage. He faces the possibility of his own death, as well as the loss of everyone on the ship. Yet, he also faces death in another way, which is most difficult for him. He has to face the death of his oldest and best friend, the part-alien whose depth of soul, wisdom, and stoic valor he respects in a superlative manner.

Through the sacrificial death of Captain Spock, Kirk begins the true journey of the hero, the mono-mythical journey of sacrifice and redemption which brings the hero to terms with himself and leads him toward true maturity. Kirk must move beyond the egotistical and arrested stage of masculine dependence on power, just as Odysseus did after his journey in the underworld to meet the sage Teiresias.

Spock is the sage for Kirk, inspiring him in various ways, leading him toward that "lost Atlantis of the co-ordinated soul" in which the transformed hero unites masculine and feminine, logic and feeling, intellect and heart, active and passive (Campbell, *Hero* 388). Mr. Spock invested overly in the masculine world of logic earlier in his career, in the '60s television series. Yet in the first *Star Trek* movie, he undergoes a transformation which ultimately effects Kirk also, through their relationship. Spock's realization that, for the gigantic brain of V'ger, the supermachine, it came to be that logic was not enough. Spock seems now to have realized the same thing.

Some of the results of the transformation beginning at that time are seen in a scene fairly early in "Star Trek: The Wrath of Khan." Kirk visits Spock's quarters. It has just been learned that someone--Kirk's old enemy Khan, it turns out--is attempting to steal the top secret project Genesis which could be perverted to use as a superweapon. Genesis is the project of Carol Marcus, Kirk's former lover, and of their son David, whom Kirk has met but once. Kirk has gone to tell Spock that he, as ranking officer, must take over the command of Spock's trainee *Enterprise*.

Kirk tells Spock that they may have a difficulty, that matters could be awry on the science research laboratory Regula I. The *Enterprise* has been chosen to check out the situation. Kirk is bothered by the fact that the present crew manning the ship is nothing but "a boatload of children." He asks Spock how good his students are and how they are likely to respond in really stressful situations. Spock answers: "As with all living things, each according to his gifts."

He adds that Kirk, of course, may take over the captain's chair. He also says that Kirk must not make the mistake of fearing to hurt Spock's feelings for, being a Vulcan, Spock has "no ego to bruise." Kirk mentions the subject of logic, and Spock's usual claim that all his own actions are dictated by it. Spock makes bold to tell Kirk that he made a mistake in accepting the promotion to Admiral that he is best as a starship captain, that to spend his time doing anything else is a waste. Spock tells Kirk, further, that logic demands "that the needs of the many outweigh the needs of the few." "Or the one?" Kirk adds. Spock then says: "You are my superior officer. You are also my friend. I have been, and always shall be, yours."

Spock would never have been able to utter these sincere words about friendship during his period of absolute devotion to logic before he met the example of V'ger. Spock has taken on something of the air of the sage. Like the ancient Teiresias, he has begun to know both life and death, to accept the failings and imperfections of human beings while still valuing the individuals.

Also, whether Spock has an ego to bruise, Kirk certainly does. His ego *is* bruised by many things, especially any suggestion that he (Kirk) has done anything less than what he could have done in a given instance of his responsibility. He is also bothered by the suggestion that a situation is without hope for him if he does his best as a commander.

The present danger is Khan, the superman gone awry, a product of twentieth-century genetic engineering. Khan is, in the dark side of things, the mirror image of Kirk. He is the resourceful, ingenious, resolute, hero. It is significant that the subtitle, "The Wrath of Khan," alludes to the intemperate Greek hero, Achilles, to whom, in his extreme revenge, Khan is parallel. His entire activity, in "The Wrath of Khan," is an attempt to avenge himself on Kirk.

In the "Space Seed" episode of the television series, the *Enterprise* finds Khan's two-hundred-year-old ship with its inhabitants in suspended animation. After recovering his strength, Khan tries to take over the *Enterprise*, and Kirk has to maroon him on a small planet. He is now free, fifteen years later, and seeks his revenge (Coon and Wilbur).

One scene which shows Kirk's positive masculine dynamism, his heroic assertiveness, is that in the "Genesis cave" experimental world of the Drs. Marcus. Khan has stolen the dangerous "Genesis device. The admiral and his team have transported to Regula I and do not know whether they can be picked up or not by the disabled *Enterprise*. Lt. Saavik asks Kirk whether they are even now playing out the Kobayashi Maru scenario, the always-fail test of character from Star Fleet Academy. Saavik is very much interested in knowing just how Kirk dealt with that test, how *he* reacted to try to prevent his ship from being captured by the enemy. Dr. McCoy tells her that Kirk was the only cadet who ever defeated the so-called "no-win scenario." It seems that Kirk had re-programmed the simulation so as to win, or as Kirk's son puts it, he cheated. Kirk received "a commendation for original thinking." In response to his masculine explanation, "I don't like to lose," Saviik says, "Then you never faced that situation--faced death." Kirk claims not to "believe in a "no-win" scenario."

Though Kirk cheated, changed the rules of the game to restore possibility of success in the Kobayashi Maru scenario, he is unable to save his cherished friend Spock who sacrifices his life to save the *Enterprise*. With the death of Spock, Kirk finally faces death. The depth of Kirk's feeling for Spock is seen, along with the complexity of his character. His character is one in which impulses related to authority and power have for a long time ruled over those related to feeling. This situation is seen in Kirk's delivery of Spock's eulogy and Kirk's confrontation with his son David Markus afterward.

The crew has come together in solemn assembly, in the words of Admiral Kirk,

> ". . . to pay final respects to one of our own. To honor our dead . . . and to grieve for a beloved comrade who gave his life in place of ours. He did not feel this sacrifice a vain or empty one. And we cannot question his choice, in these proceedings.
> He died in the shadow of a new world, a world he had hoped to see.
> . . .
> Of my friend . . . I can only say that of all the souls I have encountered in my travels, his was--the most human!" (McIntyre, *Wrath* [text from novel] 215)

With great feeling, Kirk seems to have realized what it is to face death--at least the death of his best friend. In claiming Spock as the most human of souls, Kirk is saying a great deal; perhaps he is alluding to the deep human characteristic of giving one's own life to save the life of others.

Campbell cites what he calls "a magnificent essay" by Schopenhauer dealing with the question of why self-sacrifice exists. He says that Schopenhauer argues that "such a psychological crisis [as that bringing on self-sacrifice] represents the breakthrough of a metaphysical realization, which is that you and that other are one" (*Power* 110). Many mythological traditions see the one and the other (or the many) as being unified in the noumenal world beyond time and space--however separate they may seem to be here in the phenomenal world.

After Spock's funeral, Kirk is visited in his quarters by his David Markus. David says that he agrees with Lt. Saviik in her opinion that Kirk has never really "faced death." Kirk agrees that, indeed, he *has* never faced death as in what he experienced through the death of his friend Spock. Ever the resourceful hero, he has "cheated death. I've tricked my way out of death and patted myself on the back for my ingenuity. I know nothing." However, David reminds him that he did know enough (earlier, in the Genesis Cave) "to tell Saviik that how we face death is at least as important as how we face life."

Kirk calls this mere words. David replies that "That's where ideas begin. And maybe you should listen to them." David admits to having been wrong in his earlier negative attitude toward his father and says that he is now sorry. Further, he has come to tell Kirk that he is very proud to be his son (Cf. McIntyre, *Wrath* 219-20).

With the cathartic death of Spock experienced vicariously by Kirk, and the acceptance by his son, the seeds of transformation have now been planted in Kirk's occidental masculine heroic character. Kirk has undergone the most traumatic set of events in his whole life. The change away from his staunch egotistical attitude can be seen the final scene. Kirk stands gazing at the newly created Genesis planet toward which the photon tube/coffin of Captain Spock has been fired. As the sun rises around the edge of the new planet, Carol Marcus asks Kirk how he feels. And Jim Kirk, who in the opening scenes was obsessed with his age and what he saw as the waning of his life, says, "I feel . . . young!" (Cf. McIntyre, *Wrath* 222).

The sequel to "The Wrath of Khan," "The Search for Spock," though enjoyable, is clearly inferior to the previous film. None of its scenes display the depth of character and feeling of some of those in "The Wrath of Khan." However, what does happen is that Kirk embarks on a mission to resurrect

Spock. He must bring Spock to his homeworld so that Vulcans may reunite Spock's soul (or "Katra")--which Spock has lent to Dr. McCoy--with his body (which is yet alive on the surface of the Genesis planet). In the process, Kirk has to sacrifice the beloved anima symbol, the *Enterprise*, and to endanger his career in Starfleet. In one of the last scenes, Kirk says, "What I have done, I had to do." Sarek, Spock's father, asks, "But at what cost? Your ship . . . Your son?" Kirk's answer is: "If I hadn't tried, the cost would have been my soul" (McIntyre, *Search* 295). Just after he has been revived, Spock does not know that Kirk and the other friends have risked their careers and that David has lost his life for him. He asks Kirk, though, why he would bring him home to Vulcan so that he could be resurrected. Kirk answers: "Because the needs of the one outweighed the needs of the many" (296). This comment echoes the discussion between the two in "The Wrath of Khan" when Spock hands over the reins of authority on the *Enterprise* to Kirk.

Gerrold quite rightly proclaims the psychological and mythic significance of "STAR TREK [which] is a *noble vision* of humanity in the process of achieving maturity" (202, 204). That is most certainly true of the Khan film. Kirk, the overly masculine, Odyssean hero, is transformed in facing the death--even though it is temporary death--of his friend Spock.

CHAPTER TWELVE

THE JOURNEY OF THE HERO:

CLARKE'S *SPACE ODYSSEY* NOVELS

AND THE FUNCTIONS OF MYTH

Arthur C. Clarke's *2001: A Space Odyssey* (1968) and *2010: Odyssey Two* (1982) involve recapitulations of the mythic hero journey with its metaphysical, psychological quest to come to terms with the ultimate. In particular, these works clearly serve two of the four functions of mythology pointed out by comparative mythologist Joseph Campbell: the metaphysical and the psychological. According to Campbell, the first function of traditional mythology is "the reconciliation of consciousness to the preconditions of its own existence" ("Mythological Themes" 178)--that is, the bringing of the individual to terms with the whole of which he is a part.

One aspect of the perspective set forth by the *Odyssey* novels is the place of humanity at the dawn of the twenty-first century. Behind him lie three million years of human evolution, the beginning of which is represented by the Moonwatcher episodes concerning the pre-humans at the beginning of *2001*. According to naturalist John A. Livingston, the environmental perspective needed to face the future "will demand unprecedented humility" and "willingness to see ourselves in the perspective of time of infinite duration and of events of unimaginable magnitude" (23).

A certain humility is involved in Clarke's picture of humankind as a gardening experiment performed by an alien and superior race. He implies that this super-race has gone about seeding consciousness in various species throughout the galaxy. They visited earth in the dim past, the time of the ape men, and used giant monoliths, highly advanced "teaching machines," to induce a quantum evolutionary leap in humanity's imaginative and reasoning capacity. The serious contemplation of such a conception requires great humility indeed, for it asks that we see the human species as having been fathered by a form of consciousness as much in advance of the present stage of human development as are the gods of the world's older mythologies.

This hypothetical image, not original with Clarke, has been embodied in a mass of fantasy and pseudo-scientific material of the *Chariots of the Gods* sort. This image of early human evolution is clearly parallel to cosmogonies in a number of mythologies in which the beginning of the species is related to things even more lowly than such a scientific "seeding" experiment. In more than one near eastern cosmogony, for example, the human being is fashioned from clay by the divine powers. Clarke's modern myth, however, is closer to the Hindu myth of the entire world as the dream of a deity. Here the higher intelligences, the "deities," are engaged in an enterprise involving creativity, thought, and imagination. Yet the act is, in a manner of speaking, scientific, while that of the Hindu god Vishnu is essentially spontaneous and artistic, since his dreams are the source of creation.

The "Star Gate" astronaut Dave Bowman is eventually brought through is a kind of "switching station" between dimensions or between vastly separate portions of the universe. The alien who beings have deposited the monoliths and can do what they do with Bowman have evolved beyond the need of bodies of any kind. They are presumably those who brought "reflective consciousness" to earth in the distant past and have watched over it since then.

Concerning their evolution into the state of pure inwardness, pure consciousness, Clarke says that "in all the galaxy, they had found nothing more precious than Mind" (185). They advanced technologically to the point that their machines were more subtle than their bodies, so into the machines went their vastly developing brains. And when their brains became obsolete as the seats of consciousness, they found ways to do without them. Finally, they

> learned to store knowledge in the structure of space itself, and to preserve their thoughts for eternity in frozen lattices of light. They could become creatures of radiation, free at last from the tyranny of matter. (185-86)

These beings are parallel in certain senses to the highly evolved individual on the path to (what Jung calls) individuation.

Further, the *Odyssey* novels set forth a human perspective regarding the far future. In the context of Dr. Floyd's shuttle trip to the moon early in *2001*, Clarke uses the traditional symbolism of myth: "The time was fast approaching when Earth, like all mothers, must say farewell to her children" (*2001* 66). These words echo those of one of the early twentieth-century pioneers in the theory of space flight, Konstantin Tsiolkovsky, as quoted by Carl Sagan: "'The Earth is the cradle of mankind. But one does not live in the cradle forever'" (Sagan, "Amniotic Universe" 368). Sagan himself notes "the almost mystical appeal that space flight has for us," also mentioning the image of Star Child at the end of *2001* as one of humanity, as it were, preparing to leave "Mother Earth, the world of our origins, to seek our fortune among the stars" (368). Sagan seems to imply the beginning of a new era stretching into the far future of humanity's destiny "out there" among the stars. That involves coming to terms psychologically with the ultimate through science, which, having in the past refused to broach the metaphysical questions, is now willing to look further than matter and quantitative exploration.

The perennial hero journey Joseph Campbell discusses in *The Hero With a Thousand Faces* is the mythic prototype of all journeys and questings. The hero sets off on a journey in search of his Father (39, ff), the place of his origins, the ultimate boon of knowledge about the world. The ultimate act of the journey is the atonement, or at-one-ment, with the father, the deity, the superior being to which his own being is tied. It is worth noting that this pattern crops up repeatedly in recent science fiction. One example of the pattern in a reversed sense is the quest of the robot being "V'ger" in "Star Trek: The Motion Picture," who goes back to Earth, the place of its origins, "to join with the creator." Robert Plank sees the mysterious aliens of *2001*, "the masters of the slabs," as "father figures" (137). Plank, obviously a Freudian, neglects to point out that the father as symbol in myth points to the question of the order and meaning of the world as well as to the idea of physical origination. In sending the spaceship *Discovery* to the source of the monolith's radio symbol, humanity is indeed seeking to know more about his origins--in the dim past when the strange slab was buried on the moon--*and*, perhaps partially unconsciously, he is reaching out toward the future and reunion with the intelligence which created him. Of course, both books reveal that these advanced intelligences were once creatures of flesh and blood who have now evolved to the point of being pure spirit, energy, consciousness--a close approximation to what the mystical religions describe as God (*2001*, 170-74, 184-86; *2010*, 306-08).

The last glimpse of humanity in *2010* is in the year 20,001. The point of view of the brief epilogue is that of the Europans, the form of life found on one of Jupiter's moons by the Chinese in 2010. Their evolution toward consciousness and culture dates from the transformation of the planet Jupiter into a sun by the beings behind the monolith while the recovery ship *Leonov* was on the way back from its rendezvous with *Discovery*. In the Epilogue, the people of earth are represented by "those moving lights in the sky" which the Europans speculate are kept at bay by the awesome power of the monolith which circles the planet (330-31). We may assume that humanity has reached the point that space travel outside the solar system is routine and that humanity may have outgrown some of the social and psychological problems of the twentieth and twenty-first centuries.

Yet the epilogue ends on an ominous note. It seems that those who control the monolith are deliberately keeping the two forms of conscious life in the solar system isolated from each other. At some time in the future, the two may be introduced to each other, yet such alien forms of consciousness may not be able to coexist. If such is the case, "only one of them can inherit the solar system." Clarke leaves us with a note of uncertainty, for even "the Gods" do not yet know which (*2010*, 332). Certainly, such thoughts enjoin humility and the realization that without some openness to the point of view of the *other*, war and destruction are inevitable. The hint is that humanity may soon evolve far enough in the direction of the "Lords of the Monolith" (Plank) that it can, on its own, take a friendly, even paternal attitude toward the less advanced Europans.

Besides humanity's place in a universe vast in space and time, another aspect of the "preconditions" of the existence of human consciousness has to do with that which is outside the realm of space-time. This area has in the past been the domain of the mystics rather than the scientists. In the twentieth century, however, many of the statements of the physicists are full of the same kind of paradox and feeling-toned expression found in religious documents. The experience David Bowman undergoes after his struggle with Hal, *Discovery*'s schizophrenic computer, is one fitting into the "mystical" category.

Bowman, in the space pod, moves through the Star Gate, a kind of switching station between universes and perhaps even dimensions. This part of his journey involves both the first, or metaphysical, function of myth, and the second, involving the coming to terms with the givens of the psyche. Suddenly, he finds himself in what appears to be a hotel room in America, which turns out to be a pseudo environment created by the alien Intelligences. When Bowman falls asleep, his mind is invaded by something "the full impact [of which] would have destroyed him": "Beneath that dispassionate scrutiny, he felt neither hope nor fear; all emotion had been leeched away" (*2001* 215). The force with which Bowman has come into contact sounds very like a god or a being who has united with, or reached, the ultimate in consciousness.

Indeed, the state of apotheosis, in which the mystic in his meditation or the hero in his questing becomes one with the deity, is described in both Eastern and Western traditions as a state beyond the Clashing Rocks of desire and aversion. It is a state that has transcended such oppositions, has seen beyond them (Campbell, *Mythic Image* 497). Clarke's description of the hotel suite's dissolving back into the mind of its creator (215) is reminiscent of the Hindu idea of the world as a dream, a mental play going on in the mind of a deity (Campbell, *Mythic Image* 497). In order to reach final attainment, the hero must go beyond such opposites of good and evil which arise as characters in the play; like the Buddha, he must win the combat against the demons of fear and desire, win through to the state of serenity (Campbell, *Hero* 89, ff.).

Bowman is in the hands of something near to the Hindu concept of divinity or Aristotle's idea of the contemplative God. Bowman "was watching the operation of some gigantic mind contemplating the universe of which he was so tiny a part" (216). Bowman experiences the stage of the hero journey Campbell calls apotheosis (*Hero* 149-171) by having his consciousness regress through memory all the way back to the time of his birth:

> And even as he relived these events, he knew that all indeed was well. He was retrogressing down the corridors of time, being drained of knowledge and experience as he swept back toward childhood. But nothing was being lost; all that he had ever been, at every moment of his life, was being transferred to safer keeping. Even as one David Bowman ceased to exist, another became immortal. (*2001* 216)

The new David Bowman takes the form of a child: "In an empty room, floating amid the fires of a star twenty thousand light-years from Earth, a baby opened its eyes and began to cry" (217). The parallel is clear: according to the Christ, in order for a human being to enter the kingdom of heaven, he must become again like unto a little child. The monolith appears and performs the same function for Bowman that it did for the ape humans: it causes a quantum leap in psychological evolution. It leads to something like the lordly state of wholeness Jung calls individuation. At the end of the cinematic version of *2001*, the child is portrayed as enclosed within a circle reminiscent of the mandala, the religious and psychological symbol of the completed consciousness.

Bowman, as the disembodied psychic presence born as the star child, plays a part in *2010*, but it seems unlikely that "the Gods" will soon see fit to transform humanity *en masse* in the way they have Bowman. Indeed, perhaps it is necessary for humanity to struggle on toward psychological maturity before Bowman's journey can be for anyone but the few. According to Joseph Campbell, the psychological function of myth is that which leads the individual toward wholeness and maturity and the ability to live with himself and with others ("Mythological Themes" 141).

The theme of rational humanity's schizoid nature is sounded early in *2001* after the importance of tools *and* weapons in human evolution has been indicated. Clarke mentions "the spear, the bow, the gun, and finally the guided missile." He points out that "Without those weapons, often though he had used them against himself, Man would never have conquered his world." Then, ending the "Primeval Night" section, he adds: "But now, as long as they existed, he was living on borrowed time" (*2001* 37).

One of humanity's central psychological problems is the basic insecurity of his ego which leads to defensiveness and an over-emphasis of the importance of such matters as personal pride and power--and hence to weapons, to too much competition, and to a neglect of the unconscious portion of the psyche and such faculties as feeling, intuition, and spontaneity. Modern humanity, with its pride in the power of his intellect and his guided missiles, could be, at any moment, brought to ruin by the takeover of his inner devil, that shadow containing all his darker propensities, insecurities, and paranoia.

The world *Discovery* leaves (*2001*) in search of the secret of the slab found on the moon, is one of constant crises: "In a million years, the human race had lost few of its aggressive instincts; along symbolic lines visible only to politicians, the thirty-eight nuclear powers watched one another with belligerent anxiety" (43). Because humanity can not come to terms with its shadow side, make friends with its brother the Devil, it projects the split within onto the external world, seeing the problem only "over there," in someone else, in the adversary--when the real problem is in the psychological attitude which instantly gravitates toward pointing the finger at others (Jung, *Psyche* 6-9). Such is the state of crisis in the year 2001.

Yet Dave Bowman, alone on *Discovery* after the deaths of the rest of the crew and the execution of Hal, sees, from the perspective of vast space, that the bickerings between the U.S. and the U.S.S.R. are "ludicrously parochial" (168). In a like spirit, Clarke points up the colossal irony of the petty egotistical last wishes of the last of the Chinese astronauts in *2010* who perish on Europa--when he asks that the creatures found there be named after him and that the bones of him and his crew be transported back to China (*2010* 79-80). The image of the child at the end of the first book is clearly a uniting symbol pointing toward the possibility of the resolution of warring oppositions in a fresh and vital synthesis of consciousness.

A further reference to the problem of the shadow is the narration both at the end of *2001* and in "Chapter 30: Homecoming" of *2010* where David Bowman, now a being of pure spirit, detonates an orbiting nuclear warhead on returning to earth on a reconissance mission for the lords of the monolith. This episode is a reminder of humanity's suicidal psychological immaturity which forces the maintenance of such weapons. Yet Clarke hints that the events connected with the *Leonov*'s mission, the genuine intimations of a UFO on Bowman's visit, and the dramatic events on Jupiter may change humanity, moving it in the direction of *some* degree of maturation: "History as men had known it would be drawing to a close" (*2001* 221).

Yet about all we learn about history between 2010 and 20,001 is that humanity still lives, that he has developed interstellar, or at least interplanetary, space travel. Other journeys set during that part of future history might become the burden of other Odysseys. Yet what these two novels in their essence set out to do--despite any flaws, seen mostly by those who are unable to read the books in the spirit which is at their heart--is of a mythic nature and involves the broadest of concerns and the deepest of questions. The task is completed as clearly and as successfully here as anywhere else in contemporary fiction--"science-" or otherwise.

CHAPTER THIRTEEN

MANDALAS, EVOLUTION, AND DISEMBODIED MINDS:

INNER JOURNEYS IN OUTER SPACE

Frequently, a persistent theme in space travel fiction is that of evolution--growth, process, change, onward into the far future. Much of science fiction takes place in the vistas of the future--"out there," in space. Yet sometimes, mixed with the "out there," we have the "in there," the reference to the development of depths of the psyche, mind, soul, spirit. Many writers of science fiction see humanity's future as a turning inward into the depths of the psyche, as well as a journey "out there"--*also* a place "where no one has gone before." Frequently, what Jung calls the individuation process, what Campbell calls the completion of the hero journey of myth is written large, by being projected onto the idea of the evolution of the species out there in space.

Often, whether consciously or not, many science fiction narratives employ the traditional symbolism of the hero, and, in particular the circular, spherical, or egg-like mandala, a symbol of wholeness or completion found all around the world. Applying the myth-and-archetype method points up interesting parallels to evolution at the level of the species. Psychological evolution, the road to wholeness within, termed the process of individuation by Jung, is frequently seen in narrative form when some evolution occurs taking the human or some other species beyond physical form.

Some particularly telling examples of this relationship between science fiction and archetypal psychology/myth regarding the journey toward individuation are found in Gene Roddenberry's *Star Trek* series.

In the *Star Trek* episode entitled "Charlie's Law" and first telecast on 15 September 1966, the crew of the *Enterprize* meets a seventeen-year-old who has lived since the age of three on a barren and deserted world--Thasus. As it turns out, Charlie has strong mental powers of the sort referred to as psychokinetic. However, his adolescent insecurity, lack of self-confidence, and inexperience with humanity cause him to use these powers in very destructive ways. He makes people disappear, causes another ship to self-destruct, and subverts the control of the *Enterprize*.

Finally, the ship is rescued by the boy's guardians. As it turns out, the Thasians who inhabited the planet millennia ago are still alive, living on another plane of existence. Existing in incorporeal form, they reared the boy Charlie and taught him the use of psychic powers so that he could live and protect himself on the barren planet. Yet the powers were too much for the otherwise psychologically unevolved Charlie. He has misused them, and the Thasians must take him back and repair the damage before he does more.

These Thasians represent the evolution of a species to the point of journeying so far into the psyche that consciousness moves to a plane of existence other than the corporeal. The Thasians have reached the stage of individuation or movement toward psychological completion which Jung says takes place in a reality beyond that of corporeal nature. The roughly oval shape in which the Thasian leader appears is to be related to what Jung calls the mandala, a symbol of wholeness (*Psyche and Symbol* 122). The Thasians have undergone individuation on a cultural, or racial stage. They have evolved to a another plane of being--beyond the shaky, paranoid, self-conscious world of the human ego represented (at a rather extreme level, of course) by the adolescent Charlie. Like the individual who has made some movement toward wholeness in his life of corporeal reality, the benevolent but solidly objective, thinking Thasians are as Jung described the psychically whole individual. This person is "no longer imprisoned in the petty, oversensitive, personal world of the ego, but [able to participate] freely in the wider world of objective interests." His broader, more open mode of consciousness is no longer the "touchy, egotistical bundle of personal wishes, fears, hopes, and ambitions which always has to be compensated or corrected by unconscious counter tendencies ("Relations" 127). The latter part quoted above, from Jung's description of the ego state before the evolutionary process of individuation is an apt description of the state of mind both of the paranoid, "touchy" Klingons and of the members of the Federation in the next work here discussed.

In "Errand of Mercy," first aired on 23 March 1967, the incipient war between the militaristic Klingons and the self righteous members of the United Federation of Planets represents the world of human egoism and paranoia. It represents a world in which conflict and opposition between beings is due payment (or compensation) for the inability to come to terms with the elements within the individual psyche which have been repressed--especially the shadow, as Jung calls it.

The Klingons want to establish a military base on the planet of the seemingly sheeplike Organians. Kirk and Spock claim *they* only want to protect the Organians from the Klingons, thus giving them a "choice." The Organians insist that they are in no danger from the Klingons, despite the reports of the execution of thousands of Organians in the courtyard in reprisal for the destruction of the Klingon ammunition dump--a feat effected by Kirk and Spock. When the Federation and the Klingons finally begin to fight--they are stopped by the psychic powers of the Organians who make all weapons, as well as the bodies of the enemy in each case, "too hot to handle." Both Kirk and Kor, the Klingon commander, are indignant that their war has been prevented. In the tradition of the dissolving of time and space, Jung's concept of synchronicity, the leader of the Organians claims that, "as I stand here, I also stand upon the bridge of your ship, upon the bridge of every ship, upon the home planet of the Klingon Empire, on the home planet of your Federation" (Coon 606). Thus he alludes to his ubiquitious psychic power.

The Organian leader also proclaims the evolution of his species to another plane of being. He says that at one time--eons ago--they were flesh and bone creatures like human beings. Yet for a long time they have had no need of physical bodies, that their present appearance is merely temporary and purely for the "convenience" of the humanoid visitors (607).

Although the presence of the would-be combatants is "acutely painful" (607) to them, the Organians act like guardian gods or powerful, benevolent sages--symbols of the state of the psyche Jung called wholeness.

The mandala image appears again: The two Organian council members begin to glow, to become brighter, to the point of looking "like metal statues in a furnace." Their human shape fades, and "It was as if there were two suns on the room" (Coon 607). Again, the popular television episode has produced the image of the mandala, the symbol of psychic wholeness appearing in the dreams and myths of all humankind and at all except the very first levels of his development. The circular, spherical, or egg-like shape which has no beginning and no end symbolizes pure consciousness, the wholeness on which man's life is based and toward which, at a higher level, his evolution--both that of the individual and that of the species--ever strives.

"Pure thought--or pure energy?" asks Spock: "In any event totally incorporeal. Not life as we know it at all. . . . I should guess that they are as far above us on the evolutionary scale as we are above the amoeba" (Coon 607). Spock's estimation may be a bit extreme, since psychic evolution does occur in individuals which is in certain important ways comparable to that of the Organians on the racial scale. Individuals do on occasion take the attitude toward war and paranoia that the Organians do, and certain individuals possess psychokinetic and synchronistic capabilities.

Kor, as though with a wink of the eye, tells Kirk that he is a little sad, not because of the unevolved state of his species, but because he and Kirk will not be able to have their war, after all. "I'm only sorry that they wouldn't let us fight," he sighs, "It would have been glorious" (608). This scene between Kirk and Kor is very good on screen, giving the impression of an underlying rapport between opposites of the sort frequently found in myth. This passage is related to the one a little earlier in which one of the Organian leader predicts that the Klingons and the members of the Federation will one day become fast friends and will "work together in great harmony" (Coon 607). In other words, both the Federation and the Klingons will come to terms with their main enemies--each other--and, one hopes, with the shadow within. (Indeed, this prophecy comes true in 1987 in the form of the television series *Star Trek: The Next Generation*.)

Bernard Shaw, of course, forty years before had portrayed creatures--somewhat like the Organians--who are in the process of evolving beyond the body, giving up the petty pursuits of humanity, like war and social oppression, and turning toward the pursuits of pure consciousness.[1] Shaw's rendition, however, in *Back to Methuselah*, is weak psychologically in that he conceives of the Ancients of his Utopia as striving toward a "power" which sounds rather too cerebral (in the usual negative sense of that word) to be very realistic.

At any rate, the theme *is* a recurring one in science fiction. Another example is that of the "Old Ones" of Mars in Robert Heinlein's *Stranger in a Strange Land* (1961).[2] Here, as it happens over and over again, the motif is understandable in terms not only of scientific speculation concerning the future

---

[1] Cf. Chapter 7.

[2] Cf. Chapter 14. As with Charlie and the Thasians, Michael Valentine Smith's teachers are of beings of pure consciousness--Martians who have "discorporated," that is, exited the state of consciousness in which mind is housed in physical bodies.

evolution of the race, but also in terms of psychological transformation.

CHAPTER FOURTEEN

STRANGER IN A STRANGE LAND AS MYTH:

THE CHRIST AND THE SELF[1]

Robert A. Heinlein's fantasy *Stranger in a Strange Land* (1961) is a modern extension of the age-old and universal myth of humanity, God, and the self.[2] Michael Valentine Smith, the terran reared on Mars who returns to earth with cosmic wisdom, establishes a church, and is martyred--can easily be seen as a modern embodiment of the of the same figure as that represented by the Christ, by Osiris, by Dionysus, and by other dying and resurrected gods of myth. He is an avatar of the hero-god, a mythological projection (embodiment or version) of a deeper reality. Specifically, Smith parallels the Christ figure as interpreted by Carl Jung in "Christ, a Symbol of the Self." As such, Smith as hero[3] infuses the

---

[1]This essay first appeared in *Extrapolation* 27.4 (1986): 295-303. It reappears here with the kind permission of Kent State University Press.

[2]Though the critical literature is, for the most part, conspicuously silent on *Stranger* as myth, Scholes and Rabkin comment on the general appearance of the myth of the hero in science fiction: "The most pervasive myth in our culture . . . [as clarified in] Joseph Campbell's monomyth in *[The] Hero with a Thousand Faces* (1949), is the myth of the killing of the king . . . [which initiates] the new social order [and brings] the world into a new era. The story of Jesus' Passion and Resurrection is a clear version of this myth. . . . We see versions of it in science fiction whenever a socially representative character dies for the wider society" (105).

[3]According to Jung, the Christ "is our culture hero, who, regardless of his historical existence, embodies the myth of the divine Primordial Man, the mystic Adam. It is he who occupies the center of the Christian *mandala*, who is the Lord of the Tetramorph, i.e., the four symbols of the evangelists, which are like the four columns of the throne. He is in us and we in him . . . so also

novel with mythic connotations. The novel is a projection of archetypal contents and needs onto the contemporary vision of humanity's contact with alien beings.

One of the reasons for many of the disparaging treatments of this novel is a failure by critics[4] to read it appropriately, against the background of the traditions of world mythology. Jung's theory of myth as a screen receiving the projections of the "unconscious" is also quite helpful but has been ignored.

According to Jung, the *self* is a transcendental factor which is the center of the entire psyche--including the vast "unconscious," as well as all levels of consciousness--as the *ego* is the center of the so-called "conscious" portion of the psyche. This self, along with the quest for it, is projected in the form of myths of god-heroes. To ignore these elements as context for reading this novel is a serious omission.

Heinlein's Smith, like the chief historical Occidental god-hero, the Christ, exemplifies new possibilities of consciousness based on a certain understanding of the relationship between the individual and the cosmos. As is typical of so much of modern literature *and* of myth, the novel uses the methods of exaggeration and irony in its portrayal of the deeds of Smith in this futuristic setting (circa. 2005, according to Panshin 98). Using his psychokinetic powers

---

is his heavenly kingdom" ("Christ" 36). In a general sense, such a realization could be adduced from the canonical gospel materials, but it is seen unequivocally in the non-canonical gospels. According to the voice of the quester in the *Gospel of Eve*, "I stood on a lofty mountain and saw a gigantic man and another a dwarf [sic]; and I heard as it were a voice of thunder, and drew nigh for to hear; and He spake unto me and said: I am thou, and thou art I; and wheresoever thou mayest be I am there. In all am I scattered, and whensoever thou willest, thou gatherest Me; and gathering Me, thou gatherest Thyself" (Campbell, *Hero* 39-40). Certainly the being which appears here as the large and the small, the magus, the divine hero, the voice from the other side is none other than the Christ, the symbol of the realization of the self, that fulcrum of the psyche in all beings.

[4]For example, Hume, Samuelson, Hull, and Panshin.

to dispose of that in which he "groks wrongness,"[5] with even human beings sometimes disappearing and not returning, Smith's actions seemingly represent an ironic parallel to the miraculous powers of Jesus in healing illness and resurrecting the dead. Similarly, he initiates ritual cannibalism which ironically parallels Jesus's instituting the "Last Supper." Yet if one is able to read the novel in the context of the strange yet wonderful mirror of myth, significant discoveries result.

According to Jung, in "Christ, a Symbol of the Self," the Christ--like other "culture heroes"--exemplifies the archetype of the self (36). Jung defines the self as a supraordinate entity (or content) unifying and energizing the entire psyche, a transpersonal reality to be compared with symbolic beings like the occidental God, the Hindu Atman, and the Chinese Tao or with the hero embodying or questing for the spirit of God. Coming to terms with the metaphysical reality existing within himself and as well within all things, and communicating these discoveries to his society are always the goals of the traditional hero's quest:

> The two--the hero and his ultimate god, the seeker and the found--are . . . understood as the outside and inside of a single, self-mirrored mystery, which is identical with the mystery of the manifest world. The great deed of the supreme hero is to come to the knowledge of this unity in multiplicity and then to make it known. (Campbell, *Hero* 40).

Smith fits this pattern of the hero.

Smith was reared on Mars where the intuition of the oneness of all things is universally held, not "believed" or taught or preached, but *known*. Now, having been transplanted back to his birth planet, he conveys this perennial

---

[5]"Grokking" is, according to Pielke, "intuitive insight . . . [It is also] the ability to empathize . . . to become one with a person, object, or situation" (157). Samuelson makes similar points about "grokking" (151).

realization verbally to his friends at Jubal Harshaw's home, thus: "'Thou are God,' Mike repeated serenely. 'That which groks. Anne is God. I am God. The happy grasses are God. Jill groks in beauty always. Jill is God. All shaping and making and creating together--' He croaked something in Martian and smiled" (144). The deepest level of each individual and of every thing else is here seen as one with the universal creative principle. This level is that of transcendental consciousness, that pure awareness, of which mystics in all ages and domains have spoken. In terms of the ubiquitous monomyth--based on what has been called the "perennial philosophy" (Huxley, *Perennial* vii.)--all of reality is the embodiment of the divine creative center or the world's soul. That creative center is what has been symbolized as the universal self, or God, the Christ, the Atman, or any number of mythological beings.[6]

Smith learns from the eccentric intellectual and open-minded cynic, Jubal Harshaw, that God is generally taken to refer to the universal creative principle, that which "made the world" (143). That Smith first uses his newly acquired word to tell Jubal such things as, "Thou are God" and "I am God," reveals something quite central about the relationship of Martian "grokking" and the meaning behind the monomyth.

God is one variation of the archetypal being who, in communion services throughout world myth, is dismembered and scattered forth to renew the cosmos.[7] Whether involving the eating of the god or, as with the Martians, the

---

[6]For example, as Campbell points out, in Hinduism, "It is not that the divine is every*where*: it is that the divine is every-*thing*. . . . One has but to alter one's psychological orientation and recognize (re-cognize) what is within" (*Oriental* 12-13).

[7]According to Samuelson--who seems to miss the mark: "Cannibalism is not that rare in human history--a symbolic variety is built into the Christian communion--and recalls myths of human beings partaking of the divine in order to share its strength and immortality (Orpheus, Dionysus, Freud's 'primal horde')" (163). Actually, the communion service is a re-minder of the original and ongoing act of creation by which the universal self bodies forth of itself as the

eating of the person who, like all beings, is simply one "mask of god," these rituals involve the celebration of the ongoing creation of the cosmos through the self-emptying, the sacrifice by which the deity Itself gives being to the world (Campbell, *Oriental* 9-10 ff., 28, and *Creative* 346-348, ff.).

"Thou are God" and "I am God" are clearly parallel to the "That art Thou" of the Hindu *Upanishads*. "That" (the universe around and within you) is an embodiment of the same divine being that "Thou" (you, a finite individual) "art." These expressions in their respective contexts embody the metaphysical doctrine which holds that the entire cosmos is sacrificial. The creation of the cosmos--and creation is an on-going process--is the dividing, the splitting asunder of the Deity, the original One into the many--a concept mirrored in the Christian ritual of the communion, in the crucifixion of the Christ, and in the death and dismemberment of vegetation divinities throughout the Near East. This doctrine has profound implications in terms of the way individual believers view themselves and other human beings and the way they view the world as a totality.

The phrase "Thou art God" is the central chant of Smith's Church of All Worlds, the communistic, anarchic organization that Smith himself establishes (341). This society is reminiscent, in important ways, of the early Christian community, except for such traits as its true and all-embracing innocence and freedom from such forces as the Jewish and Roman tendencies to disparage sexual openness.

The phrase "Thou art God" also represents "the universe proclaiming its self awareness" (341). Yet Ben Caxton, Jill's friend, the newswriter, says,

---

cosmos. The god-hero, like the Christ, who presides over the institution of the rite, embodies the self in an exemplary manner. Campbell speaks of "this hidden Being of beings particularly in certain heroic individuals, who thus stand as epiphanies" (*Creative* 200).

echoing other expressions,[8] "The universe is a thing we whipped up among us and agreed to forget the gag" (339). Smith tells Jubal that "'Thou art God and I am God and all that groks is God, and I am all that I have ever been or seen or felt or experienced. I am all that I grok. Father, I saw the horrible shape this planet is in and I grokked, though not in fullness, that I could change it'" (419). The "All that groks is God" (662), whether intended as such by Heinlein or not, is an echo of Blake's "every thing that lives is holy" (*Marriage of Heaven and Hell*). Blake's poetry, in fact, contains a non-institutionalized embodiment of the same *philosophia perennis* as that lived by Michael Valentine Smith. As does Blake's poetry with its fanciful pantheon, Heinlein's novel projects archetypal significances concerning the relation of individual to cosmos onto his extrapolation of humanity's fantasy of visits from other worlds.

Smith, like the culture hero represented in the Christ or the Buddha, returns to his own world after receiving his apotheosizing realization on Mars. Presumably, he wishes to bring an ultimate boon to his home world--yet it is one in which the mass of humanity is not yet ready for enlightenment. His experiences on the other world of Mars exemplify the birth of the individual's awareness of the self that dwells in all things. That self is ultimately the center of consciousness and of the unconscious, as well as what the physicists call energy, that is often symbolized by light.

Appropriately, just before Smith is martyred at the hands of angry institutional religionists, he appears in the sunlight as a "golden youth," his clothes having miraculously vanished (428). In myth, the self is frequently symbolized as "a marvelous youth," signifying life's renewal, "a creative *elan*

---

[8]Watts speaks of the universe as a "game of hide-and-seek, positive-and-negative" in which, "explicitly (that is, on stage) the light and the dark are enemies, but implicitly (off stage), they are not only friends . . . [and] co-conspirators, but constitute a unity" (*Beyond Theology* 72). Coomaraswamy speaks of the opposites of this world as being "of one mind behind the scenes" (*Hinduism and Buddhism* 7).

vital," and a renewed spirituality filling all things with life and power (von Franz 199). All these qualities are associated with what Jung calls the archetype of the self. The self is that transcendental center that lies deeper than the ego. The source of all our deepest, most precious inspirations, it is the divine element in us which energizes the life of the individual, infusing it with cosmic of divine life.

The Old Ones of Mars, Smith's mentors, never appear in the novel. They are described as magus figures in the pattern of what Jung called the "wise old man" (von Franz 196, 198). They symbolize the heightened spirituality of those few who have gone the road toward full realization of the self. The Old Ones of Mars are beings who have died or "discorporated" and become one with pure life, energy, being itself. They represent serenity of a sort seen more often in the East than in the West, the calm, intuitive way to realization of the ultimate.

In the other-world scenes after "his glorious resurrection," Smith, though he embodies much of their spirit, is not to be found with the Old Ones, the calm, slow, contemplative spirits who, if they were to take human form, might remind one of old Zen monks. Rather, in the dimension beyond death, he shares the company of "Archangels" Foster and Digby, founder and missionary, respectively, of the Fosterite religious sect.

The Fosterites are reminiscent of some of the more Dionysian of the Protestant fundamentalist sects with their snake-handling, emotional responses to music and oratory, and "writhing and foaming" frenzy (249). Some unconventional aspects of the Fosterites are somewhat reminiscent of that other sect indigenous to America, the Mormons. Their positions on sexual freedom and suicide, however, would have a place in few Protestant sects.

Foster's new revelation proclaims the message of the historical Jesus as, simply, that God wants us to be happy by opening ourselves to love. As another character, Patricia Paiwonski, observes that

> "By 'love' he [God] didn't mean namby-pamby old-maid love that's scared to look up from a hymn book for fear of seeing a temptation of the flesh. If God hated flesh, *why did He make so much of it?* God is no sissy. He made the Grand Canyon and comets coursing through the sky and cyclones and stallions and earthquakes" (288).

She goes on to say that such a God could hardly be displeased with the free display of sexuality. Sexuality is, of course, one of the symbol systems associated with the mythological divine love bringing together all things in cosmic unity.

Despite its openness to the genuine life of the feelings, the Fosterite church is full of commercialism and showmanship smacking of old-West charlatanry and, in the musings of the narrator, is treated satirically as a particularly American compensatory movement, with the implication that it grows out of the neurosis of America:

> The culture known as "America" had a split personality throughout its history. Its laws were puritanical; its covert behavior tended to be Rabelaisian; its major religions were Apollonian; its revivals were almost Dionysian. In the twentieth century (Terran Christian Era) nowhere on Earth was sex so vigorously suppressed--and nowhere was there such deep interest in it. (289)

The split is between the demands of the social self, which desires possessions and status, and those of the deeper self we share with all other individuals and with the universe.

While Foster seems to have shared in such a realization at some level, he has set up an institution which perpetuates some of the same old problems that he criticizes. Yet--with his God who is immense, unfathomable by human reason, and as ambiguous as being itself--he too sets forth a religion which is one more, necessarily imperfect, embodiment of the *philosophia perennis*. For his God is also the one who embodied himself symbolically in a human son, the Christ, the culture hero--thereby representing in his all-encompassing love the transpersonal self at the center of the cosmos.

205

Actually, then, the Christ of the Fosterite revelation represents the same mythic essence as does the man from Mars, despite Foster's and his followers' trickery and commercialism. No human thing--certainly no religion or philosophy--ever is or can be perfect. We should no more expect Smith or the Fosterites to be free from flaw or contradiction than we do the Jesus of the Western Christian tradition.

Smith causes Digby, leading missionary of the church, to "go away" while they are alone after the latter has tried to exploit the presence of the "Man from Mars" before a mass of worshippers in the Archangel Foster Tabernacle (252-55, 263-64, 267).

Yet Smith is, after all, somehow inspired to found the Church of All Worlds, which shows some kinship with Fosterism in its attitude toward sexual matters. Indeed, one of the charter members, Patricia Paiwonski, the snake charmer and former stripper, is a former Fosterite who says that the two faiths in no way conflict (337).

Yet Smith's church is more cosmic and universal than is Fosterism with its carnival tactics. It attracts members through the charismatic powers of Smith and the inner circle and by the compelling nature of the "Thou art God" centerpiece of Martian theology. The appeal of the Fosterites, however, at least in tone, is to the provincial rather than to the cosmic.

Nevertheless, in keeping with the many ironies and the parody-like tone of the novel, Smith is found, in the dimension beyond death, with Archangel Foster and Junior Archangel Digby. Foster appoints Digby as Smith's assistant. Digby does not know Smith, as far as he can remember--"Of course, out of so many when-wheres--" he shrugs. "No matter. Thou art God," says Smith, who also (in this other dimension) does not seem to remember their coming together in the room near the tabernacle when Smith caused Digby to discorporate. Foster, interested that these two should get down to work, rejoins, "Certainly, Thou art

God--but who isn't?" After pushing back "his halo," Smith gets to work, seeing "a lot of changes he wanted to make" (437-38).

The rapport, in the transcendental realm, between the saintly charlatan Foster and the man from Mars is significant. It is clearly parallel to what Jung calls the path of the middle way between extremes, the balancing of the opposites without which--according to Blake, Heraclitus, and a multitude of others--there is no progression.

Smith is, after all, through one line of descent, the son of the "Christian" but essentially de-Christified West. The "can do" spirit and manipulative attitudes toward matters of science and technology which have triumphed since the Renaissance set the stage for the eruption of such a sect as Fosterism, with its neurotic combination of litany and libido. Smith's final comment recalls the Protestant and Western scientific "works/work" tradition.

He is, however, also the spiritual descendent of the intuition-oriented culture of Mars, which represents what is known on earth as the Eastern way of contemplation. As In *Memories, Dreams, Reflections*, Jung says:

> Western man seems predominantly extraverted, Eastern man predominantly introverted. The former projects the meaning and considers that it exists in objects; the latter feels the meaning in himself. But the meaning is both without and within. (317)

One side of Smith's heritage is Western, extraverted, and tends to be ego-oriented and possessive at least to the point of making things happen. The other side, represented by the Martians, parallels the attitudes of the Orient, its introversion, and its concern with metaphysics rather than physics.

Michael Valentine Smith, Extraordinary Everyman, represents the compensatory force toward the realization of opposites--whether they be the "in here" and the "out there," the feminine and the masculine, or universal and the individual. He also represents the Christ, the hero who is brave enough to embrace both sides of experience and to see and live and communicate to others the realization of the *self* that lies deep within the human psyche as well as within all things.

He comes to earth as a stranger totally absorbed in the almost shamanistic ways of the Old Ones, his discorporated masters from Mars. Becoming involved in the lives of a few earthlings, he groks an even deeper and more general "wrongness" than that of the physical violence he encounters in the police at Jubal Harshaw's home. He establishes his Church of All Worlds for those who value as he does the vision of totality and oneness. His martyrdom is a cheerful one, and he is apotheosized to a realm beyond time and space in which he and Digby, the religious enemy whom he made to disappear, are at one. He thus exemplifies the aspect of the deep self which knows its opposite, its enemy, as the other side of itself.

Many of the attacks on, and disparagements of, this novel point to what critics term the "thinness of its ideas" (Hume 105), "its solipsism" (Samuelson 171-73) its "extreme cynicism" (Hull), or the "pointless religion" (Panshin 101-02) presumed to make up a major portion of the novel. To indulge in such "commentary" is to have remained ignorant of the formidable and ubiquitous traditions in myth, religion, and philosophy that appear significantly within the novel and represent an appropriate context against which to read the novel.

This work is a modern rendition of the ubiquitous myth of the divine self which embodies itself in all of creation, and--in a special, exemplary sense--in the hero, in this case in Michael Valentine Smith. Smith--despite inevitable human flaws--points toward what Huxley calls "the impossible paradox and supreme truth" that "reality shines out of every appearance, that the One is totally, infinitely present in all particulars" (*Doors* 119). To fail to see the novel's status as "modern myth," is to misread it by ignoring its context in these traditions. Thus to fail is also to be left with what Coomaraswamy referred to as no more "than a dilettante knowledge" of the work (*Art* 75).[9]

---

[9]Also, says Coomaraswamy, a critic must "sacrifice himself . . . must cease to be a provincial . . . must universalize himself . . . [and] assimilate whole cultures . . . strange to him" (*Art* 30).

CHAPTER FIFTEEN

INNER AND OUTER SPACE/THE MYTH OF THE UFO:

SELF AND SHADOW IN CRICHTON'S *SPHERE*[1]

Michael Crichton's *Sphere* (1987) participates in the modern myth of the UFO in its portrayal of a quest for the secrets hidden in what at first seems to be an alien spacecraft discovered at the bottom of the Pacific Ocean. However, it turns out to be an American craft, from sometime well into the twenty-first century, that has travelled to the stars and through time and contains a silver sphere of unknown, possibly of alien origin. The sphere's mystery, the powers it ultimately exhibits, and the symbolism of its shape--associate it with what Jungians think of as the god and the devil within, the archetypes of the self and the shadow. In portraying these timeless archetypes, this science fiction novel is highly mythic--containing variations on symbols universal and ubiquitous in the human past the world over. Thus, here myth transforms itself again and lives on even in the world of modern technology and speculation about the future and about outer and inner space--even in the form of a "thriller" remaining for three months on the *New York Times* best-seller list.

Crichton tells his story from the third-person point of view of Norman Johnson (at 53), a psychology professor called to be a member of the investigatory team concerning this crash in a remote portion of the Pacific. As a psychologist, Norman has helped to investigate airline crashes in the past repeatedly (4). However, when Johnson reaches the crash site, he is amazed to

---

[1]This essay first appeared in *POMPA* (1989): 99-111. It reappears here with the kind permission of the Mississippi Philological Association.

find that the matter of the site is shrouded in the utmost secrecy. Navy Colonel Harold C. Barnes, the "Project Commander" (9), informs him that it is "a *spacecraft* crash site" (11)--the crash estimated as having occurred at least three-hundred years ago (12).

The novel serves the function of modern myth in keeping with a number of Jung's statements in *Flying Saucers: A Modern Myth of Things Seen in the Sky* (1959). There Jung points out that great masses of Christians no longer believe in the Christian mythology in any deep manner. Related to that vacuum, Jung finds "a political, social, philosophical, and religious conflict" to have "split the consciousness of our age" (414). Jung argues that in the period starting after World War II, many people typically have projected their need for a living mythology into fantasies about outer space. They do this because their earthly religions and governments have failed them. The world has become so threatening, world leaders so undependable, that people have turned to the sky where once great gods and goddesses resided (*Flying Saucers* 320).

That is, the old mythological systems in the form of religions like Christianity are failing in the age of "better living through science," "mega-death," and the cold war and post-cold war periods. Yet the same archetypal needs and situations are being spoken to by a new mythology, that of "outer space." Thus, in approaching the modern novel containing UFO's or aliens or space travel, we should expect the reframing of the same archetypal mythic materials, the same psychological problems, in the context of the world of science and technology.

In this version of the myth, the archetypes of the self and the shadow--which in Christian mythology were expressed in the forms of the God and the devil--appear in modern form in the magical sphere (found in the crashed ship) and its effects on the human psyche (or reflections *of* the human psyche).

After the civilian members of the "Anomaly Investigation Team" have been brought together, Norman learns that the craft was found recently (the novel is set in the present, the late '80s) by a ship laying a communications cable when the cable was sheared (31). The huge rocket-like craft shows a technology unknown at present on earth--although it involves a kind of technology experts think may exist from ten to fifteen years in the future (33). It has been decided that the crashed craft has been "on the planet at least three-hundred years," perhaps five-hundred or even five thousand (34).

The mythological framing of the scenario is emphasized by the fact that Norman's Odyssean descent to the lower world where a laboratory has been set up in an undersea habitat is accomplished in a submarine called *Charon V*. Norman and Ted Fielding, the astrophysicist member of the team, pay the pilot for good luck as though they were dead souls being ferried by Charon across the river Styx (49). The hell-like nature of the situation is intensified by the fact that soon after the team starts its investigation, a typhoon arrives in that area of the Pacific, communication are lost, and ultimately all surface support vessels have to leave the area.

Though the assumption has been that the half-mile long spacecraft is of alien origin, when the team members enter the craft, they find that it is not. The original suspicions of mathematician/logician Harry Adams are confirmed: the labels inside the craft are in English. The craft seems to have materialized from the future in that location three-hundred or more years ago (66). The date near the serial number is 2043 (79). Harry theorizes that the craft went through a black hole and thus traveled through both space and time (100-01). Though a speculation and not an empirically verified fact, this scenario qualifies as an element of modern myth, as it tends to fulfill, in general, Joseph Campbell's requirement of a living myth's congruence with the scientific thought of the time (221-22).

It is Ted who first discovers the sphere inside the craft (103-04). "Large, perfectly polished and silver," it is "about thirty feet in diameter." At first, it appears to have "no markings or features of any kind." Norman, however, notices "an odd shifting iridescence, faint rainbow hues of blue and red." On the far side of the sphere, they discover "a series of deep, convoluted grooves, cut in an intricate pattern into" its surface. Norman finds the pattern arresting, though he does not know why (104). Thus, the sphere has that typical arresting effect of the mythological symbol.[2]

Ted thinks the sphere is the instrument by which some form of intelligent life has attempted to communicate with other beings across the vastness of space (105). Harry thinks the sphere is hollow and contains something and is frightened by the fact (107). Colonel Barnes is preoccupied with the idea of eventually blasting open the sphere, if necessary, to see what is inside (108), thinking of it in a purely adversarial manner.

Zoologist Beth Halpern, who has serious fears about her own ego, imagines the possibility of a long series of attempts to get the sphere open, culminating in the use of a nuclear device, all to no avail--"One great frustration for mankind" (109). Thus to some degree, the sphere functions here as the gold doubloon does in Herman Melville's *Moby Dick* (Chapter XCVIII). Several characters see the sphere, each giving it a different meaning based on his own fears, desires, or preoccupations--as is the case with any true symbol.

Harry is the first to open and enter the sphere. When he emerges, he is changed psychologically. He has lost what Norman thinks of as a "slow sarcasm," having replaced it with a "speedy, overly cheerful quality" and a "laughing indifference to everything" (155). At first, Harry says he does not remember what happened to him in the sphere. Later he declares that "It was wonderful, and beautiful. Something about lights, swirling lights" (154). He only remembers that the idea came to him as a sudden intuition as though it were an inspiration: "I just

---

[2]The "individual human being" can appear in dreams as a sphere, indicating the parallel between the little circle or sphere of the ego, and the great circle or sphere of the self (Cf. Jung, "Individuation" 302).

remember this sudden insight, this certainty about how it was done" (155), but he has lost the conscious knowledge of how.

Soon after Harry's excursion into the sphere a number of sea animals invade the area around the undersea habitat: bioluminiscient squid, shrimp, jellyfish, and a gigantic squid. Some of these animals have anomalous physical characteristics, and all seem peculiarly out of place there. Also, at one point, Norman encounters a black sailor he at first thinks has been sent down to the habitat by the military. This sailor has about him a "flatness" which Norman finds "odd" (220). It turns out that Harry has seen him too and found him to be "dull . . . kind of boring" (221).

It is decided about the black crewman, as about all the unusual sea animals, that "he came from the sphere," as Ted puts it, "Or at least, he was *made* by the sphere" (221). Another development since Harry's entrance into and emergence from the sphere is that the sphere, it seems, or something inside it which calls itself Jerry, has been communicating with the crew through the computer terminal. The first manifestations on the computer screen were in the form of numbers which at first seemed random and then turned out to have a design. Ultimately, came language in code, which code was eventually broken. The "alien," or whatever was revealing itself, identifying itself as "Jerry" and proceeding to converse with the team in very simplistic language. The style seems to indicate a childlike mentality. Like the typical science fiction alien, it is fond of the term "entity" (187).

Ted thinks that Jerry is able to "create things . . . animals." He does not identify this "Jerry" with the giant squid but does think that this force somehow made the squid that attacked them (221). Ted thinks that the attack was an accident, that the squid attacked the cylinders of the habitat, thinking they were its mortal enemy, a whale.

Norman thinks it more likely that it is Jerry himself who is hostile. Soon afterward the squid continues its attacks, and it, or one or another form of sea creature, eventually kills everyone in the habitat except for Norman, Harry, and Beth (232).

At one point, Jerry says that "THE ENTITY SQUID IS A MANIFESTATION," adding that he/it finds it difficult to manifest the squid. It becomes clear that the other anomalous animals were also manifestations provided by Jerry. Jerry seems to think that all the separate human beings living in the habitat are also "MANIFESTATIONS" things made, presumably by some other immaterial "entity" (259).

Soon Beth notices that Harry has regained the same psychological traits he had before his short trip into the sphere: "the same old Harry--arrogant, disdainful, and very, very intelligent" (257). The reasons for these changes are unclear. Jerry begins to use here and there particularly colloquial expressions, like "HEY MAN GET OFF MY BACK" (262, 264).

Norman begins to wonder why Jerry decided to manifest himself as a squid (264). He realizes that just before the squid first appeared, the crew had been discussing the giant squid in *Twenty Thousand Leagues Under the Sea*--which had frightened Harry when he was a child. Norman realizes that it was Harry who broke the numerical code, making it possible for them to communicate with Jerry. As Norman is playing around with the code, hoping to discover something, he discovers a mistake in the translating of the name Jerry, a mistake of one letter: the name is really "*Harry*" (266).

Beth and Norman get together and put together a variety of facts: the animals as well as the computer messages started appearing *after* Harry came out of the sphere; it was *Harry* who held special memories about a giant squid; "Jerry" only communicates with them when Harry is in the room; the black crewman appears "just as Harry is having a dream of being rescued" (269) (Harry, by the way, is also black). In the middle of one of the attacks of the squid, Harry was knocked unconscious, then the squid disappeared. Norman theorizes that while inside the sphere, Harry gained the power to make his thoughts real, even to make manifest things he merely imagines (270-71).

Norman brings up the subject of Jungian psychology (272), giving an explanation of the shadow archetype that is quite accurate:

> Jung suspected there was an underlying structure to the human psyche that was reflected in an underlying similarity to our myths and archetypes. One of his ideas was that everyone had a dark side of his personality, which he called the 'shadow.' The shadow contained all the unacknowledged personality aspects--the hateful parts, the sadistic parts, all that. Jung thought people had the obligation to become acquainted with their shadow side [sic]. But very few people do. We all prefer to think we're nice guys and we don't ever have the desire to kill and maim and rape and pillage. (273)

Norman thinks that all the "manifestations" have been projections, comings-to-life of various aspects of Harry's shadow side.

Norman decides to talk with Jerry again, knowing that he will be talking to a part of Harry (278). Norman tries to convince Jerry to stop attacking the crew of the habitat with manifestations. Jerry reacts with what must be the deep-seated (unconscious) attitude of Harry:

> YOU SHOULD NOT BE DOWN HERE IN THE FIRST PLACE. YOU PEOPLE DO NOT BELONG HERE. . . . ARROGANT CREATURES WHO INTRUDE EVERYWHERE . . . YOU HAVE TAKEN A GREAT FOOLISH RISK AND NOW YOU MUST PAY THE PRICE. YOU ARE AN UNCARING SPECIES WITH NO LOVE FOR ONE ANOTHER. (281)

When Norman tells Jerry that it is he who is unfeeling, Jerry reacts with the threat: "I WILL KILL YOU ALL" (281).

While Harry is asleep, Norman and Beth decide that if Harry dreams, he might manifest monsters from his dreams,[3] so they decide to give him an

---

[3] In the 1950s film "Forbidden Planet," partially based on Shakespeare's *Tempest*, the concept arises of "monsters from the Id." While the highly intelligent Prospero character is asleep, the

anesthetic to produce a dreamless sleep (283-84). However, while going to do so, Norman finds "two female Navy crewmen" outside where Harry is sleeping--"handsome, black, and muscularlooking." Though he has the syringe ready, Norman leaves without applying it (286). The giant squid attacks again, Harry is awakened, and Norman tells him that he is causing the attack and must stop it. Harry rejects that idea, but Beth is able to apply the syringe of anesthetic, so the attack halts (289-91).

Beth starts displaying erratic behavior such as carrying out a fixed idea of wiring explosives around the crashed space ship so that if "something starts to come out of that sphere" the whole ship can be exploded (295). Despite the fact that Harry is anesthetized, Jerry shows up again on the computer screen with "I WILL KILL YOU" (303) while Beth is outside the habitat on the way back from the ship. Norman goes outside and rescues her. A mass of sea snakes come inside with them, but neither is seriously injured.

A little later, Norman remarks to Beth, "With your hands full of snakes, you looked like Medusa." Beth's lack of recognition of the mythological reference elicits thoughts in Norman that constitute one of the key passages in the novel involving the theme of the UFO as a myth of modern times. He marvels at the fact that once

> every educated Western person knew these figures from mythology and the stories behind them intimately--as intimately as they knew the stories of family and friends. Myths had once represented the common knowledge of humanity, and they served as a kind of map of consciousness. (309)

But today an individual like Beth, even though highly educated in a technical sense, knows very little about myths. Norman thinks that it is as though modern

---

rescue ship that has recently arrived from earth is attacked by grotesque monsters. The Prospero character has gained this psychological characteristic after discovering the records of the "Krael," the ancient race once inhabiting the planet, which destroyed itself through the psychic powers of its own imagination.

humanity thinks "the map of human consciousness" is now different," but Norman wonders if it really is (309).

Indeed, according to Jungian psychology and to the work of Joseph Campbell as well, the psyche itself has not changed much at all. The same instincts and archetypes are still there in the unconscious to be contended with. In works like this one, the "myths we live by," though really the same always in their basic patterns, merely have been updated and have appeared in modern dress. In fact, the very scenario which Norman and Beth have been living through in this novel is one of those myths in modern dress. Norman realizes a portion of this idea when he tells Beth that "Perhaps these are our new myths. Dorothy and Toto and the Wicked Witch, Captain Nemo and the giant squid" (310).

The computer screen starts printings words--"I WILL KILL YOU NOW (310)--even though Harry still sleeps. Also, Norman realizes that Beth has armed explosives around the habitat as well as around the space ship. He accuses her of making the recent manifestations (of the squid and the threats on the computer). She says that he is the one causing these manifestations.

In other words, it seems to be possible that the (inner) shadow side of either one or both of them is, like Harry's, projecting real threats into the (outer) environment (311). Beth and some of Norman's own thoughts and memories make a fair case that Norman could be responsible, at least partially (311-14). He offers the negative argument that he, unlike Harry, has not been inside the sphere. Beth's rejoinder is that he really has but that he merely does not remember (314). She points out other facts, such as the fact that his own middle name happens to be "Harrison" (315). Norman realizes the clear possibility that she could be correct, that no one is exempt from the "blindness about self"[4] which causes the ego to ignore the shadow (316-18).

By watching the video tape made by the camera trained on the sphere, Norman discovers that Beth herself has been in the sphere (320). Norman realizes that Beth, "with her lack of self-esteem, her deep core of self-hate," has become obsessed with power but at the same time perhaps unconsciously wants to kill herself (321-2). While they are arguing over the intercom, she turns off the life support system and locks him in one room of the habitat (322). He escapes by going outside the habitat with an air bottle and entering through another airlock. He immediately puts on his diving suit and goes into the space ship (326-9).

He realizes that Beth must have gotten the sphere to open simply by imagining it as open. He does the same, and the sphere opens. He sees darkness and then "something like fireflies," "a dancing, luminous foam, millions of points of light, swirling around him." He sees in it no structure "and apparently no limit." He sees it as "a surging ocean, a glistening, multifaceted foam" and feels "great beauty and peace" (331).

After he has adjusted to his surroundings, he feels a presence and asks, "Anybody here?" "*I* am here," says a loud voice. When Norman asks who this voice is, it says, "*I am not a who.*" "Are you God?" Norman asks. "*God is a word*," comes the reply (232). The replies to Norman's questions indicate that the presence is not from another planet or another civilization. Norman realizes that he is communicating in thoughts (telepathically) with the presence. The sphere itself, though, *does* come from both another civilization and from another time. Norman continues to think that the presence must or should be "God": "I'm

---

[4]Here "self" must be taken primarily to mean "ego": what is referred to essentially is the blindness of the ego to the fact of the projections of the shadow, one of the archetypes of the collective unconscious--blindness to the fact that what one blames in the outer world is partially that shadow within which one refuses to see. Of course, the phrase could also refer to a blindness to the archetype of the self as well [something quite beyond the ego].

afraid I am not very knowledgeable about religion. I'm a psychologist. I deal with how people think. In my training, I never learned much about religion" (333).

The presence tells Norman that it and Harry and Norman and even Jerry "*spring from the same source.*"[5] It tells Norman he already has "*the power to make things happen by imagination*" (334). The presence goes into a long speech starting, "*On your planet you have an animal called a bear.*" It makes the point that the imagination is the greater part of what is specifically human intelligence:

> *This is the gift of your species and this is the danger, because you do not choose to control your imaginings. You imagine wonderful things and you imagine terrible things, and you take no responsibility for the choice. You say you have inside you the power of good and the power of evil, the angel and the devil, but in truth you have just one thing inside you--the ability to imagine.* [italics in the original] (355)

The voice goes on the say that it hopes Norman has enjoyed the "speech," intended for an upcoming meeting of psychologists and social workers in Houston. Then Norman becomes confused, and the voice asks whether he thought he was conversing with "God." Wondering who this voice is, he is told that it is none other than himself. The first of the paragraphs just quoted is, of course, parallel, in some respects, to the statement made by Jerry (281) about the "arrogant species" which inhabits the wrong place. This time, instead of being prompted by someone's shadow side, the statement seems to be prompted by the deep self in Norman, with which the sphere, as a kind of psychological "enzyme" or "mirror,"[6] has put Norman into direct contact.

---

[5]This "*same source*" is, in Jungian terms, the self, which is universal and transpersonal, and is, by Jung, likened to the Christ and to the Hindu Atman (Cf. "Christ" and "Commentary/Secret").

[6]At one point in the novel, Beth theorizes that perhaps the sphere acts as a kind of mental enzyme (292), and Norman, while they are in the decompression chamber, calls it "a sort of mirror for us" (363).

The sphere--or, rather, the superior consciousness within it, which is also within Norman--coincides with a universal pattern for the symbolic expression of the archetypal self or what Jung calls "the God within." Jung notes repeatedly the congruence of the typical shape of the UFO--spherical or saucer/disc-like--with the archetypal image of the mandala, or magic circle (338). According to Jung, "ritual mandalas"

> express either the totality of the individual in his inner and outer experience of the world, or its essential point of reference. Their object is the *self* in contradistinction to the *ego*, which is only the point of reference for consciousness, whereas the self comprises the totality of the psyche altogether, i. e., conscious *and* unconscious. ("Individuation" 389)

In this novel as modern myth-text, the sphere--as a variation on the mandala--functions as a symbol of the self--as well as being an "unidentified" alien something, perhaps a former UFO.

Further, the lack of recognizable structure, the oceanic aspect, and the limitlessness of the "foam" (331) also point to the transpersonal and infinite aspects of the self. Norman notices the godlike nature of the sphere and the being he meets therein. Concerning the "fireflies," or "millions of points of light," light is again and again all over the world associated with the supreme godhead or with beings which form a part of it. In particular, Jung notes that "globular luminosities . . . with remarkable consistency, are regarded as 'souls' in the remotest parts of the world" ("Individuation" 294-95). "Soul" is frequently used to imply "whole human being" or "individual."

After Norman returns to the habitat, he tries to disconnect Beth's explosives but by mistake starts the timer (339-40). Despite his knowledge of the shadow, Norman starts to take the submarine and leave Beth and Harry to their fates. Yet even as he is in the process of leaving, he recognizes facts in keeping with Jungian psychology: "Left unattended, the irrational side of man had grown in power and scope." "Complaining about it," he realizes, "didn't help either. All those scientists whining in Sunday supplements about man's inherent destructiveness and his propensity for violence, throwing up their hands" (342). Norman knows that the "responsibility began with each individual person, and the choices he made" (343).

As he starts to ascend, Norman thinks about the tendency in human beings never to explore their unconscious sides. However, "as a psychologist, Norman had some acquaintance with his unconscious. It held no surprises for him." He thinks that unlike Beth and Harry, he is a person whose unconscious contains no "monsters." Suddenly, he realizes how wrong he is about that, that right now he is in the grips of the shadow side which is forcing him cruelly to leave Beth and Harry on the bottom of the ocean. This realization is perhaps the major climax of the novel (345).

Norman goes back, but at this point, Beth is so much in the grips of the self-hate caused by her shadow side that she tries to force him to leave, presumably wishing to commit suicide. Harry, suddenly awake and lucid, presumably brought forth from his deep slumber by Norman's power of imagination, incapacitates Beth (253), and the three of them escape before the explosion occurs (353-60).

After the three are safe (and while they are in the decompression chamber and have had no contact with other people), they decide not to reveal the power given to them by the sphere. They decide to "imagine away" all the evidence of the sphere's existence and the power it conveyed--a power too dangerous to the world in its primitive psychological state, the power even "to overcome your enemies simply by imagining it had happened" (361). Norman says that "The sphere was built to test whatever intelligent life might pick it up, and we simply failed the test" (362). They do not wish any group or government to search the crash area for the seemingly alien, and perhaps indestructible, silver sphere.

However, Norman later decides that the sphere might be totally unrelated to the attempt to explore other life forms or the concept of somehow testing life, that it may be pure accident that it has the serious effect it does on these twentieth-century individuals. He realizes that they really know nothing at all about the sphere or where it originated, only that it is "sort of a mirror for us" (363). They fashion a story to substitute for what really happened and decide to imagine, on the count of three, that the story they have fabricated is what really happened. Their story contains no reference to a sphere. Of course, the plan works.

The effect of the experience each of the three main characters has with his own shadow side is presumably enduring in that it is not something limited to the conscious and cognitive side of the psyche. The value of the power of imagination is associated, at least in regard to Norman's excursion into the sphere, with an insight or intuition hailing from the self or true center of the psyche. It represents a theme persistent in the modern myth of UFO's and space travel: the idea that in an extremely desperate situation, even in one like that at the end of the twentieth century, things can improve if only enough people imagine other alternatives.

CHAPTER SIXTEEN

MYTH AND HISTORY IN NOVELS BY

HOYLE AND LEGUIN

The value of continued, constant, and unprecedented growth in technical facility, economic wealth, and the control of externals seems to be an ideal for many of those in power today. Government subsidized futurists find their province in predicting the direction and speed of such change. Yet the unthinking acceptance of technological progress, and the willingness to use whatever powers knowledge gives us, without due consideration of the *long-range* consequences--but in deference to egotism and the profit motive--is the sin of Faust.

Such attitudes have brought us to our present state of ecological crisis including the possibility of a nuclear war which would mean the end of life on this planet. The question now is how long we can go on the way we are going.

Thus have our times been called apocalyptic. To many who look for a way out of the present impasse, some reckoning based on the ancient symbol science of astrology seems appropriate. The age of Pisces, whose beginning coincided with that of the Christian era, is in the process of transforming itself into the new and more vital Age of Aquarius--the next cycle of 2000 years. William Irwin Thompson suggests that we are living on the "edge of history," that history as we know it is, in one way or another, coming to an end--with the rationalism and historicism of the last few centuries of the Christian era to be superceded by a return to "mythic consciousness" and a new valuation of the revelations of the unconscious depths (Thompson, *Edge* 82-89). Kenneth Boulding, thinking along similar lines, agrees that we are on the threshold of a change comparable to the beginning of agriculture. He speaks of pre-civilization, civilization, and the new era of post-civilization involving a world society unknown in historical times (Boulding 39-42). In fact, *many* argue that attitudes contrasting sharply with those of the Christian, civilized or *city-oriented*, technological West, will somehow be dominant in the era now emerging.

Seen as especially likely to change are attitudes concerning the meaning of history, purpose, and progress. These "new" attitudes are closely related to the Eastern myths and to Western mythologies predating Christianity and holding a cyclical view of nature and the cosmos. They are also similar to the authentic eschatological, Hebrew myth of the paradise regained.

In keeping with such possibilities, certain science fiction novels between 1950 and 1980 show significant significance regarding this theme. Myth is useful in understanding these novels and seeing their relationship both to our rationalistic and progress oriented heritage and to the archetypal truth that life runs in circles.

In a study of science fiction and myth, Casey Fredericks reminds us that "scientific positivists," whose views of reality still reign, argue that "whatever myths might do, they *must* involve a return to outmoded thinking or social action" (Fredericks 34). Fredericks adds that "This supposed retrograde evolution caused by myth is then judged objectionable from the viewpoint of intellectual or social progress" (34).

Fredericks himself, though, holds a very limited view of myth and actually sides with the positivists when it comes to the Christian/scientific emphasis on the supremacy of history. He finds such criticism of myth

> especially appropriate in the face of Mircea Eliade's advice to contemporary Western man to abandon "the terror of history" (really "the fear of change") and return to a more archaic stratum of belief in supratemporal "archetypes," which are quasi-Platonic, static models of conduct represented in ancient myths and religions. (34-35)

225

Fredericks cites Phillip Rahv's view that modern humanity's sensibility has little if anything in common with that of humanity in ancient times (35-36). Such a view is, of course, the converse of the Jungian hypothesis which sees the human psyche as being built up out of all the "archetypal" experiences of his past. Surprisingly, in his attempt to support his position, Fredericks quotes--out of context--Joseph Campbell, whose works on myth are in essential agreement with the many of the findings of both Eliade and Jung (36). Yet Fredericks claims that Jung's view of myth "is completely unacceptable to most contemporary myth scholars" (41). To some degree, he may be right about that--which is so much the worse for the contemporary myth scholars of whom he speaks.

Presumably, to illustrate the "backward" views of Eliade, Jung, and other "out of step" "proponents of myth," Fredericks quotes a long passage from Eliade's *Cosmos and History*:

> It is not inadmissable to think of an epoch . . . when humanity, to ensure its survival, will find itself reduced to desisting from any further "making" of history in the sense in which it began to make it from the creation of the first empires, will confine itself to the repeating of prescribed archetypal gestures, and will strive to forget, as meaningless and dangerous, any spontaneous gesture which might maintain "historical" consequences. It would even be interesting to compare the antihistorical solution of future societies with the paradisal or eschatological myths of the golden age of the beginning or end of the world. (Fredericks 34-35; Cf. Eliade 153-54)

Then, Fredericks--approvingly--cites Rahv's view that if such is what is involved in "'taking myth seriously,' then indeed we must think badly of myth" (34).

Yet, Eliade's view is of value even from the perspective even of a "rationalist" like Voltaire who claims that history is "the sum of the crimes and follies of mankind." A rational analysis could find much of the thread of what Eliade calls "history in the sense in which it [humanity] began to make it from the creation of the first empires" to be motivated by the greed, selfishness, and the egotistical bumblings of men of narrow attitude and limited perspective.

Further, it is worth noting that Eliade's world beyond history and progress is a world that is actually portrayed in proto-Christian myth in the Hebrew Old Testament--the world of which the prophets speak, in which the lion lies down peaceably with the lamb, in which the fierce argument between God and Satan is envisioned as being ended. This world is beyond, outside of, the world of "Holy Wars," of capitalism versus communism, and of history and technology. This world beyond history is incomprehensible to the views on which most of the actions and policies of any "Christian nation," or any typical modern Western individual, are based.

Yet this paradigm of reality is an element of the vital, really ignored aspect of proto-Christian myth. This world beyond history has much in common with an element appearing in a number of other mythologies: the time *in illo tempore*, the time "of the beginnings" discussed by Eliade (91). In Jungian terms, the time *in illo tempore*, the Eden of the Christian myth, is a symbol for the collective unconscious.

The "terror of history" experienced by modern humanity, Jung has shown in a number of places to be a function of humanity's ignoring the collective unconscious in ways which were not possible in more mythically based cultures. Examples of the theme abound in Jung's works, Volume 10 of *The Collected Works* being a particularly fertile area, especially the essay (published separately as well) *The Undiscovered Self: Past and Present*. Openness to the unconscious involves a different perception of time than that of time as linear--that of time as a circle.

However, linear time, "historical consciousness," and the idea of progress through science and technique are intimately related to Judaeo-Christian culture. The idea of the "historical" purpose of the Hebrew people, even the ideas of social and moral progress in a universal sense, are inherent in Moses and the prophets.

Christianity *is a historical religion*, placing great value on change in the sense of the unprecedented event. The Jewish idea of the Messiah involves the appearance of a historical personage at a particular time whose career and mission imply a change in history and the subsequent movement toward an "eschaton" or end to history, a time of peace, justice, and perfection. A potent New Testament example appears at the opening of that most marvelously syncretistic gospel attributed to John. The Greek idea of the Logos, the informing principle of reason, knowledge, wisdom, the "Word" is introduced in a particularly Jewish way--in terms of its unique incarnation at a point in "history." "The Word," in the sense of scientific "logos," has fueled history in the West during the last five-hundred years.

The Judaeo-Christian, scientific Western *ideas* of history sharply contrast with the emphasis on the cyclical nature of time central to most other mythologies and with the vision of the Hebrew paradisal myth. These mythologies might be termed examples of "perennial myth," since they embody in such a "pure" form the archetypal themes of the collective unconscious bearing the imprint of humanity's perennial interactions both with itself and with the natural world since time immemorial. This category includes major elements of mythologies from Greece, Rome, and Asia Minor. Actually, it includes aspects of the myth and ritual structure of Christianity on its esoteric side and certainly elements from the myth systems behind three other high religions--Hinduism, Buddhism, and Taoism. It is at positions closer to these mythological systems than to Christianity that some of the more interesting of the recent science fiction novels have arrived.

Astronomer-science fiction novelist Sir Fred Hoyle portrays what Eliade might call an "antihistorical solution" in a future society in *October the First Is Too Late* (1966). Hoyle's protagonist, a musician named Richard, enters a society some 4,000 years in the future where the three people he meets show him a cinematographic version of the history of the past 4,000 years. During that time, cycles of prosperity, expansion, and growth are followed by catastrophic collapses in the form of wars causing all but the extinction of the species. Humanity has recovered from each collapse only to forget the "lessons of the past" and to go through the same *enantiodromia*, the same reversal of opposites: expansion--saturation point and instability--and then sudden collapse--after which a new expansion began the cycle again (Hoyle 171-77).

In order to escape the "agony of the past" (177), the people of this distant future have rejected history and the belief in the value of linear progress. Now their society does not change.

Dick's friend and fellow traveller physicist, Dr. John Sinclair, though, describes the human beings of this future thus:

> We're in a fossilized society. They've decided, completely as a matter of policy, that they're not going to change. They're not going to seek after progress. They're satisfied with the way life is. For them this may be fine but to us it would be a living death. We have a drive that forces us toward further achievement. Of course it may be quite illusory, probably it is. But being the way we are I think we would find it very much an imprisonment. (185)

In keeping with his views as a scientific positivist, Sinclair does return to his own time, 1966.

Yet the culture of the future Sinclair rejects closely parallels Eliade's humanity of the future which strives "to forget, as meaningless and dangerous, any spontaneous gesture which might maintain 'historical' consequences." Though the image of Hoyle's future society is rather sketchy, aspects of it seem to bear out Eliade's parallel to a paradise beyond history. No trace of any kind of political structure in the ordinary sense appears. The people of that time live on only one small part of the earth's surface and have no desire to expand. Though they do seem to enjoy a high degree of technical control of their environment, they do not wish for more.

The viewpoint of this static but happy society is contrasted to the technological striving for progress. John and Dick have also witnessed the much further future (parallel structurally to Wells's *The Time Machine*), a future in which the human race has become extinct and when the earth is covered by an undifferentiated "Plain of Glass" caused by the sun's going into the supernova stage. The white-haired man who has acted as host to the visitors from the past tells John:

> "You have in mind an ultimate El Dorado, which some day you may attain. . . . You have seen the final state of the Earth, out there in the great Plain of Glass. Perhaps you may think we could escape to some other planet moving around some other star. Yet that star too will die. So it will be for our entire galaxy. Ultimate continuity, in a physical, material respect is impossible." (181)

He goes on to outline the "Creative Evolution" hypothesis that a "huge intellect" is being constructed from the evolution of creatures on countless planets throughout the universe. In such a cosmos, the importance of most individuals would be nil; duplication would occur on an enormous scale: "Perhaps in one case in a thousand a new facet may emerge" (181). The people of this society, though, have made the decision that the agony of the historical aspect of any such evolutionary "plan" is not justified by the hope of that final El Dorado coming at the end of a linear process. Thus this society has, to use Eliade's language, opted for an "antihistorical solution." It has chosen paradise, a world where historical change is not a factor.

Dick opts to spend the rest of his life in that world. Unlike his friend John, the technocrat, Dick is a true musician and understands life to be really quite similar to a piece of music. The purpose of the music is not found in reaching the end but in the process of the movement, from one to the next, of each bar and each note--like the worlds of nature and of myth, in which the "eternal return" rules.

In *The Lathe of Heaven* (1971), Ursula LeGuin tells the story of a young man who has "effective dreams" (15-18). George Orr *dreams* that a certain condition exists and then awakens to find that now, *after* his dream, it really does. A power-crazed psychiatrist gets hold of George and systematically uses hypnosis and George's dreaming power to manipulate reality in the name of "progress."

From George's point of view, the psychiartist only succeeds in causing all manner of havoc both in George's life and in the world at large. It only takes one of Orr's dreams induced by Dr. Haber to wipe out masses of people, cities, anything that gets in the way of Haber's views as to what progress should be. Orr revolts: "Please, stop using my dreams to improve things, Dr. Haber. It won't work. It's wrong. I want to be *cured* [of "effective dreaming"]" (81).

Haber has been playing the alternative histories game by way of trial and error with a total disregard for individuals. "You can't go on changing things, trying to run things," says Orr. Haber, with the fervor of a technocratic positivist, replies: "You speak as if that were some kind of moral imperative." He asks also, "Isn't that man's very purpose on earth--to do things, change things, run things, make a better world?" (82).

Indeed, the novel seems to imply that humanity's "purpose" is not as clear as all that, that to decide what Haber has decided is the height of presumption. The source of the novel's title appears in a quotation from Taoist mystic Chuang Tse which is used as epigraph to one of the chapters: "To let understanding stop at what cannot be understood is a high attainment. Those who cannot do it will be destroyed on the lathe of heaven" (30). The admonition is essentially the same as the one embodied in the mythic vision concerning *hubris* in the plays of the Greek dramatists of the classical period, Sophocles and Aeschylus.

George counters Haber's views in terms in keeping with the philosophy behind perennial myth:

> Things don't have purposes, as if the universe were a machine, where every part has a useful function. What's the function of a galaxy? I don't know if our life has a purpose and I don't see that it matters. What does matter is that we're a part. Like a thread in a cloth or a glass-blade in a

field. It *is* and we *are*. What we do is like wind blowing on the grass." (82)

Haber replies contemptuously: "You're of a peculiarly passive outlook for a man brought up in the Judaeo-Christian-Rationalist West. A sort of natural Buddhist. Have you ever studied the Eastern mysticisms, George?" (82-83).

"No," says George, "I don't know anything about them. I do know that it's wrong to force the pattern of things. It won't do. It's been our mistake for a hundred years" (83). That is, the way of the West during the last century is madness whether from the point of view of Eastern philosophies or even that of "right moral reasoning" in the Western sense.

Haber views history in Christian, technological terms, emphasizing plan, purpose, and progress, seeing history in linear terms, as though it were moving toward some perfectly ordered end. Orr's view is close to the one held by Eliade and the proponents of perennial myth. It is at bottom a religious view involving an attitude of humility and awe in the face of the immensities and mysteries of humanity and nature. He is willing to ignore history and the possibility of engineering it and to live peacefully in the paradise of the present, but is horrified at that strange sense of justice of Haber's which rivals that of the Empire-builder or Prince alluded to by Eliade. "The end justifies the means?" thinks Orr, questioningly. "But what if there never is an end? All we have is means" (83). Those who think purely in terms of history and progress really do, if they are consistent, side with Machiavelli and Eliade's egotistical tyrants.

Both of these novels are entertaining stories which air clearly and in some depth the problem of history as we face it today. As Joyce's Stephen Dedalus says, "History is the nightmare from which I am trying to awake." This century really is a kind of nightmare, and all really rational accounts indicate that without some apocalypse involving the revelation of a new consciousness, all sorts of nightmares are quite possible in the future. The question is: Will we continue to march blindly into the dark, ignoring "the terror of history"? Or will we draw back from the brink of chaos and form some new synthesis of consciousness including an acceptance of nature, the nature of the eternal return of natural cycles, without totally rejecting science but embracing consciousness/the unconscious intellect in its most comprehensive perspective?

AFTERWARD:

WHERE NOW AND WHAT ELSE?

These essays collectively show something of the value to be found in the application of Jungian and comparative mythological materials to questions of UFOs and to science fiction narratives. In no way is this volume deisgned to be comprehensive.

Time travel, for example, touched on only in the final two chapters, could be approached in a whole string of works--specifically, from the perspective of Jungian psychology and comparative myth. Similarly, another area which has been only briefly dealt with here (mainly in Chapter 2) concerns the matter of items written by or about contactees or abductees. Such works frequently claim to be autobiography or investigative reporting. Orfeo Angelucci is only one of many certainly worth discussing; others include Whitley Striber and Bud Hopkins.

If asked why anyone should be interested in these materials, the answer is that these items are part of the fantasy fabric (some would say myth) of the present time, for they embody much in the way of the psychological drama of contemporary humanity and deal with many of the universal questions as they present themselves in our era--especially with the psychological aspect of those questions.

Both the artist and the literary critic try to bring light where there was darkness, to suggest an order where there was chaos. Certainly, science fiction is one of the art forms dominant during the present. A great deal may be learned from it when it is understood from the Jungian and perspective and from the viewpoints of comparative mythology.

WORKS CITED

Aldiss, Brian W. *Trillion Year Spree*. New York: Atheneum, 1986.

Amis, Kingsley. *New Maps of Hell: A Survey of Science Fiction*. New York: Brace, 1960.

Auden. W.H. "September 1, 1939." *Chief Modern Poets of Britain and America*. Vol 1. Fifth Ed. Sanders, et al. New York: Macmillan, 1964. 366-68.

Blair, Karin. *Meaning in Star Trek*. New York: Warner Books, 1979.

Blake, William. *The Marriage of Heaven and Hell. The Complete Prose and Selected Poetry of John Donne and William Blake*. Ed. Robert Silliman Hillyer. New York: Modern Library, 1941.

Bloch, Robert. "Wolf in the Fold." *Star Trek: The Classic Episodes*. Adapted by James Blish. Vol. 2 (1968) New York: Bantam, 1991. 147-78.

The Bhagavad Gita. Trans. Juan Mascaro. Baltimore: Penguin, 1970.

Boulding, Kenneth. "After Civilization, What?" *The Bulletin of the Atomic Scientists* (Oct. 1982): 39-48.

Bova, Ben. "The Role of Science Fiction." *Science Fiction: Today and Tomorrow*. Ed. Reginald Bretnor. Baltimore: Penguin, 1975. 3-16.

Campbell, John, Jr. *"Who Goes There?" and Other Stories*. New York: Dell, 1939.

Campbell, Joseph. *The Hero with a Thousand Faces*. Princeton: Princeton UP, 1973.

___. *The Inner Reaches of Outer Space: Metaphor as Myth and Religion*. New York: Alfred Van Der Marck, 1986.

___. *Joseph Campbell: The Power of Myth, with Bill Moyers*. Ed Betty Sue Flowers. New York: Doubleday, 1988.

___. *The Masks of God: Creative Mythology*. New York: Penguin, 1976.

___. *The Masks of God: Oriental Mythology*. 1976.

___. *The Masks of God: Primitive Mythology*. Viking, 1969.

___, assisted by M.J. Abadie. *The Mythic Image*. Princeton: Princeton UP, 1974.

___. "Mythological Themes in Creative Literature and Art." *Myths, Dreams, and Religion*. Ed. Joseph Campbell. New York: Dutton, 1970. 138-75.

___. *Myths to Live By*. New York: Bantam, 1973.

Capra, Frijof. *The Tao of Physics: An Exploration of the Parallels Between Modern Physics and Eastern Mysticism*. Berkeley: Shambhala, 1975.

Clarke, Arthur C. *Childhood's End*. 1953. New York: Ballantine, 1980.

Clarke, Arthur C. *Rendezvous with Rama*. New York: Ballantine, 1973.

Clarke, Arthur C. *2001: A Space Odyssey* (based on the screenplay of the MGM film by Stanley Kubrick and Arthur C. Clarke). New York: New American Library, 1968.

___. *2010: Odyssey Two*. New York: Ballantine, 1982.

Clareson, Thomas D. (A Transcription of) MLA Forum on 29 December 1968: "Science Fiction: The New Mythology." *Extrapolation* 10 (1969): X-69 - X-115.

Coomaraswamy, Ananda K. *Christian and Oriental Philosophy of Art*. New York: Dover, 1956.

___. *Hinduism and Buddhism*. Westport, Connecticut: Greenwood Press, 1971.

___. "Who is Satan and Where is Hell?" *Disguises of the Demonic: Contemporary Perspectives on the Power of Evil*. Ed. Alan M. Olson. New York: Association Press, 1975. 57-68.

Coon, Gene L. "Errand of Mercy." *Star Trek: Classic*. Vol. 1 (1966) 593-608.

___ and Carey Wilbur. "Space Seed." *Star Trek: Classic*. Vol. 1 (1969) 537-54.

Crichton, Michael. *Sphere*. New York: Ballantine, 1987.

Davies, Paul. *God and the New Physics*. New York: Simon & Schuster, 1983.

Dostoyevsky, Fyodor. *The Brothers Karamazov*. 1880. Trans. Constance Garnett. New York: Signet, 1957.

___. *Crime and Punishment*. 1866. (Norton Critical Edition) Ed. George Gibian. Trans. Jessie Coulson. 1953. New York: Norton, 1975.

___. "The Dream of a Ridiculous Man." 1877. *Dostoyevsky: "Notes from Underground," "White Nights," "The Dream of a Ridiculous Man," and Selections from The House of the Dead*. Trans. Andrew MacAndrew. New York: Signet, 1961. 204-26.

Eliade, Mircea. *Cosmos and History: The Myth of the Eternal Return*. Trans. Willard R. Trask. New York: Harper and Row, 1959.

Eliade, Mircea. *The Sacred and the Profane: The Nature of Religion*. Trans. Willard R. Trask. New York: Harcourt, Brace, and Javanovich, 1959.

Ehrlich, Max. "The Apple." *Star Trek: Classic*. Vol. 1. 1967. 201-20.

Farmer, Philip José. "My Sister's Brother." *The Classic Philip José Farmer: 1952-1964* (*Classics of Modern Science Fiction* Series, Vol. 4; general editor, George Zebrowski). Ed. Martin Harry Greenberg and Isaac Asimov. 1960. New York: Crown, 1984. 158-213.

___. *The Dark Design*. New York: Berkley, 1977.

___. *The Fabulous Riverboat*. 1971.

___. *The Lovers*. 1961. New York: Ballantine, 1979.

___. *The Magic Labyrinth*. Berkley, 1980.

___. *To Your Scattered Bodies Go*. 1969.

Fiedler, Leslie. "The Criticism of Science Fiction." *Coordinates: Placing Science Fiction and Fantasy*. Eds. George E. Slusser, Eric S. Rabkin, and Robert Scholes. Carbondale: Southern Illinois UP, 1983. 1-13.

Fontana, D.C. "Charlie's Law." *Star Trek: Classic*. Vol. 1 (1966) 161-81.

___ and Nathan Butler. "This Side of Paradise." *Star Trek: Classic*. Vol. 1 (1967) 555-70.

Franz, M.-L. von. "The Process of Individuation." *Man and His Symbols*. Ed. C.G. Jung. Garden City: Doubleday, 1964. 158-229.

Fredericks, Casey. *The Future of Eternity: Mythologies of Science Fiction and Fantasy*. Bloomington: Indiana UP, 1982.

Galbreath, Robert. "Ambiguous Apocalypse: Transcendental Versions of the End." *The End of the World*. Eds. Eric S. Rabkin, Martin H. Greenberg, and Joseph D. Olander. Carbondale: Southern Illinois UP, 1983. 53-72 (notes: 176-80).

Gerrold, David. *The World of Star Trek*. Revised. New York: Blue Jay, 1984.

Göethe, Johann Wolfgang von. *Faust: Part One and Part Two*. Trans. Charles E. Passage. New York: Bobs-Merrill, 1965.

Goodrich, Peter H. "The Lineage of Mad Scientists." *Extrapolation* 27.2 (Summer 1986): 109-14.

Grof, Stanislav, with Hal Zina Bennett. *The Holotropic Mind: The Three Levels of Human Consciousness and How They Shape Our Lives*. New York: HarperCollins, 1993.

Hartwell, David. *Age of Wonders: Exploring the World of Science Fiction*. New York: Walker, 1984.

Heinlein, Robert A. *Stranger in a Strange Land*. 1961. New York: Berkley, 1981.

Homer, *The Odyssey*. c. 850 B.C.E. Trans. E.V. Rieu. Baltimore: Penguin, 1967.

Howard, Thomas. *The Achievement of C.S. Lewis*. Wheaton, Illinois: Harold Shaw, 1980.

Howes, Allen B. "Expectation and Surprise in *Childhood's End*." *Writers of the Twentieth-First Century: Arthur C. Clarke*. Ed. Joseph Olander and Martin Harry Greenberg. New York: Taplinger, 1977. 149-71.

Hoyle, Fred. *The Black Cloud*. New York: Signet, 1957.

___. *October the First Is Too Late*. New York: Harper & Row, 1966.

Hull, Elizabeth. "Justifying the Ways of Man to God: The Novels of Robert A. Heinlein." *Extrapolation* 20.1 (1979): 38-49.

Hume, Kathryn. *Fantasy and Mimesis*. New York: Metheun, 1984.

Huntington, John. "From Man to Overmind: Arthur Clarke's Myth of Progress." *Writers: Clarke*. 211-22.

Huxley, Aldous. *The Doors of Perception; Heaven and Hell*. New York: Harper & Row, 1963.

Huxley, Aldous. *The Perennial Philosophy*. New York: Harper & Row, 1970.

Johnson, Robert A. *We: Understanding the Psychology of Romantic Love*. San Francisco: Harper and Row, 1983.

Jung, C.G. *Answer to Job. The Portable Jung*. Trans. R.F.C. Hull. New York: Viking, 1971. 519-650.

___. "Archetypes of the Collective Unconscious." *The Archetypes and the Collective Unconscious. The Collected Works of C.G. Jung*. Vol. 9 Pt. 1. Second Edition. Trans. R.F.C. Hull. 1959. Princeton: Princeton UP, 1969. 3-41.

___. "Commentary on The Secret of the Golden Flower." *Psyche and Symbol*. Ed. Violet S. de Laszlo. Trans. R.F.C. Hull. Garden City: Doubleday, 1958. 302-51.

___. "Christ as a Symbol of the Self." *Psyche and Symbol*. 35-60.

___. "Flying Saucers: A Modern Myth of Things Seen in the Sky." *Civilization in Transition: C.W.* Vol. 10. 1978. 307-433.

___. *Memories, Dreams, Reflections*. Rec. & Ed. Aniela Jaffe. Revised. Trans. Richard and Clara Winston New York: Random House, 1965.

___. "On the Nature of the Psyche." *On the Nature of the Psyche: C.W.* Vol. 8. Trans. R.F.C. Hull. Princeton: Princeton UP, 1973.

___. "Psychological Aspects of the Mother Archetype." *Archetypes*. 73-110.

___. *Psychological Reflections*. Ed. Jolande Jacobi and R.F.C. Hull. Princeton: Princeton UP, 1974.

___. "Psychology of the Child Archetype." *Psyche and Symbol*. Ed. Violet S. de Laszlo. Trans. Cary Baynes and R.F.C. Hull. Garden City: Doubleday, 1958.

___. "The Relations Between the Ego and the Unconscious." *The Portable Jung*. Ed. Joseph Campbell. New York: Viking, 1974. 70-138.

___. "A Study in the Process of Individuation." *Archetypes*. 290-354.

___. "The Special Phenomology of the Child Archetype." *Psyche and Symbol*. 131-47.

___. *The Undiscovered Self: Past and Present. Civilization in Transition: C.W.* Vol. 10. 1978. 245-305.

Keen, Sam. "Man and Myth: A Conversation with Joseph Campbell." *Voices and Visions*. New York: Harper and Row, 1976. 67-86.

Ketterer, David. *New Worlds from Old: The Apocalyptic Imagination, Science Fiction, and American Literature*. Bloomington: Indiania UP, 1974.

King, Stephen. *Danse Macabre*. New York: Berkeley, 1981.

Klass, Philip J. "Alien-Abduction Tales, Books Spark Author Rivalries." *The Skeptical Inquirer* 12 (Fall 1987): 21-22.

LeGuin, Ursula K. *The Lathe of Heaven*. (1971) New York: Avon, 1973.

Leitch, Donavan. "Atlantis." Recorded by its author. A Mickie Most Production. New York: Epic Records, CBS, 1968.

Lewis, C.S. *The Abolition of Man*. 1943. New York: Macmillan, 1962.

___. *Out of the Silent Planet*. 1943. 1965.

___. *Perelandra*. 1944. 1965.

___. *That Hideous Strength*. 1946. 1965.

Livingston, John A. *One Cosmic Instant: Man's Fleeting Supremacy*. New York: Dell, 1973.

MacLaine, Shirley. *Out on a Limb*. New York: Bantam, 1983.

Matheson, Richard. "The Enemy Within." *Star Trek: Classic*. Vol. 1 (1967) 101-29.

Maupassant, Guy de. "The Horla." c. 1880. *Selected Short Stories*. Trans. Roger Colet. New York: Penguin, 1980. 313-44.

McIntyre, Vonda N. *Star Trek III: The Search for Spock*. New York: Pocket Books, 1984.

___. *Star Trek II: The Wrath of Khan*. 1982.

Melville, Herman. "Chapter XVIII: The Doubloon." *Moby-Dick*. 1851. New York: Peebles, 1976. 366-71.

Moorman, Charles. *Arthurian Triptych: Mythic Materials in Charles Williams, C.S. Lewis, and T.S. Eliot*. New York: Russell & Russell, 1960.

Neumann, Erich. "Art and Time." *Man and Time: Papers from the Eranos Yearbooks*. Trans. Ralph Manheim. Ed. Joseph Campbell. Princeton: Princeton UP, 1973. 3-37.

Panshin, Alexei. *Heinlein in Dimension*. Chicago: Advent, 1968.

Pielke, Robert G. "Grokking the Stranger." *Philosophers Look at Science Fiction*. Ed. Nicholas D. Smith. Chicago: Nelson-Hall, 1982. 153-63.

Plank, Robert. "Fathers and Sons in A.D. 2001." *Writers: Clarke*. 121-48.

___. "Some Psychological Aspects of Lewis's Trilogy." *Shadows of Imagination: The Fantasies of C.S. Lewis, J.R.R. Tolkien, and Charles Williams*. Ed. Mark R. Hillegas. Carbondale: Southern Illinois UP, 1979. 26-40.

Rabkin, Eric S. *Arthur C. Clarke: Starmont Reader's Guide* 1. Series ed. Roger C. Schlobin. Mercer, Washington: Starmont, 1980.

___. "Genre Criticism and the Fantastic." *Science Fiction: A Collection of Critical Essays*. Ed. Mark Rose. Englewood Cliffs: Prentice-Hall, 1976. 89-101.

Roddenberry, Gene. *Star Trek: The Motion Picture* (novel based on the screenplay by Harold Livingston and story by Alan Dean Foster). New York: Pocket Books, 1979.

___ and Don Ingals (story by Jud Crucis). *Star Trek: Classic*. Vol. 1. 1967. 345-73.

Russell, Jeffrey Burton. *Mephistopheles: The Devil in the Modern World*. Ithaca: Cornell UP, 1986.

Samuelson, David N. "*Childhood's End*: A Median Stage of Adolescence?" *Writers: Clarke*. 198-210.

___. "*Stranger* in the Sixties: Model or Mirror?" *Critical Encounters: Writers and Themes in Science Fiction*. Ed. Dick Riley. New York: Ungar, 1978. 144-75.

Sagan, Carl. "The Amniotic Universe." *Broca's Brain: Reflections on the Romance of Science*. New York: Ballantine, 1979. 353-68.

___. *Contact*. New York: Simon & Schuster, 1985.

___. *Cosmos*. New York: Random, 1980.

Scholes, Robert. *Fabulation and Metafiction*. Chicago: U of Illinois P, 1979.

___ and Eric S. Rabkin. *Science Fiction: History; Science; Vision*. New York: Oxford UP, 1977.

Shaw, Bernard. *Back to Methuselah: A Metabiological Penteteuch*. Middlesex: Penguin, 1971.

Shaw, George Bernard. *Man and Superman: A Comedy and a Philosophy*. *Masters of Modern Drama*. Ed. Block, M. Haskell, and Robert Sledd. New York: Random House, 1969.

Spies, Adrian. "Miri." *Star Trek: Classic*. Ed. Blish with J.A. Lawrence. Vol. 1 (1966) 251-76.

Stapledon, Olaf. *Last and First Men and Star Maker*. New York: Dover, 1931, 1937.

Stohl, Jerry. "The Corbomite Maneuver." *Star Trek: Classic*. Vol. 1 (1967) 65-99.

Sturgeon, Theodore. "Amok Time." *Star Trek: Classic*. Vol. 1 (1967) 115-28.

Talbot, Michael. *The Holographic Universe*. New York: HarperCollins, 1991.

___. *Mysticism and the New Physics*. New York: Bantam, 1981.

Tanzy, Eugene. "Contrasting Views of Man and the Evolutionary Process: *Back to Methuselah* and *Childhood's End.*" *Writers: Clarke.* 172-95.

Taves, Ernest. "Communion with the Imagination" (review of Whitley Strieber's *Communion*). *The Skeptical Inquirer* 12 (Fall 1987): 90-96.

Thompson, William Irwin. *At the Edge of History.* New York: Vintage, 1972.

___. *Darkness and Scattered Light: Speculations on the Future.* Garden City: Anchor, 1978.

Toms, Michael. "A Conversation with Joseph Campbell." Voices and Visions Radio Series. San Francisco: New Dimensions Foundation, 1982.

Watts, Alan. *Beyond Theology: The Art of Godmanship.* New York: Random House, 1973.

___. *Myth and Ritual in Christianity.* Boston: Beacon, 1968.

___. *The Two Hands of God: The Myths of Polarity.* New York: Collier, 1974.

Wilson, Colin. *Bernard Shaw: A Reassessment.* New York: Atheneum, 1969.

___. *The Mind Parasites.* Berkeley: Oneric Press, 1983.

___. *The Philosopher's Stone.* Berkeley: Wingbow, 1979.

The UFO Phenomenon (*Mysteries of the Unknown*). The editors of *Time-Life* Books. Alexandria, Virginia: *Time-Life* Books, 1987.

Vallee, Jacques. *Dimensions: A Casebook of Alien Contact.* New York: Ballantine, 1988.

Wyndham, John. *The Midwich Cuckoos.* 1957. New York: Ballantine, 1976.

Yeats, W.B. "The Second Coming." *Chief Modern Poets.* 121.

INDEX

Abolition of Man, The; see Lewis, C.S. 141
Achilles, 176
Acteon, 138
Adam and Eve, 102, 103, 144
Aeschylus, 230
Ahab; see Melville
Aldiss, Brian, 148; *Trillion Year Spree*, 55; *Billion Year Spree*, 55n
Amis, Kingsley; *New Maps of Hell*, 55
Angelucci, Orfeo; *Secret of the Saucers, The*, 46ff
Aquarius, 36, 223
Aquinas, St. Thomas, 76
Argüelles, José, and Miriam; *Mandala*, 37
Arnold, Kenneth, 25n
Arthurian, 16, 144, 146
Arthurian Triptych; see Moorman, 143
Asimov, Isaac, 56
Atman, 199, 200, 219
Atman-Brahman, 161
Auden, W.H.; "September 1, 1939," 38
Augustine, 16
Babel, Tower of, 76, 176
Back to Methuselah; see Shaw, George Bernard
Bacon, Roger, 16
Ballantine, 68
Baum, Frank L., 165
Beatles (rock group), 10
Beowulf, 76

Bergson, Henri, 133, 142
Bernal, J.D., 90
Bethlehem, 37
Bhagavad Gita, 133
Bible, 30, 31, 35, 50, 54, 152
Billion Year Spree; see Aldiss
Blair, Karen; *Meaning in Star Trek*, 121, 171n
Blake, 23, 206; *Marriage of Heaven and Hell, The*, 122n, 202
Blatavsky, Madame, 48
Bloch, Robert, 124
Boulding, Kenneth, 223, 224
Bova, Ben, 58
Brahman, 5, 84, 133
Broad, C.D., 84, 160
Brothers Karamazov, The; see Dostoyevsky
Bruno, Giordano, 13, 16
Buddha, the, 47, 101, 102, 186, 202
Buddhism, 54, 134, 227
Buddhist, 102
Buddhists, 61, 101
Campbell, John, 73
Campbell, Joseph, 4-6, 10, 12-14, 29, 30, 39, 53, 58, 60, 62, 101, 157, 165, 177, 181, 186, 187, 191, 200, 201, 211, 217, 225; *Creative Mythology* (*The Masks of God*), 6, 201; *Hero with a Thousand Faces, The*, 4, 5, 8, 10, 31, 63, 100, 135, 158, 163, 166, 174, 183, 186, 198, 199; *Inner Reaches of Outer Space, The*, 39, 53,

60, 61n; *Mythic Image, The*, 186; "Mythological Themes in Creative Literature and Art," 8, 12, 35n, 44, 101, 132, 181, 187; *Myths to Live By*, 31, 39, 54, 60-62; New Dimensions Radio (with Michael Toms), 62; *Oriental Mythology (The Masks of God)*, 200, 201 *Power of Myth, The* 101n, 102, 177; *Primitive Mythology (The Masks of God)*, 138
Capra, Fritjof, 137
Carter, President Jimmy, 28n
Catholic, 127
Chariots of the Gods, 182
Christ, 16, 17, 21, 26, 47, 67, 79, 100, 102, 122, 143, 145, 186, 197, 200-02, 204-06, 219
Christian, 16, 26, 30, 31, 34, 35, 40, 42, 74, 76, 80, 93, 102-04, 117, 125-28, 135, 141-44, 146-48, 152, 200, 201, 205, 206, 210, 223, 224, 226, 231
Christianity, 14-17, 21, 30, 31, 34, 35, 48, 53, 54, 101, 148, 210, 224, 227
Clareson, Thomas, 56
Clarke, Arthur C., 41, 55, 86, 93, 103, 152, 153, 158, 160, 182, 185, 188; "2001: A Space Odyssey" (movie), 57, 60, 62; *2001: A Space Odyssey*, 57, 74, 146, 152, 181ff; *2010: Odyssey Two*, 46, 146, 181ff; *Childhood's End*, 27, 74, 112, 146, 151ff; *Rendezvous with Rama*, 31, 89ff
Coleridge, Samuel Taylor, 109, 123

Conrad, Joseph; *Heart of Darkness*, 142
Coomaraswamy, Ananda K., 67, 202, 208; "Who is Satan," 101; "Christian and Oriental Philosophy of Art," 67, 207-08; *Hinduism*, 133
Coon, Gene L., 193ff
Coon, Gene L., and Wilbur, Carey, 176
Copernicus, Nicholas, 13, 16, 91
Cosmo-Christianity, 93, 94
Crane, Stephen, 97
Crichton, Michael; *Sphere*, 209ff
Crispin, John; *V* (novel), 74
Dante; *Inferno,* 126n, 127n
Darwin, Charles, 17, 46
Darwinism, 34
Davies, Paul; *God and the New Physics*, 82
"Day the Earth Stood Still, The" (movie), 33
Del Rey, Lester, 56
Devil, 17, 36, 65, 67, 74, 101, 102, 104, 124-28, 135, 143, 152, 157-58, 187, 209, 210
Diana, 138
Dickens, 4
Dionysian, 127, 203
Dionysus, 197
Donavan; see Leitch
Dostoyevsky, Fyodor, 17, 109; *Brothers Karamazov, The*, 104, 106; *Crime and Punishment*, 108n, 138; "Dream of a Ridiculous Man, The," 102ff; *Possessed, The*, 111
Dunn, J.W., 164
"E.T." (the movie), 77
Eden, 107, 108, 226
Einstein, Albert, 3, 20, 49, 54, 61

Eliade, Mercea; *Cosmos and History* 225-227, 231
Emerson, Ralph Waldo, 161
Eros, 64
Eve, 126, 144
Eve, The Three Faces of; see *Three Faces of Eve, The*
Exodus, 76, 156
Exorcist, The, 126
Extrapolation, 55, 197
Farmer, José Philip; *Lovers, The*, 163ff; *Riverworld* (series), 50; "My Sister's Brother," 112ff
Fascism, 53
Fatima, 32
Faust (Göethe), 17-19, 21, 102, 105, 148
Faustus, Doctor; see Marlowe
Feinberg, Gerald, and Robert Shapiro; *Life Beyond the Earth*, 82
Fiedler, Leslie, 59
Finny, Jack; "Invasion of the Body Snatchers" 112
Fontana, D.C., 121n, 192
"Forbidden Planet" (movie), 215
Frankenstein (Shelley), 32
Franz, Maria-L. von, 64, 65, 203
Fredericks, Casey; *Future of Eternity, The*, 54n, 58, 224, 225
Freeman, Jerry, 56
Freud, Sigmund, 125, 184
Fuller, Buckminister, 39, 60
Future of Eternity, The; see Fredericks
Galbreath, Robert, 59
Galileo (Galileo Galilei), 13
Genesis, 76, 99, 103, 117
Gerrold, David; *The World of Star Trek*, 179
God, 2, 5, 12, 16-18, 23, 34, 35, 47, 67, 75, 80, 95, 100, 142, 143, 152, 156, 157, 161, 184, 186, 197, 199, 200, 203, 204, 210, 218, 219, 220, 226, 233
Göethe, Johann von Wolfgang, 105, 135
Goodrich, Peter, 148, 149
Gospel of Eve, 198
Govinda, Lama Anagarika, 137
Grof, Stanislav; *Holotrophic Mind*, 24n
Hull, Elizabeth, 207
Hardy, Thomas, 97
Hartwell, David; *Age of Wonders*, 59
Heart of Darkness; see Conrad
Heinlein, Robert; *Stranger in a Strange Land*, 113n, 195, 197ff
Hell, 117, 126, 211
Heraclitus, 206
Hermeticism, 42
Hindu, 14, 133, 152, 157, 161, 182, 186, 199, 201, 219
Hinduism, 48, 50, 54, 84, 134, 200, 227
Hitler, Adolf, 35, 124, 153
Holy Grail, 16, 49
Homer, 41
Odyssey, 171
Howard, Thomas, 147, 148
Howes, Allen B., 154
Hoyle, Sir Fred, 75-77, 79, 81, 84, 86, 88, 223, 227; *Black Cloud, The*, 46, 75ff, *October the First Is Too Late*, 227ff
Hume, Kathryn, 207
Huntington, John, 151

Huxley, Aldous, 160, 207; *Doors of Perception*, 84, 160, 207; *Heaven and Hell* 137; *Perennial Philosophy, The*, 6n
Iliad, The, 32
Isaiah, 152
Islamic jihad, 40
Jack the Ripper, 124, 126-128
James, William, 133
Jehovah, 40
Jesus, 26, 50, 93, 101, 199, 203, 205
Joad, C.E.M., 133, 142
John (Gospel of), 227
Johnson, Robert A., 22
Jove, 40
Joyce, James, 231
Judeao-Christian, 54, 226, 227
Jung, C.G., 8, 9, 11, 22, 24, 26, 32, 36, 37, 41, 43, 45ff, 55ff, 62, 67, 73, 75, 76, 79, 80, 84, 98, 100, 116, 118, 121, 122, 131ff, 135ff, 141, 143, 151ff 160, 163ff, 172, 183, 186, 191, 193ff, 203, 206, 215, 219, 220, 225, 226; *Answer to Job*, 122n; "Archetypes of the Collective Unconscious, The," 9, 167; "Christ, a Symbol of the Self," 161, 197ff, 209; "Commentary on *The Secret of the Golden Flower*," 219; *Flying Saucers: A Modern Myth of Things Seen in the Sky*, 26, 28ff, 40ff, 44ff, 48, 51, 53, 58, 59, 65, 66, 75, 78, 84, 88, 151, 153, 210; "Individuation, A Study in the Process of," 220; *Memories, Dreams, Reflections*; 75, 84, 206; "Nature of the Psyche, On the," 137; *Portable Jung, The* 9, 24, 119; *Psyche and Symbol*, 188, 192; *Psychological Aspects*, 135; *Psychological Reflections*, 163, 165; *Psychology and Alchemy*; 75; "Psychology of the Child Archetype, The," 9; "Relations Between the Ego and the Unconscious, On the," 161, 165, 171, 193; "Special Phenomenology, (The . . . of the Child Archetype), 69n, 152; *Structure and Dynamics of the Psyche, The*, 84; *Undiscovered Self, The*, 152, 153, 155, 226
Jupiter, 83, 115, 184, 188
Kali, 157
Kant, Immanuel, 24
Keen, Sam, 62
Kent State University Press, 197
Ketterer, David; *New Worlds for Old*, 57
King, Stephen, 112; *Danse Macabre*, 73
King Arthur, 145
Krishna, 5
LeGuin, Ursula, 55n, 56, 223; *Lathe of Heaven, The*, 229ff
Lewis, C.S., 103, 114; *Abolition of Man, The*, 141; *That Hideous Strength*, 103, 141ff; *Out of the Silent Planet*, 103, 143, 144; *Perelandra* 103, 144
Leitch, Donavan; "Atlantis" (pop song), 25
Livingston, John A., *One Cosmic Instant: Man's Fleeting Supremecy*, 181

Lovecraft, H.P., "The Color Out of Space," 112
Lovers, The; see Farmer, José Philip
Lucifer, 17, 124, 125, 143
Lyell, Charles, 17
Machiavelli, 231
MacLaine, Shirley, *Out on a Limb*, 50
Madonna (film star), 10
Man and Superman; see Shaw, George Bernard
Marlowe, Christopher, *Faustus, Doctor*, 2, 16, 17, 18, 122n
Mars (planet), 112, 202, 205-207
Matheson, Richard, 119
Maupassant, Guy de, "Horla, The," 109ff
McIntyre, Vonda N., *Search for Spock, The*, 179; *Wrath of Khan, The* 174, 177, 178
Melville, Herman, *Moby Dick* 18-20, 212
Mercury (planet), 92, 93
Merlin, 141, 146-149
Messiah, 227
Metamorphoses; see Ovid
Midwich Cuckoos, The; see Wyndham
Milton, John, 101, 127
Mind Parasites The; see Wilson
Mississippi Philological Association, 151, 209
MLA forum on SF: The New Myth, 56
Monkees (rock group), 10
Monroe, Marilyn, 10
Moorman, Charles, *Arthurian Triptych*, 143ff
Moses, 156, 164, 168, 226
Nature, 17, 68, 72
Nazi, 88, 138, 141, 142
Neumann, Erich, 67, 68, 121
New Maps of Hell; see Amis

New Testament, 227
New York Times, 209
Newton, Isaac, 3
Nietzsche, Friedrich, 10, 31n, 35
Odin, 41
Odysseus, 172, 173, 174, 179, 211
Old Testament, 17, 148, 226
Orpheus, 200
Orwell, George, 163
Osiris, 197
Out/Silent Planet; see Lewis
Oversoul, 160
Ovid, *Metamorphoses*, 54
Pandora, 35, 96
Panshin, Alexi, 199, 207
Perelandra; see Lewis
Pielke, Robert G., 199
Pisces, 36, 223
Plank, Robert, 147, 184, 185
Pluto (planet), 139
Pohl, Frederick, 56
Pope, Alexander, 97
Presley, Elvis, 10, 45
Prince (rock personality), 10
Promethean, 111
Protestant, 203, 206
Rabkin, Eric S., 146, 153, 156
Rahv, Phillip, 225
Reagan, President Ronald 28n
Renaissance, 16, 34, 126, 206
Roddenberry, Gene, 39n; *Star Trek* (original series), 18, 22, 39, 51n 61, 77, 103, 118, 121, 124, 128, 171, 172, 176, 191ff; "Star Trek: IV: The Voyage Home," 74; "Star Trek: The Motion Picture," 61, 74, 174, 184; *Star Trek: The Next Generation* (1987-94 series), 39, 195; "Star Trek II: The Wrath of Khan," 171ff; "Star Trek III: The Search for Spock," 171ff

Rolling Stones, (rock group) 10
Russell, Jeffrey Burton, 127n
Sagan, Carl, 20, 88, 183; *Contact*, 75, 84ff
Samuelson, David N., 151, 199, 200, 207
Satan, 125, 126, 142, 143, 145, 226
Scholes, Robert, 146; *Fabulation and Metafiction*, 79
Schopenhaur, Arthur, 177
Schrödinger, Erwin, 54
Science Fiction Studies 55
Secret of the Saucers, The; see Angelucci
Shakespeare; *Hamlet*, 50; *Tempest, The*, 215
Shaw, George Bernard, 140, 142, 195; *Back to Methuselah* 131ff, 195; *Man and Superman* 70, 131, 133
Silverberg, Robert 56
Sophocles, 230
Space Odyssey; see Clarke
Spengler, Oswald, 16
Spenser, Edmund, 79
Stapledon, Olaf; *Star Maker, The*, 103
Stohl, Jerry, 173
Sturgeon, Theodore, 121
Suvin, Darko, 56, 57
Swift, Jonathan, 32
Talbot, Michael; *Holographic Universe, The*, 24n
Tantric Buddhist, 137
Tanzy, Eugene, 153
Tao, 12, 133, 199
Taoism, 134, 227
Teiresias, 174, 175
Terran, 165, 166
Terrible Mother, 68, 72
That Hideous Strength; see Lewis
"Thing, The" (movie), 73
Thompson, William Irwin, 223; *At the Edge of History*, 223; *Darkness and Scattered Light*, 36
Three Faces of Eve, The, 120n
Time/Life Mysteries of the Unknown, 25n
Tsiolkovsky, Conrad, 90
Twenty-Four Philosophers, Book of the, 5
Upanishads, 201
Vallée, Jaques, 24n
Venus (planet), 124, 144
Verne, Jules, 32; *Twenty Thousand Leagues Under the Sea*, 214
Virgil, 41
Virgin Mary, 47
Voltaire, 225
Von Franz; see Franz, von
War of the Worlds, The; see Wells, H.G.
Watts, Alan W., 16, 202; *Beyond Theology*, 202; *Hinduism and Buddhism*, 202; *Myth and Ritual in Christianity* 6, 15
Wells, H.G., 32, 69, 132; *War of the Worlds* 33, 47, 73, 110
Wells, Orsen, 33
Wilbur, Carey; see Coon
Wilson, Colin, 118, 131, 132, 134, 137, 140; *Bernard Shaw: A Reassessment*, 134; *Mind Parasites, The*, 108, 112ff; *Philosopher's Stone, The*, 112, 134
World War I, 32, 34
World War II, 34, 35, 38, 39, 43, 45, 46, 55, 101
"Wrath of Khan, The"; see Roddenberry, Gene
Wyndham, John; *Midwich Cuckoos, The*, 46, 58, 63ff
Yeats, 37, 38
Zelazny, Roger;

Lord of Light, 54n
Zeus, 41